$10.00

BARENTS SEA

Bear Island

North Cape

Altenfjord

Tromsoe 70°

Murmansk

Lofoten Islands Harstad
Narvik

Vestfjord

Archangel

cle

Trondheim

60°

Bergen
ord
Horten Oslo
Stockholm
stiansand
Gothenburg
Skaggerak Kattegat
BALTIC SEA
Jutland Copenhagen
goland
Bight Kiel Gdynia
Danzig
Brunsbuttel The Belts
Lubeck Swine
aven Jade Hamburg
uiden Elbe
dam
ls
50°

Rome
40°

TERRANEAN

SEA
15° 30°

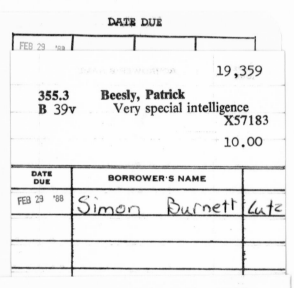

19,359

355.3   **Beesly, Patrick**
B 39v   Very special intelligence
                                 X57183

Very Special Intelligence

Very Special Intelligence

The Story of the Admiralty's Operational Intelligence Centre 1939–1945

By Patrick Beesly

With a Foreword by
Admiral of the Fleet
the Earl Mountbatten of Burma
KG, PC, GCB, OM, GCSI, GCIE, GCVO, DSO

1978
DOUBLEDAY & COMPANY, INC.
GARDEN CITY, NEW YORK

FIRST PUBLISHED IN GREAT BRITAIN 1977 BY
HAMISH HAMILTON LTD
COPYRIGHT © 1977 BY PATRICK BEESLY
ALL RIGHTS RESERVED
PRINTED IN THE UNITED STATES OF AMERICA
LIBRARY OF CONGRESS CATALOG CARD NUMBER 77-82615
ISBN 0-385-13206-9
FIRST U.S. EDITION

'All the business of war, and indeed all the business of life, is an endeavour to find out what you don't know by what you do; that's what I call guessing what was at the other side of the hill.'

WELLINGTON

'A great part of the information obtained in war is contradictory, a still greater part is false, and by far the greater part is of doubtful character.'

CLAUSEWITZ

'Amid the torrent of violent events one anxiety reigned supreme. Battles might be won or lost, enterprises might succeed or miscarry, territories might be gained or quitted, but dominating all our powers to carry on the war, or even to keep ourselves alive, lay our mastery of the ocean routes and the free approach and entry to our ports.'

WINSTON CHURCHILL

Contents

CONTENTS

Illustrations

Endpaper maps by Patrick Leeson

Author's Note and Acknowledgments

THIS BOOK describes the work of the British Admiralty's Operational Intelligence Centre from 1939 to 1945 and gives an account of the maritime war against Germany, as seen through the eyes of the staff of O.I.C. In order to make this intelligible to the general reader, I have felt obliged to sketch in something of the strategic and operational background, even though these aspects of the war have been exhaustively and far more ably chronicled by other writers.

I have not attempted to deal with the part played by O.I.C. in the war in the Far East and the Pacific where the Germans were barely involved and where O.I.C.'s role was an indirect one. Nor have I covered the Mediterranean, despite the fact that German intervention in that theatre vitally affected the course of operations, and that the victories of Matapan and Taranto and the air, surface and submarine attacks on Axis convoys owed a tremendous amount to the rapid supply of accurate intelligence. O.I.C.'s Mediterranean section did, indeed, supply the Commander-in-Chief Mediterranean with much information and with their assessment of its significance, but there was also an Intelligence Centre at Alexandria, and later at Algiers and Caserta. Moreover, the Admiralty did not have the same opportunities for exercising direct control over operations as it did in Home waters, and our knowledge of the British day-to-day plans and movements was not nearly so complete. However, my principal reason for this omission is that, in my opinion, the successes and failures of each of the three services in the Mediterranean, in the intelligence field as much as in the operational, had such a bearing on one another, that it would be impossible to deal adequately with the maritime side in isolation. Mediterranean intelligence is a subject which deserves a book to itself.

One of the unexpected pleasures in writing *Very Special Intelligence* has been the great kindness and help which I have received from so many people, some of them previously quite unknown to me. I owe a great debt to my old chief and friend, Vice-Admiral Sir Norman Denning, K.B.E., C.B. It was at his prompting that I first wrote the three articles for *The Naval Review*, from which this book has been developed, and I have continued, throughout, to rely heavily on his recollection of events which took place between thirty and forty years ago. I am also particularly indebted to Captain S. W. Roskill, C.B.E., D.S.C., Litt.D., F.B.A., R.N. Although I was not, at the outset, personally known to him, he could not have been kinder in reading many of the chapters in draft and not only pointing out errors of fact, but in making many other suggestions about style and treatment, which have been quite invaluable to a tyro embarking on his first venture into authorship. I need hardly say how often I have consulted the four volumes of his official history of *The War at Sea*. Another historian, and a friend from O.I.C. days, Lieutenant-Commander Peter Kemp, O.B.E., R.N. has also read much of the book in draft, has tried to guide me along the right paths and has encouraged me to persevere when I began to fear that I was attempting something beyond my capabilities. Vice-Admiral Brian Schofield, C.B., C.B.E., a wartime Director of the Admiralty's Trade Division, with personal experience of O.I.C. and himself an historian, has also been most helpful with comments and suggestions.

It is not possible here to thank all the former members of O.I.C. and related departments who have spent time and trouble in giving me their recollections and impressions, but I must mention Captain Henry Denham, C.M.G., R.N., Captain Geoffrey Colpoys, C.B.E., R.N., Captain Kenneth Knowles, U.S.N., Commander R. A. Hall, O.B.E., R.N., Commander Patrick Barrow-

AUTHOR'S NOTE AND ACKNOWLEDGMENTS

Green, R.N., Commander George Clements, R.N., Sir Clive Loehnis, K.C.M.G., Eric Fiske, Esq., Hubert McMicking, Esq., John Foster, Esq., Mark Hewitt, Esq., E. H. Bissett, Esq., Lady Winn, Dr. Margaret E. C. Stewart, Mrs. Gwen Clark, Miss Barbara Brice, Miss D. I. Salmon, Miss Elizabeth Gant and Mrs. Cynthia Church.

In Germany, Professor Dr. Jürgen Rohwer of the Bibliothek für Zeitgeschichte has most generously given me the benefit of his unrivalled knowledge of the German Navy and the Battle of the Atlantic, while Gross-Admiral Karl Dönitz, Konter Admiral Eberhardt Godt and Kapitän zur See Hans Meckel have replied in the most friendly way to my inquiries.

Mrs. Mary Pain's expertise in research among naval records has been invaluable, and I am also grateful to Dr. Kitching and his staff in the Rolls Room of the Public Records Office for their invariable help and courtesy.

My grateful thanks are due to Her Majesty's Stationery Office for allowing me to quote material from S. W. Roskill's *The War at Sea*, and to the publishers Weidenfeld & Nicolson for quotations from Dönitz's *Memoirs*, and D. McLachlan's *Room 39*.

Finally, I would like to thank Yvonne Van der Byl, Caroline Lakin and, in particular, Judy Morgan for producing the typescript.

The entire manuscript of this book has been submitted to the Ministry of Defence to ensure that there has been no breach of the Official Secrets Act. I must, however, make it clear that I alone am responsible for any opinions expressed and for the accuracy or inaccuracy of the statements made.

Foreword

by Admiral of the Fleet the Earl Mountbatten of Burma,
KG, PC, GCB, OM, GCSI, GCIE, GCVO, DSO

IN 1968 I wrote a foreword to the late Donald McLachlan's classic book about Naval Intelligence, *Room 39.* In *Very Special Intelligence* Patrick Beesly, because of his own wartime experience and a considerable relaxation of security restrictions, has been able to expand and elaborate the short account which McLachlan gave of the work of one of the most important sections of the Intelligence Division, the Operational Intelligence Centre.

O.I.C., like its First World War predecessor, Room 40, handled decrypted enemy signals or 'Special Intelligence', as they were known. I can well remember the conviction expressed in 1939 by officers with knowledge of Room 40's activities that its successes would immediately be repeated. Few of them unfortunately shared my fears that as a result of the Admiralty's refusal to adopt my very strong recommendation of machine ciphering, it would be our own codes and ciphers, rather than those of the enemy, that would be the first to be broken. Indeed, one of the lessons of Beesly's book is the astonishing over-confidence displayed by both the British and Germans (and in fact by all nations) in the security of their ciphering arrangements.

Although in fact the Operational Intelligence Centre was a Naval organization the sources of information upon which it relied were many. The O.I.C. served not only the Royal Navy but

also the Royal Air Force and it worked, as the book shows, in intimate co-operation with its opposite numbers in Ottawa and
Washington, thereby assisting our Allied Forces as well.

By the time I was appointed Allied Commander South East
Asia in 1943 I was well aware, both from my service at sea as Captain (D), 5th Destroyer Flotilla, and as Chief of Combined Operations, of the immense value of the work which the O.I.C. was
doing, and of the paramount necessity for an efficient Intelligence
staff to serve in my Headquarters in Kandy. I was equally convinced that the best results would only be obtained by a fully integrated inter-Allied and inter-Service staff.

I was extremely fortunate in securing as my first Director of Intelligence Major General Lamplough, a Royal Marines officer who
was at that time the Deputy Director of the Intelligence Division
in the Admiralty. 'Lamps' knew all the tricks of the trade and he
and his Deputy, Brigadier General Pape of the United States
Army, soon welded their mixed British-American staff into a
highly efficient team which was of immense assistance to me in
the many and wide ranging decisions which I had to make. My
Army, Air Force and Naval Commanders-in-Chief continued to
maintain their own individual intelligence staffs who also did an
excellent job, though such a complex set-up led to some inevitable
duplication.

Twenty years later, with the Prime Minister's approval, I set
about the difficult task of creating a unified Ministry of Defence.
It was quite clear to me that a completely integrated inter-Service
Intelligence Staff was essential. It would not only save manpower
but would in fact give better results. By no means everyone agreed
with me so it was crucial to have the right man as my first Deputy
Chief of Defence Staff (Intelligence).

As First Sea Lord I had been instrumental in getting Ned Denning (now Vice-Admiral Sir Norman Denning) appointed as the
Director of Naval Intelligence. He was a member of the Supply
and Secretariat branch of the Navy and this was the first time a
non-Executive officer had been put up for the post. This proposal
met with considerable opposition from those who wanted to see
the appointment go, as it traditionally had, to an Executive officer
of operational experience. By then Admiral Sir Charles Lambe
had been nominated to succeed me as First Sea Lord and I con-

sulted him. He strongly supported the appointment and Ned Denning went on to become one of the finest DNIs the Navy has ever had.

Denning, who was the principal architect of the Operational Intelligence Centre and, quite rightly, figures so largely in this book, was one of the earliest supporters of the idea of joint intelligence. I therefore chose him for the important new appointment as DCDS (Intelligence). Once again he did a superb job and he and his successors have fully proved the validity of my argument that Intelligence, like Defence itself, is indivisible.

Patrick Beesly's own wartime experience of the Operational Intelligence Centre has enabled him to study the O.I.C. secret records available in the Public Records Office in great depth. This has resulted in a full and factual account of the maritime war against Germany, as seen through the eyes of the O.I.C. staff, which will fascinate its readers.

Preface

TWENTY YEARS after the end of the Second World War
Gross-Admiral Karl Dönitz was asked whether 'he felt, during the
Battle of the Atlantic, that he had opposed to him a single commanding mind reading his own. Not, he replied, until Horton
took over the conduct of the anti-U-boat war at Liverpool in November, 1942'. It was a well-merited tribute to that great Admiral,
Sir Max Horton, but it displayed a pardonable ignorance of a department of the Naval Intelligence Division which in fact was the
nerve centre not only of the struggle against the U-boats but of
the whole maritime war against Germany. This small, under-
staffed and over-worked department was the Admiralty's Operational Intelligence Centre. Its work was so secret that, although it
has been referred to in complimentary terms by many wartime admirals such as Sir Andrew Cunningham and by naval historians
such as Captain S. W. Roskill, it was only at the end of 1975 that
the first carefully selected batch of its files was released to the
Public Records Office. In consequence no detailed and factual account of its aims and achievements has previously been possible.
The object of this book is to try to repair this omission.

Abbreviations

A.C.N.S.(H.)	Assistant Chief of Naval Staff (Home).
A.C.N.S.(F.)	Assistant Chief of Naval Staff (Foreign). (See note on Admiralty.)
A.C.N.S.(U.T.)	Assistant Chief of Naval Staff (U-boats and trade).
A.M.C.	Armed Merchant Cruiser.
A.N.C.X.F.	Allied Naval Commander-in-Chief Expeditionary Force. (Invasion of France).
A.O.C.-in-C.	Air Officer Commanding-in-Chief. (Coastal, Bomber and Fighter Commands, R.A.F.)
A.O.C.	Air Officer Commanding. (Groups of R.A.F. Commands.)
A.S.D.I.C.	Anti-Submarine Detector Indicator Committee, which gave its name to a device for detecting submerged objects. (Now known as Sonar.)
A-S.W.D.	Anti-Submarine Warfare Division (British).
A.S.W.O.R.G.	Anti-Submarine Warfare Operations Research Group (U.S.).
B.d.U.	Befehlshaber der U-boote. (Flag Officer U-boats.)
B.P.	Bletchley Park. Wartime home of Government Code and Cipher School.

C.I.A.	Central Intelligence Agency (U.S.).
C-in-C.	Commander-in-Chief.
C.O.	Commanding Officer.
COMINCH	Commander-in-Chief U. S. Fleet and Chief of Naval Operations.
D.C.D.S.(I.)	Deputy Chief of Defence Staff (Intelligence).
D.C.N.S.	Deputy Chief of Naval Staff. (See note on Admiralty.)
D.D.I.C.	Deputy Director Intelligence Centre. (Head of O.I.C.)
D/F	Direction Finding (Radio).
D.N.I.	Director of Naval Intelligence.
D.S.D.	Director of Signal Division.
E-boats.	Enemy boats. British term for German M.T.Bs. or P.T. boats.
E.G.	Escort Group.
F.21.	U. S. N. Operational Intelligence Centre.
First L.	First Lord. (See note on Admiralty.)
First S.L.	First Sea Lord. (See note on Admiralty.)
G.A.F.	German Air Force.
G.C. & C.S.	Government Code and Cipher School.
G.R.T.	Gross Registered Tonnage.
H/A	High Angle, anti-Aircraft gun.
H/F	High Frequency.
H/F D/F	High Frequency Direction Finding (U.S. Huff Duff).
I.D.	Intelligence Division.
M/F	Medium Frequency.
M.T.B.	Motor Torpedo boat (U.S. P.T. Boat).
N.I.D.	Naval Intelligence Division.
O.I.C.	Operational Intelligence Centre.
O.K.M.	Oberkommando der Marine. (German Admiralty.)
OP.20	U.S. Operational Intelligence Centre. (See also F.21.)
O.S.S.	Office of Strategic Services.
P.R.U.	Photographic Reconnaissance Unit of R.A.F.
R.A.F.	Royal Air Force.
R.C.N.V.R.	Royal Canadian Naval Volunteer Reserve.

ABBREVIATIONS

R.N.	Royal Navy.
R.N.V.R.	Royal Navy Volunteer Reserve.
R.N.Z.N.V.R.	Royal New Zealand Naval Volunteer Reserve.
S.K.L.	See Kriegs Leitung. (German Naval Staff.)
S.O.E.	Special Operations Executive. (British counterpart of O.S.S.)
S.O.(I.)	Staff Officer (Intelligence).
U-boat.	Untersee Boot. (Submarine.)
U.K.	United Kingdom of Great Britain and Northern Ireland.
U.S.A.	United States of America.
U.S.N.	United States Navy.
V.C.N.S.	Vice-Chief of Naval Staff. (See note on Admiralty.)
V.H.F.	Very High Frequency.
V.I.P.	Very Important Person.
V.L.R.	Very Long Range (Aircraft).
W.R.N.S.	Women's Royal Naval Service. Equivalent of U. S. WAVES.
Y. Station.	Station monitoring and recording foreign wireless transmissions.
W/T	Wireless Telegraphy.

Convoys Mentioned

GUF.	Gibraltar	U.S.A. Fast.
GUS.	Gibraltar	U.S.A. Slow.
HX.	Halifax	U.K. 10 knot.
JW.	U.K.	North Russia after November 1942.
MKS.	North Africa	U.K.
ON.	U.K.	North America. 10 knot.
ONS.	U.K.	North America. 7 knot.
PQ.	U.K.	North Russia up to November 1942.
QP.	North Russia	U.K. up to November 1942.
RA.	North Russia	U.K. after November 1942.
SC.	Halifax	U.K. 7 knot.
SL.	Sierre Leone	U.K.
WS.	U.K.	Middle East troop convoys.
UGS.	U.S.A.	Gibraltar. Slow.
UGF.	U.S.A.	Gibraltar. Fast.

Very Special Intelligence

1

Astute Men

THE SECOND World War was in so many ways merely a continuation of the First that it is not surprising to find that the origins of O.I.C. go back to the earlier conflict and that it owed its creation to an officer, Admiral Sir William James, who in 1917 had been in charge of its famous predecessor Room 40 OB., and who, by 1936, was occupying the position of Deputy Chief of the Naval Staff. There were considerable differences between the two organizations but as O.I.C. benefited greatly from the experience and the mistakes of its pioneer parent, some assessment of Room 40's strengths and weaknesses must be attempted.

Room 40 OB., so called because of the number of the room in the Old Block of the Admiralty which it occupied, was, in essence and for most of its existence, a cryptanalysis bureau. Thanks to the invaluable gift from our Russian allies of a German Naval Signal book recovered after the sinking in the Baltic of the German cruiser *Magdeburg*, the tiny section had, by the end of 1914, begun to decrypt a whole series of the enemy's codes and ciphers. Although it did not become an integral part of the Naval Intelligence Division until 1917 it was responsible to that legendary character, Admiral Sir Reginald Hall, perhaps the best known Intelligence chief in history. It was 'Blinker' Hall, the Director of Naval Intelligence, and not the Foreign Office, who master-

1

minded the handling of the notorious Zimmerman telegram, which finally brought the United States into the war in April 1917. Nevertheless, although Room 40 decrypted a variety of diplomatic messages, both enemy and neutral, its primary task was of course to serve the Navy and it is with this side of its work that we are concerned.

Room 40's activities were kept so secret that very few officers, either in the Admiralty or in the Grand Fleet were aware of them. Although, thanks to its staff's ability to read German naval wireless signals, it knew more about the procedures and intentions of Admiral Scheer's High Sea Fleet than any other department in the Royal Navy, it was not allowed to communicate direct with Jellicoe and the Grand Fleet. Indeed all it was permitted to do was to pass to one or other of the handful of officers of the Operations Division who were privy to its existence the translated text of the German signals which it had decrypted. Despite Room 40's background knowledge of these signals, it was left to the chosen few in Operations to assess the significance of each message placed in front of them and to decide whether or not to pass it on to Jellicoe. The officers concerned were neither trained intelligence officers nor experts on the Imperial German Navy. It is scarcely surprising that when it came to the crunch they failed lamentably to make the best use of the priceless information with which they had been presented.

There was, of course, no precedent for dealing with intelligence of this nature. Indeed the very idea of a Naval Staff had only recently been forced on a reluctant Navy by the First Lord of the Admiralty, Winston Churchill. Room 40 was only formed at the outbreak of war. It was not part of the accepted Establishment, but was staffed for the most part by gifted amateurs. Some were naval paymasters, but others schoolmasters from Dartmouth, dons from the universities, or clerics. It was inconceivable to the very great majority of naval officers of that era (Hall was one of the few exceptions), that anyone not trained and brought up as an Executive officer of the Service could possibly be entrusted with the interpretation and dissemination of information upon which the tactics and movements of the Grand Fleet might have to depend. That was a task which could only be performed by regular officers of the Executive Branch.

The crux of the intelligence problem, so far as Jellicoe was concerned, was how to ensure that the Grand Fleet could be sailed from Scapa Flow, where it was based to avoid danger from U-boats, in sufficient time to catch and engage the German High Sea Fleet during the course of the latter's brief and infrequent sorties into the southern North Sea. The time and distance factors were such that both fleets had to leave their respective bases practically simultaneously if there was to be any hope of a successful interception. Only Room 40's cryptanalysts could possibly provide Jellicoe with sufficiently timely warnings, and in the case of the Battle of Jutland they did exactly that. Thereafter grave faults in the handling of intelligence contributed significantly to the fact that Jutland was not the second Trafalgar for which the Royal Navy had so ardently been longing and which Britain had confidently expected.

Early on May 31, 1916, the High Sea Fleet began to emerge from the Jade and the Elbe with the intention of surprising Beatty's battlecruisers before Jellicoe and the main body of the Grand Fleet could intervene, and in the hope of luring the latter into a U-boat trap. More than twelve hours earlier, however, Room 40 had detected signs of the impending sortie and Jellicoe had been duly alerted. As a result he was in fact at sea and steaming south two hours before the first of Scheer's ships left harbour. So far so good.

Around noon that day, the Director of the Operations Division, Captain Thomas Jackson, came into Room 40 and inquired where the direction finding stations placed call sign DK, the call sign normally used by the German Commander-in-Chief. He was told, quite correctly, 'In the Jade'. Jackson turned on his heel and left the room. Had he asked where Admiral Scheer was at that particular moment, he would have received a very different answer, for everyone in Room 40 knew that, when Scheer put to sea, he transferred call sign DK to the shore command in Wilhelmshaven and himself used another one in an effort to deceive the British. Quite unknown to Room 40, Jackson then proceeded to signal Jellicoe and Beatty that the main German Fleet was still in the Jade, its intended sortie apparently postponed due to lack of reconnaissance by its Zeppelins. By this time, in fact, Scheer had been steaming north for more than ten hours. Both Jellicoe and Beatty

3

were, therefore, taken very much by surprise when, less than four hours after the receipt of Jackson's wretched and ill-conceived signal, they found themselves confronting not just the German battlecruisers, but the whole of the High Sea Fleet. Their faith in the reliability of the Admiralty as a source of intelligence about the enemy was shattered.

To be fair, the surprise was mutual and Scheer only managed to extricate his battered ships from a desperate situation by brilliant tactics. Even then, but for the lateness of the hour at which the two main fleets made contact with each other and the poor visibility prevailing, the afternoon would probably have ended in a heavy defeat for the Germans. As it was, although they had inflicted rather more damage than they had suffered, they had taken a severe pounding, they were still out-numbered and had, unlike Jellicoe, no wish to renew the struggle on the following day. Their only hope was to find a way during the night round the British, who were between them and their bases, in order to make good their escape.

Scheer had a choice of four routes home. Jellicoe selected as the most probable one on which to base his own dispositions one which, in the event, Scheer rejected. This however would not have mattered if only the British Commander-in-Chief had been supplied with, and had believed, all the information that was now becoming available to Room 40. At 9:58 P.M., Jellicoe was sent a signal giving him the position and course of the rear of the German Fleet but unfortunately the navigation of the German ship upon which this signal was based was faulty and she was not in fact where she reported herself to be. Jellicoe knew that the position signalled to him by Operations Division was substantially wrong and this, coming on top of the earlier mistake, finally destroyed what remnants of trust he had left in the reliability of the Admiralty's information. When fifty minutes later, he received a further message informing him that the German Fleet had been ordered to return to port and which gave a course indicating the route likely to be followed, he ignored it, preferring to rely on his own assessment of the probabilities. He continued to steam in a direction which gradually took him further away from Scheer, who was thus enabled to slip round the British rear and escape.

So much for the information which Operations did pass to

Jellicoe. It was not however the end of the sorry story. Shortly after decrypting the signals mentioned above, Room 40 intercepted a message from Scheer requesting a dawn reconnaissance by Zeppelin of the Horns Riff, the channel by which he planned to return. This and subsequent signals which made the Germans' intentions crystal clear were faithfully passed by Room 40 to Operations but they got no further than the desk of the Duty Officer. Next morning the British scoured an empty sea. Scheer was safely back in Wilhelmshaven. It was not until several years after the war that Jellicoe even learned of the existence of these vital signals.

The main reason for the intelligence failure at Jutland was quite simply that Room 40 was not permitted to act as an operational intelligence centre. The dissemination of the information which it produced, and which it alone fully understood, was the responsibility of a small group of officers who were neither trained nor equipped to make proper use of it. The subsequent Naval Staff Appreciation of the battle remarked that there was 'a policy of secrecy, amounting to an absolute obsession . . . vitally important information was only sent to the Chief of the War Staff and Director of Operations, who passed or did not pass it on. The section that was responsible for such information was the only section able to "vet" it in the light of continuous and cumulative intelligence. It was clearly the function of the Intelligence Division to keep the Commander-in-Chief supplied with information as to the movements of the High Sea Fleet and this it did not do because its function had been withheld'.

Admiral James makes an illuminating comment in his biography of Hall.* The latter recognized the need to turn Room 40 into 'an intelligence centre as distinct from a cryptographic bureau. But the time was not ripe for making such a radical proposal to the Naval Staff, and Hall could do nothing until next year'. Such was the strength of naval prejudice and conservatism.

When the change was made, in the spring of 1917, Room 40 ceased to send raw intercepts to the Operations Division and began instead to feed them with all relevant facts in the shape of reasoned appreciations of German intentions and movements. Even then it was still left to Operations to decide what practical

* See W. James: *The Eyes of the Navy*, Methuen.

use to make of Room 40's deductions, what to pass out and what to ignore. It was an improvement but it was not the final answer, and some of the faults lay within the Intelligence Division's own organization.

These weaknesses were clearly apparent at least to some of Room 40's more junior staff. Some time after the war two papers† were produced by one or more of them, containing detailed criticism and suggestions which were to prove of great value to the young officer who in 1937 was charged with the creation of our Operational Intelligence Centre. It is therefore worth quoting at some length from them.

The first was entitled 'Naval Traditions and Naval Intelligence'. It began by questioning the fitness of the Executive Officers of the Navy for intelligence duties. 'He is a man of action and never at a loss. He must make up his mind on every occasion instantaneously and without hesitation, and he must be prepared to take on *any* job at a moment's notice. Now just in these characteristics lie his strength and his weakness. They make him the finest ship's officer in the world, but they render him unsuitable for work that requires administrative, organizing (if it implies more than "telling off" parties to work) or reflective capacity, and what is more they *prevent him from realizing that there is any kind of work that he cannot do*'.‡

There were of course exceptions to this rule, but to expect the average Executive officer to change the habits and attitudes drilled into him over ten years or more during a mere two-year appointment to the Admiralty was expecting the impossible. There was however one class of regular officer who was, by the nature of his Service training and experience, already largely fitted for Intelligence duties, and that was the Paymaster.* Other branches specialized; why should not some Paymasters specialize as Intelligence officers? 'The Navy would thus possess a trained permanent

† *Denning Papers*. Alistair Denniston, who subsequently became the head of the Government Code and Cipher School, was probably the author or co-author of these papers.

‡ The italics are those of the writer of the paper.

* Officers of the Accountant Branch used the rank prefix of Paymaster. This Branch was responsible for pay, stores, victualling and clothing and for administrative, secretarial and legal duties in ships and on the staffs of Flag officers. The Branch has now become part of the General List.

staff at sea and in the Admiralty for work which in its very essence requires long training and permanent appointment, and the relief of senior posts would thus no longer entail loss of continuity and efficiency'.

The paper concluded by attacking the evils of the water-tight system, not only in the wartime Intelligence Division, but in the Admiralty as a whole. 'Operations Plans and Intelligence have proved, in time of war, absolutely inseparable. For every activity at sea, intended or under way, the fullest knowledge of enemy habits and movements is necessary. To keep each of these departments in a separate box is therefore to fly in the face of experience. The fullest results can only be achieved by some arrangement which enables those of each department, who are concerned, from different angles it is true, but with work on identical spheres or subjects, to co-operate closely. Only so will the outcome of their labours represent, not merely the individual opinions of specialists but the broad and final verdict, arrived at by weighing every aspect of the problem under consideration in the light of the knowledge which can be brought to bear by each department'.

The second and rather longer paper was headed 'Naval Intelligence Organisation. (Based on an historical analysis of the 1914–18 War)'. It started by pointing out that although much thought had been devoted to analysing the course of the various engagements at sea during the late war, and the reasons for success or failure, the actions of the Admiralty had not been subjected to the same careful scrutiny, and that because its performance could not be compared, as could that of a ship, with an actual or potential opponent, no attempt was made to improve its efficiency. 'Thus from decade to decade, while the shape, size and composition of ships are developing beyond recognition, while the whole theory of naval warfare and every problem connected with it have undergone radical transformation, it is possible for the organizations of the Admiralty, on which in the end depends the efficiency of the Service, to remain almost unaffected by new methods and ideas—simply for lack of ventilation'. And yet modern technology had inevitably resulted in greater power and responsibility being concentrated in the Admiralty at the expense of the Commanders-in-Chief at sea and overseas.

Turning then to the Intelligence Division the paper made a number of serious criticisms of its wartime organization. It seemed incredible to the author (or authors) that up to May 1917 the section which provided the best and most reliable information about the enemy's fleet, Room 40, was not even an integral part of the Intelligence Division. Even after this was achieved, contact between its staff and those of other sections of N.I.D. which dealt with other valuable source material was far from close. For example, it was not until the autumn of 1917, when the unrestricted U-boat campaign was at its height, that the officer responsible for tracking U-boats had access to Room 40's records. The 'German' section of N.I.D., which dealt with captured documents, the interrogation of prisoners of war and so on never did gain full access. It was obvious, at least to the junior officers concerned, that these three sections should be combined into one, but 'a central body, collating and distributing the results of all Intelligence Division activities remained only a dream of those subordinates who had bitter experience of working in blinkers'.

Another criticism was that there were too few staff to deal with the growing number of duties which they had to perform. Originally all decrypted signals were passed through to the Operations Division. Then as the volume grew, only those which seemed of immediate and overriding importance could be dealt with in this manner. To try to overcome this weakness a daily summary, the War Diary, was produced, but this had to be done by the duty watchkeepers in between their other and more pressing tasks, and there was no one who could take an overall view and decide what was really important and what was not essential. Indeed there were no records, no cross indexing, and what was not of immediate operational interest went into the waste paper basket. In consequence, for a long time no study was made of German activity in the Baltic and a priceless source of information on the German Fleet's habits and tactical procedures was completely ignored.

Nevertheless, the authors did recognize that even as early as August 1916 the organization was incomparably better than that of any other power, or of the British War Office, and they summed up as follows: 'Shortly before the Armistice, then, the Intelligence Division was beginning to set its house in order. The section dealing with enemy W/T had become decentralized without loss

of unity, with br   vith routine, cryptography, directionals, the mome   nd cumulative intelligence. The
barriers between th   tions were breaking down, and
a scheme was on foot   their activities in one department. The conception of   ody in the Division to receive
and to distribute between ev   on, and to establish close and
permanent liaison with other   tments inside or outside the
Admiralty, which at this point   that might establish contact
with I.D.—that conception had the conclusion of the Armistice got no further than the minds of subordinates, but in the
analogy of other reforms we may infer that sooner or later the
forces of progress would have triumphed'.

Perhaps reforms would have come, but within a short time of
the conclusion of hostilities Room 40 had been disbanded and the
Naval Intelligence Division reduced, like the sea-going fleet, to a
shadow of its former self. Hall's position of unparalleled and
largely independent power had aroused alarm and jealousy in
many quarters in Whitehall. The Foreign Office, for one, was determined that no future Director of Naval Intelligence should
ever again be capable, as Hall had been, of exerting such influence
on events outside the purely naval sphere. Much of his organization, including those of his brilliant cryptanalysis team who did
not choose to return to their pre-war careers, was therefore transferred to the Secret Service under the control of the Foreign
Office, while the secrecy which had surrounded Room 40 throughout the war continued in peacetime to inhibit any reasoned and
detailed examination of its achievements. By the mid-thirties,
when it began to dawn on the politicians and the public that the
'War to end War' had signally failed to guarantee such a utopian
state of affairs, there was precious little left of an organization
which, despite its shortcomings, had contributed immensely to
the Allied victory and had become the envy of every other informed intelligence department in the world.

For most of the twenties and thirties the Naval Intelligence Division, although technically remaining the senior division of the
Naval Staff, became something of a backwater and appointments
to it were not generally sought after by ambitious officers but were
filled instead, more often than not, by those serving out their last
two or three years in the Navy before retirement. It is not there-

fore very surprising that when, in 1936, the Abyssinian crisis nearly involved Britain in war with Italy, 'Bubbles' James, the Deputy Chief of Naval Staff, with memories of his own two years as head of Room 40 from 1917 to 1918, became seriously concerned about the ability of the Division to cope with an emergency.

He had good reason for alarm. There was little left of Hall's fabulous organization. The Division was now organized into a number of so-called 'Geographical Sections', each dealing with a particular country or group of countries. These sections were, on the whole, reasonably well informed about foreign naval construction and coast defences, but they were neither interested in nor equipped to collect or disseminate information about the organization, dispositions and movements of foreign fleets. So far as this sort of 'operational' intelligence was concerned the situation was very little better than it had been when 'Blinker' Hall's father had been appointed to the newly created post of Director of Naval Intelligence in 1892. A single officer, and he on a part-time basis, formed what was called the Movements Section. His information was quite inadequate and mostly out of date. Large old-fashioned ledgers were used in which to enter in longhand the last known whereabouts of Japanese, Italian and German warships based on reports from Naval Attachés, Consuls and Reporting Officers. These reports were often months old and only once a quarter was an O.U. (Official Use Book), giving the supposed dispositions of foreign navies, issued to the Fleet. The Section did not even subscribe to Lloyds' List, which would at least have provided a daily and highly accurate record of the movements of all the world's merchant ships. Reports of the movements of warships from the Secret Service were virtually non-existent. There were only five Direction Finding Stations in operation, two in the U.K., one in Malta and two in the Far East. The possibility of locating ships at sea was therefore even more remote than that of obtaining up-to-date information about them when they were in port.

Cryptanalysis was, as we have seen, no longer a responsibility of the Naval Intelligence Division of the Navy. It was now the responsibility of what was euphemistically called the Government Code and Cipher School which occupied a building in Broadway off Victoria Street. Fortunately its head, Commander Alistair

Denniston, and a number of his staff were old Room 40 hands: Dilly Knox, a truly brilliant cryptanalyst; Edward Travis†; Nigel de Grey, who had helped to decrypt the Zimmerman Telegram; 'Nobby' Clarke, who had been on duty at the time of Jutland, these and others knew what naval operational intelligence was all about and were anxious to avoid the mistakes and weaknesses which had prevented Room 40 realizing its full potential. Despite this, no real thought seems to have been given to the problem of how such information as might become available in time of war was to be supplied to the fleet and the watertight compartments which had bedevilled Room 40 were if anything tighter now that G.C. & C.S. was both administratively and geographically separated from the Admiralty.

What James wanted was an intelligence centre of the type that Room 40 was gradually becoming in 1918. He could not count on its having the same priceless flow of decrypted enemy signals, but there were other sources of information if only they could be organized and the right men detailed to handle the results. 'There is,' he wrote in a minute to the Director of Naval Intelligence, Rear-Admiral Troup, 'a great field of work with directionals, reports from agents, own ships etc., and if astute men are put on to this work, there is no doubt in my mind that very soon a valuable form of operational intelligence will be built up.' Troup was as handicapped as any other senior officer at that time by the financial restrictions imposed on the three services by the continued enforcement by the Treasury (and the Government) of Winston Churchill's 'Ten Year Rule'.‡ His main concern was to avoid any increase in his establishment which might incur additional expenditure and one can only conclude that it was from a wish to avoid depleting the staff of his existing sections rather than from any conviction that the individual concerned was the ideal man

† Later in the war, Travis was to take charge at Bletchley Park which then specialized in armed services traffic, while Denniston returned to London to take charge of diplomatic and commercial decrypting.

‡ The 'Ten Year Rule', first instituted in 1919 and made self-perpetuating by Churchill in 1928, instructed the Service Departments, when preparing their annual estimates, to do so on the basis that Britain would not be involved in a war with any major power for ten years. It was particularly inhibiting for the Navy since the time required from the commencement of the design of a new major warship until its acceptance into service was, in peace time, anything from six to eight years.

for the job, that, in June 1937, he entrusted the task to a new-comer to the Division, Paymaster Lieutenant-Commander Norman Denning.

Whatever his reasons, Troup could not have made a better choice. Denning came from a remarkable family. Two brothers did not survive the First War but of the three who did one is now Lord Denning, the Master of the Rolls, the second is now Lieutenant-General Sir Reginald Denning, K.C.V.O., K.B.E., C.B., while 'Ned' eventually retired from the Navy in 1965 as Vice-Admiral Sir Norman Denning, K.B.E., C.B., after serving as the twenty-seventh and penultimate Director of Naval Intelligence and Lord Mountbatten's first Deputy Chief of the Defence Staff (Intelligence). He was indeed the 'astute' man demanded by James, a born intelligence officer and, as it turned out, the 'Father' of the O.I.C.

He started work in the summer of 1937 with one clerical assistant, Charlie Pace, no remit except the D.C.N.S.'s minute, no particular experience of intelligence, no office of his own and virtually no organization on which to build. He had, however, a free hand, he was on his own and he did not have to attempt the difficult task of changing existing Admiralty institutions. He was able to start from scratch.

He first spent four weeks at G.C. & C.S., where he received much good advice from Denniston and the others. They could not, however, provide him with much else. Apart from the administrative staff and the cryptanalysts, there was a Naval Section whose duty it was to supply specialist advice on naval subjects and to act as a link with the Admiralty. This section was making attempts to identify and trace the call signs used by Italian and German warships with the help of the Direction Finding (D/F) stations but it was not using the bearings to pinpoint ship positions; indeed with so few stations in operation this would not have been easy. Some decrypting of Italian codes was being achieved, but nothing could be done with the German ciphers. Denning returned to the Admiralty and examined the Room 40 files which were gathering dust in an attic. There he found the two papers mentioned already and he studied them carefully. He began to see the problems with which he was faced even if he could not as yet provide the answers. It was clear that Room 40 had been too secret, too remote for most of its existence from the rest of N.I.D. and from Operations and Plans. But cryptanalysis of foreign naval messages was now the responsibility of an entirely separate and non-naval department. It was not, any longer, even housed in the Admiralty. It had less connection with the day-to-day affairs of the Navy than Room 40 had in 1916. If the regular Executive branch had then distrusted the 'backroom boys', who were after all in daily touch with at least some of the Operations Division officers, what would they now feel about information supplied to them by an anonymous band of 'mystery merchants' who were not controlled by the Navy and whose personalities and capabilities were totally unknown to the Naval Staff? If Room 40 had, for far too long, worked in isolation from the rest of N.I.D., how could intelligence which G.C. & C.S. might supply in the future be co-ordinated with that from other sources received direct in the Admiralty, and how could all this be evaluated and made acceptable to the Naval Staff and the fleet? Equally, the cryptanalysts must not be allowed to work in an ivory tower of their own. They must be kept in touch with the Navy's needs and with the day-to-day realities of its current operations and future plans. How were close relations to be established with Plans and Operations? Where was the central point, into which information from every possible source should be fed, to be established? Should one build on G.C. & C.S.? They had the only nucleus of trained and experienced staff. If not, how was staff for the embryo section to be obtained? How was the new organization, wherever it was located, to establish relationships with the other services, the Army, the R.A.F., the Diplomatic Service, let alone with all those new ministries and departments which, judging by 1914–1918 experience, would soon be established if war did break out? One thing, at least, was quite clear. Intelligence could only be passed to ships at sea by means of the Naval W/T network, a fact, incidentally, which is often ignored by non-naval critics of the Admiralty's handling of intelligence.

By the summer of 1937 the Spanish Civil War was already twelve months old and Denning was being called on to supply intelligence about it before he had had time to develop the requisite organization. The two tasks had to be performed simultaneously. The Nationalists, greatly aided by four submarines transferred to them by Mussolini and by others still manned by Italian crews, had established a partially effective if not strictly legal blockade of Republican ports. The international naval patrols to enforce maritime law and prevent acts of 'piracy', created by the Nyon Agreement, were being strictly applied by the Royal Navy and to a lesser extent by the French, but the Germans and Italians were operating with blatant bias towards Franco. It became of great importance to the British Admiralty to establish the numbers and locations of the 'pirate' submarines and to keep track of the German and Italian ships in Spanish waters. Denning was getting reports from British warships and consuls and reporting officers in both Nationalist and Republican territory but these alone would not supply a complete and up-to-date picture.

Fortunately G.C. & C.S. were having some success in tracing and identifying call signs and with the decrypting of some Italian and Nationalist codes, but they were still not interested in fixing ship positions from bearings received from the Naval D/F stations. Nor was anyone in the Admiralty, for this had been part of Room 40's work and in effect had been transferred to G.C. & C.S. with that organization. Denning quickly arranged for the bearings to be sent to him as well as to Broadway and began attempts at 'D/F plotting'. He also started a modern card index system with proper cross-referencing in place of the old ledgers, made arrangements to take Lloyds' List and keep in close touch with Lloyds, and rigged up a plot on the walls of the office of the Assistant Director of Naval Intelligence in which he had his desk. On this plot he recorded the latest position of all the ships, naval and mercantile, in which he was interested and, as James had predicted, was soon able to build up a much more accurate record of what was going on at sea than had previously been possible.

One of the decrypted messages he received from G.C. & C.S., which bore on the position at the time of an 'incident' of a 'pirate' submarine, brought to a head an important point of principle. The intercepted signal was corrupt and could not be completely unbuttoned, and G.C. & C.S., passed to Denning their interpretation of its meaning, not the original translated text. It so happened that Denning, with up-to-date information from sea available to him in the Admiralty, but not to G.C. & C.S., was able to see that the latter's rendering of the meaning of the signal was wrong. He therefore pressed strongly that if messages were intercepted even in incomplete or incomprehensible form they should nevertheless be sent to him, after translation, exactly as received, and that it should be left to him to evaluate their true significance. At a meeting presided over by Troup and attended by Denniston and Travis, this was approved and thereafter the Operational Intelligence Centre, as Denning's two-man section was now called, became the co-ordinating centre for *all* information from whatever source with full responsibility for analysis and evaluation. This was one valuable principle established.

Early in 1938 further discussions took place about the functions and locations of the Naval Section of G.C. & C.S. The section was largely staffed by naval officers and, apart from being the link between G.C. & C.S. and the Admiralty, seemed to Denning to be the only source of trained Intelligence staff on which he was likely to be able to call. He suggested that, 'the most suitable organization of O.I.C. should be based on the experience of the Intelligence Section of the Naval Section of G.C. & C.S. modified as practical experience in the Admiralty seemed to require'.* He was in fact proposing that it be transferred to the Admiralty. There was however a feeling in certain quarters at G.C. & C.S. that in the event of war they should resume Room 40's full role, and in any case Denning's suggestion would have left the cryptanalysts without their specialist advisers and their direct link with the Admiralty and knowledge of its requirements. For the time being, despite the attractions of having such a body of trained staff in O.I.C., it was decided to leave things as they were, although Denning remained of the opinion that some such move would have to be made if war were to occur.

A little later in 1938 another question of principle had to be settled. As and when intelligence became available how was it to be communicated to the fleet? Was this to remain a prerogative of the Operations Division as it had been in the late war and as it had remained since then, or should it be the responsibility of the department which, it was now agreed, was going to collect, collate and analyse it, namely O.I.C.? Denning, despite some misgivings on the part of Troup, secured the backing of Admiral James and authority was given for O.I.C. to communicate direct not only

* Denning Papers.

with authorities inside and outside the Admiralty but also with the Commanders-in-Chief and ships at sea. At first all such signals had to be taken to and signed personally by the Director of Naval Intelligence but later on signals were originated and despatched by O.I.C. without reference to higher authority. This was one of the most significant, and for O.I.C.'s future success, vital changes in procedure compared with that in force in Room 40. After twenty years a central body to collect and evaluate, and perhaps even more important to promulgate, all information from all sources had at last been established. 'The forces of progress' had indeed triumphed.

The pace was now beginning to quicken and the pressure on Denning to increase. The Nationalists seemed more and more likely to emerge as the victors in Spain, while Germany was supplanting Japan as Britain's most dangerous and probable opponent in the event of war. Troup was reluctantly forced to the conclusion that the two-man staff of O.I.C. must be augmented. 'The officer in charge,' he wrote in a minute to the Second Sea Lord, 'who joined the Division in June last, has been unable to get a single day's leave since joining, until last week, when special arrangements had to be made by borrowing an officer temporarily from G.C. & C.S. . . . This officer reported that the work is more than it is possible for the existing staff to cope with.'† The civil side were however quicker off the mark than the Second Sea Lord. An Assistant Clerical Officer, Miss Gwen Nash, arrived to help Pace, but it was nearly another six months before Lieutenant-Commander Patrick Barrow-Green, recently retired as unfit for sea duty, joined Denning. He then took over Italian, Spanish and Japanese intelligence, leaving Denning in overall control to concentrate on the Germans. Other retired officers, amongst them Lieutenant-Commander Peter Kemp, who was to head the team of D/F plotters throughout the war, were interviewed and earmarked, ready to be called in as soon as a real emergency should arise.

Apart from more staff, the most urgent requirement, for which Denning had been pressing for some time, was for the expansion of the Direction Finding organization. The control and administration of the D/F and Y stations (the latter monitored and

† Denning Papers.

recorded foreign W/T transmissions for G.C. & C.S.) was the responsibility of a combined Signals and Intelligence Section, D.S.D./N.I.D. 9. In its new head, Commander Humphrey Sandwith, Denning found a valuable ally who quickly appreciated the need for an increase in the number of stations so as to improve the network's ability to obtain more reliable ship fixes, and to concentrate on this work rather than on the detection of call signs. This was even more desirable because there were now strong indications that the Germans and Italians would abandon the use of call signs in the event of war. Between them Denning and Sandwith put forward to their respective Directors, and through them to the Board of Admiralty, proposals for far more stations and for a considerable increase in the personnel to man them. It was a time-consuming business and it was not until after Munich that the Treasury could be persuaded to provide sufficient funds for the purchase of more modern equipment, some of it from America. Even by September 1939 only six H/F (High Frequency) and four M/F (Medium Frequency) stations were in operation in the United Kingdom, three in the Mediterranean, and still only two in the Far East. To obtain approval, in the face of the usual Treasury obstruction, for the necessary increase in manpower was an equally slow process. A proposal to establish a Civilian Shore Wireless Service to man the stations and so release regular naval ratings and petty officers to handle the great increase ashore and afloat in naval signalling, was first put forward in May 1938 but was not finally sanctioned until January 1939.‡ Britain was to pay dearly in the first twelve months of the war for this and many other cases of peacetime parsimony, but at least Denning and Sandwith had managed to set the wheels in motion so that some progress could be made.

As the tension over Czecho-Slovakia grew in the late summer of 1938, staff previously earmarked for O.I.C. were called in and the department was put on a war footing. Admiral Troup recognized the importance of O.I.C. and presumably felt that the officer in charge of it should be from the Executive Branch, for he transferred Commander W. L. G. Adams from another section of N.I.D. O.I.C. was as ready as could be expected for the Munich crisis and was able to follow with some accuracy the movements

‡ See McLachlan: *Room 39*. Weidenfeld & Nicolson.

of German ships in Spanish waters and elsewhere. Their dispositions did not indicate that they were anticipating war, at least at sea, and at the last moment the *Deutschland*, for example, had to steam off hurriedly into the Atlantic but was successfully tracked by O.I.C., to the vicinity of Madeira. At the end of September the location of most of the German Fleet and of their larger merchant ships was accurately known (after the crisis was over, Troup was congratulated by the Foreign Office on the reliability of the information supplied by O.I.C. which was apparently in sharp contrast to that emanating from some other organizations).

Munich finally convinced the Government that war with Germany was probable, if not inevitable, and the rearmament programme was at last speeded up. O.I.C. benefited from this loosening of the purse strings, and plans were made for the construction in the Admiralty basement of an underground complex to house O.I.C., a Lower War Room for Operations, the Trade Plot and the War Registry, the civilian-manned unit which received, logged and distributed what was to become a vast flood of incoming and outgoing signals. 'Perfect' communications were called for, with internal distribution of signals by pneumatic tube, and external teleprinter links to Naval Home Commands, Coastal, Bomber and Fighter Commands of the R.A.F. and to G.C. & C.S., the latter direct to O.I.C. This work was only just completed by the time war broke out, indeed faults in the primitive air conditioning system caused a temporary retirement to the old quarters for a few days at the beginning of September. Nevertheless it was a considerable achievement to have planned and created this nerve centre in the short space of seven months, and Admiral Troup must be given a large share of the credit for seeing that O.I.C. was so suitably housed.

In January 1939, Troup was relieved as D.N.I. by Rear-Admiral John Godfrey. Godfrey, like his famous predecessor Hall, who was to give him much useful advice and help, was a practical and successful seaman. He, too, was a somewhat unusual naval officer, a man of wide interests, great energy and determination, an innovator and original thinker and not one of those who considered that what had been good enough for Nelson was necessarily good enough for the Royal Navy of 1939. Less inhibited than Troup had been by Treasury restrictions, he brought new energy and

ASTUTE MEN

drive to the expansion of O.I.C. and the Division as a whole. He was a term mate of Sir Tom Phillips, the new Deputy Chief, or Vice-Chief as he was soon to be called, of Naval Staff, and probably owed his selection to the future First Sea Lord, Sir Dudley Pound, under whom he had served recently in the Mediterranean and previously in Plans Division. Godfrey recognized that he would not be able to adopt the independent position that Hall had achieved, but he saw that the Intelligence Division would almost certainly be confronted with a whole range of problems which had not existed in Hall's day. A tremendous amount of rebuilding would have to be accomplished in a short space of time and, if he was to be free to devote himself to this task, he would have to delegate and devolve in a way that had been quite foreign to 'Blinker' Hall who liked to keep all the threads in his own fingers. Very early on he obtained Phillips' and Pound's backing for this policy and one of the first areas in which it was implemented was in the O.I.C. Adams had, by this time, been relieved there by Commander Geoffrey Colpoys, but Godfrey, realizing the key role O.I.C would have to play, a Division within a Division so to speak, felt that its head must be an officer equal in rank and seniority to the Directors of the Operations, Trade and Anti-Submarine Warfare Divisions with whom he would have to deal, and be capable of holding his own with the Assistant Chiefs of Naval Staff and even with the Vice-Chief. Failing this Godfrey himself would constantly be called on to deal with the day-to-day and hour-to-hour problems which were bound to arise in an organization dealing with 'operational' intelligence.

He recalled that, in 1917, when as a staff officer from the Mediterranean he had been shown, while on a visit to the Admiralty, something of the mysteries of Room 40, he had encountered 'a contemporary of mine, Jock Clayton, who was one of the watchkeepers, so nothing seemed more natural than that he should become the head of O.I.C. . . . A man of unruffled calmness, impossible to rattle and with very shrewd judgement, he had been placed on the retired list as a rear-admiral and had hoped to spend the war at sea as a convoy commodore. He was, therefore, not at all pleased with my idea, which would relegate him to the basement of the Admiralty for the duration; however, he soon became reconciled and gained everybody's confidence, including that of the

First Sea Lord and the V.C.N.S. I leaned on him heavily and was very glad to have as a colleague someone of my own age and standing, and an ex-navigator'.* Clayton was appointed to serve in the rank of Captain as Deputy Director Intelligence Centre (D.D.I.C.), in the event of war. ('Deputy Director' referred to his position in the Intelligence Division as a whole, not to his position in O.I.C.) Clayton spent March in the O.I.C. familiarizing himself with his new appointment. He was well satisfied with the plans that Denning had made and suggested no changes.

The officers recalled for duty at the time of Munich had returned to civil life when the crisis subsided, and Denning and his tiny staff had once more become jacks of all trades, dealing with surface ships and submarines of all nationalities, taking their turn at watchkeeping, analysing reports from the Secret Service and the Foreign Office or trying their hands at D/F plotting as the circumstances demanded. It is true Barrow-Green had tended to specialize on the Italian and Japanese, but he had stood in for Denning and Denning had looked out for him when necessary. Denning realized that further specialization was needed, but that the organization must be a flexible one. Early in 1939, in a paper on the development of O.I.C., he wrote 'The organization suitable for carrying out this most important function (operational intelligence) at its maximum efficiency must—like the British Constitution—grow from experience gained not only in peace but also in war. What was deemed suitable during the last war may not—except perhaps for large scale modifications—be suitable for any large scale war in which we are involved'.† He went on: 'Operational Intelligence depends for its information upon many varied sources, and only careful and unhurried examination by persons steeped in knowledge of certain foreign Naval Forces can properly weigh and assess the relative merits of reports.'‡ In July he put forward plans for the establishment of a team of specialist D/F plotters. 'Experience has shown,' he wrote, 'that it takes at least three months before a D/F plotter can be considered sufficiently experienced to deduce reasonably accurate data from D/F plotting and avoid jumping to false conclusions. . . . Although the

* See Godfrey: *Memoirs*. Typescript.
† Denning Papers.
‡ Ibid.

rudiments of D/F plotting can be acquired in a very brief space of time, owing to the vagaries of H/F D/F bearings, it is from practical experience that the only value can be obtained; otherwise, in fact D/F plotting may give rise to highly dangerous situations'.*
Lieutenant-Commander Peter Kemp was therefore recalled a second time from his job as a leader writer on *The Times*, and set about the task of interviewing and earmarking two or three civilians so that a twenty-four-hour watch system could be brought into force. This was the beginning of a small unit, whose strength never exceeded seven men and women, which as experience was gained and the number of D/F stations was increased would provide some of the best, and at times the only reliable, information available to O.I.C.

Equally important was a decision to create a special section to deal with all information about the movements of enemy submarines which, as Germany was now certain to be the principal enemy, were referred to as 'U-boats' irrespective of whether they were German, Italian or Japanese.

To head this new section, Godfrey again cast back to Room 40 and chose an officer who had performed this task in 1917. Paymaster Captain Thring, although over sixty, was well equipped to start the revived section off on the right lines; he possessed a highly sceptical and analytical mind and a stubborn integrity which was not to succumb to browbeating from superiors in the Admiralty or the optimistic blandishments of juniors afloat. One of the civilian staff earmarked to assist Thring was a rising barrister, Rodger Winn, who was eventually to take over from him and develop the 'art' of U-boat tracking into something undreamed-of in Room 40.

Denning could see that still further specialization was necessary. There was a clear need for better information about potentially hostile merchant ships. Not only would this be required by the fleet in order to enforce the blockade which would certainly be imposed as soon as war broke out, but it might also provide advance indications of a coming emergency. The sudden withdrawal from their normal routes and ports-of-call of a potentially hostile power's principal merchant ships might well be the first sign of a period of tension leading to war. Denning had seen this happen

* Ibid.

when the Japanese seized Shanghai, but during the Munich crisis he had had to rely largely on the services of a member of the staff of the Board of Trade and on information from Lloyds. This had served well enough but O.I.C. must obviously have its own plot and records. Between March and June, 1939, a Merchant Shipping section was established, with a direct telephone line to Lloyds and with close links with the Baltic Exchange and the Board of Trade. By September this plot showed accurately the daily position and movements of all German, Italian and Japanese merchant ships of more than one thousand registered tons, and fully proved its worth as soon as war broke out.

Nor was the air side forgotten. A section was created to act as a link with the Air Ministry's Intelligence Department so as to provide the Fleet with the best available information about the location and movements of the German Air Force. The Navy certainly failed to realize the full implications of the increase in the potential of the aeroplane and under-estimated the role which air power was going to play in the coming war, but it should not be accused of not being 'air minded' (Britain was, in 1939, laying down more aircraft carriers than any other power), and this applied as much to O.I.C. as to the rest of the Navy.

One last development needs to be noted. In accordance with plans made to evacuate various government departments from London in the event of war, G.C. & C.S. moved at the beginning of September to a large country house in Buckinghamshire, Bletchley Park, known thereafter to all in the 'secret' by its initials, B.P. The need, which had exercised Denning's mind for so long, to reinforce O.I.C. by transferring to it the staff of the Naval Section, was, thanks to recruitment for O.I.C. itself, less pressing, but the problem of keeping contact between G.C. & C.S. and O.I.C. was now rendered more difficult by the former's move to Bletchley. It was solved, for the time being, by leaving a small party of the Naval Section, under Lieutenant-Commander M. G. Saunders, in O.I.C. as a liaison section.

In August 1939, therefore, when O.I.C. was mobilized and put on a war footing under the pretext of a large scale 'Coast Defence Exercise', it had a staff of thirty-six men and women. It was headed by Rear-Admiral Clayton serving in the rank of Captain with Commander Colpoys as his Deputy. There were four principal sections, the Italian and Japanese Section under Barrow-Green: the D/F plotters under Kemp: the Submarine Tracking Room under Thring: and the German surface ship section, and other sub-sections, under Denning. The latter, by virtue of his pioneer work and experience was recognized as third in the line of command and automatically assumed responsibility for liaison with all outside departments including B.P.

How far did this meet the request made by Admiral James two and a half years earlier? To what extent had the weaknesses of Room 40 been recognized and overcome? How ready was the new O.I.C. to meet the test of war?

O.I.C formed an integral part of the Intelligence Division with a Deputy Director of the Division in charge of it. It had the backing of the First Sea Lord and the Vice-Chief of Naval Staff. It was the recognized centre for the collection, co-ordination and evaluation of all information bearing on the movements and intentions of enemy maritime forces, whether this information originated with the cryptanalysts at B.P., with agents of the Secret Service, or with reports from warships or merchant ships at sea, or with the aircraft of the R.A.F. flying over it, or with the D/F stations listening to the enemy W/T transmissions. It had authority to communicate direct with any other division in the Admiralty and with commanders-in-chief and the fleet at sea. It was in touch with the R.A.F., the Army and Foreign Office and would establish contact as soon as they were created with new Ministries such as Shipping and Economic Warfare. It was adequately, if not perfectly, housed in an underground complex beneath the Admiralty with an efficient communications system.

All this was a considerable achievement in just over two years. If the Germans, Italians and Russians used the Spanish Civil War for experiments in new methods of land and air warfare (although only the Germans seem to have drawn the right conclusions), the British certainly obtained a less premeditated benefit in the intelligence field. O.I.C.'s existence and its rapid growth were a direct result of that conflict, a factor perhaps as valuable to Britain in its way as the experiences of the Stukas and Panzers of the Condor Legion were to the Germans.†

For this result Denning was largely responsible. James, Troup,

† See Roskill: *Naval Policy between the Wars*. Vol. II. Collins.

Godfrey, Clayton, Adams, Colpoys and Sandwith had all made their contributions, but in its essentials O.I.C. was Denning's 'baby'. That most of the staff were only partially trained and inexperienced was inevitable. Expertise in operational intelligence could only be gained once the shooting started. But the organization was in being, equipped and ready to receive, sift, evaluate and promulgate any information that might come to it. Unfortunately, through no fault of O.I.C.'s, information was the one commodity that, for the next twelve months, was going to be lacking. The sources on which O.I.C. had hoped to rely were not immediately able to supply the intelligence which it had been designed to handle.

2

The First Twelve Months.
A Lean Time

THE SITUATION at sea on September 3, 1939 had many similarities with that prevailing on August 4, 1914. The British Fleet, although smaller than it had been twenty-five years earlier, nevertheless outnumbered the forces at the disposal of Admiral Raeder, the Commander-in-Chief of the German Navy, to an even greater extent, and there could be no question of Germany being able to challenge the British blockade which was immediately imposed.* Hitler had promised Raeder that there would be no war with Britain before 1944, and had he kept this promise the situation might well have been very different, for Raeder had produced a plan, the 'Z' Plan, which would have given him a truly formidable fleet by that date. As things were, all that he could hope to do was to protect his own coasts and to wage a *'guerre de course'* with U-boats, warships, merchant raiders and mines against British shipping in the North Sea and the Atlantic.

Certain factors greatly complicated the task of the Royal Navy and went a good way to reducing the overwhelming superiority which it appeared to possess. Before the war the Chiefs of Staff had warned the Government that, with France as her ally, Britain had the necessary maritime strength to deal with Germany, but

---

* In fact a 'blockade' was not officially imposed to avoid offending the still-neutral Italy and the United States, but as Britain exercised 'belligerent rights', it came to the same thing.

that if Italy joined her Axis partner the situation would become much more difficult, and that Britain certainly would not be able to take on Japan in addition to the other two powers. Even relative to Germany alone, too many of the British ships dated from the First World War and were obsolescent. The Germans, on the other hand, had rebuilt their fleet from scratch, and, ignoring treaty limitations, had considerably exceeded the permitted tonnage for their heavy ships so that they were in many ways superior even to their modern British counterparts, let alone to twenty-year-old veterans like the 'Mighty' *Hood*.

Secondly Britain was then, as she still is today, completely dependent for her existence on being able to maintain the regular and uninterrupted flow of her seaborne trade. On any one day in 1939 there were likely to be upwards of 2,500 British ships at sea 'on their lawful occasions', and in addition many hundreds of foreign vessels carrying goods to or from the ports of the United Kingdom. The initiative rested with the enemy, who, provided he could evade British patrols and reach the Atlantic without being detected, could attack British communications on any ocean in the world.

Far too little attention had been paid in the inter-war years to the problems of trade protection. Over-confidence in the efficacy of the Asdic,† combined with a failure to study thoroughly the lessons of the Imperial German Navy's unrestricted U-boat campaign, had led the Naval Staff to believe that the main threat to trade would come from surface raiders. This threat did indeed materialize but it was, in the end, more easily overcome than the attack by the U-boats, which for the second time in twenty-five years was to bring Britain to the very edge of disaster. The Royal Navy had far too few destroyers and other vessels with the range and endurance necessary if our ocean convoys were to be given even a modicum of protection against the U-boats.

Another grave weakness sprang from the long wrangle with the Royal Air Force about the control of maritime aircraft. The result of this twenty-year argument was that neither service had correctly thought out the true role and capabilities of aircraft in a war at sea, and insufficient attention had been given to their strategic and tactical use and to the development of suitable types of ma-

† A device for detecting submerged submarines using echoes.

chines and of the most effective weapons with which to arm them. It was to take over two years of war to put this right and was to cost thousands of seamen's and airmen's lives.

This, however, was all in the future. In September 1939 France was an ally. The English Channel was impassable to the Germans and, once again a small British army was transported to France without any interference from the enemy. The Germans had only two routes by which to enter or leave the Atlantic: that between Scotland and Iceland, or the Denmark Strait between Iceland and Greenland. Once again the British battle-fleet, the Home Fleet as it was now named, was based on Scapa Flow. Once again a Northern Patrol of cruisers and armed merchant cruisers was rapidly established to intercept any homeward-bound blockade runners and to detect any attempt by the Germans' pocket battleships, which had been specifically designed for commerce raiding, to break out. The Northern Patrol was remarkably successful in enforcing the commercial blockade of Germany, but Admiral Forbes, the Command-in-Chief, required accurate and speedy intelligence if he was to position the Home Fleet so as to ensure an interception of heavy German warships. The situation was exactly the same as it had been in Jellicoe's and Beatty's day except that the 'cutting off' position was now a good deal further north.

If the Navy failed before the war fully to appreciate the precise nature of the threat to British merchant shipping that was going to develop, at least it did not make the mistake of under-rating the value of the convoy system. In 1917, this had been forced on a reluctant Board of Admiralty both by pressure of events and by Lloyd George, the Prime Minister. In 1939, it was brought into force immediately, but many months were required before all ships considered suitable could be included, and indeed throughout the war ships over a certain speed (fifteen knots for most of the time, but at one period as little as thirteen knots) were excluded and continued to run independently. Owing to the shortage of flotilla craft with sufficient endurance, convoys could only be given anti-submarine escort to a point some three hundred miles west of Ireland. They then continued with only an ocean escort, usually a single armed cruiser (A.M.C.), while the anti-submarine escort waited and met an inward bound convoy and brought it back to Britain. But, to start with, the U-boats themselves could not operate far to the west, so this was not of such great importance. Here also accurate information about the U-boats' whereabouts and future movements would have been of vital importance.

It must be admitted at once that O.I.C. was not over-successful for the first twelve months of the war in providing the intelligence for which it had been created. The basic reason for this failure did not lie so much with any fault in its own organization as in the inadequacy at this time of all the sources of its information, which, it must be remembered, it did not itself control. Virtually nothing except some very tentative studies of the patterns of German W/T traffic was available from Bletchley. The D/F organization was still far from complete and the type and scale of both surface and U-boat warfare was such that wireless traffic was restricted and gave little scope for many fixes. Agents' reports were equally scanty. The best of these came from a black market dealer in silk stockings with a contact in the German Naval Post Office, who from time to time was able to give the address of mail for certain ships, thus providing some fragmentary clues to their whereabouts. It was very hard, if not impossible, to distinguish deliberately planted rumours from scraps of genuine information, and the débâcle at Venloo, when the British agents Best and Stephens were seized by the Gestapo, effectively disrupted the Secret Service's Dutch and German network.

What might have saved the day would have been regular, extensive and efficient air reconnaissance. This also was conspicuous by its absence. Aerial reconnaissance was not, of course, a new conception; indeed it was the very first use to which armies and navies had put aircraft in the First World War, and reconnaissance for the fleet has remained one of the prime functions of maritime aircraft right up to the present day. On the Western Front, in 1918, hundreds of aircraft were engaged on photographic reconnaissance duties and the art of interpreting the pictures obtained was developing fast. In the inter-war years, the R.A.F. was preoccupied with maintaining its independence from the other two services and was starved of money. Photographic reconnaissance, if not entirely forgotten, had a very low priority. The aircraft in use for this purpose at the outbreak of war was the

Blenheim. It had neither the speed nor the range to enable it to penetrate far over enemy territory and heavy losses were soon being incurred. Moreover the cameras and film in use were equally unsuitable, and modern equipment and trained personnel to interpret such photographs as could be secured were also lacking. With considerable foresight however, not long before the war the Secret Service had set up a clandestine organization, run by an extraordinary character called Sidney Cotton, to operate an ostensibly private aircraft, a Lockheed 12A, in flights to and from Germany. The Lockheed was fitted with hidden cameras and Cotton's unit obtained much useful information, including excellent photographs of the German ships at Wilhelmshaven only two days before war was declared. Three weeks later Cotton's small organization was incorporated into the R.A.F., but it remained highly secret and for months encountered much obstruction and jealousy from certain sections of the Air Staff. Cotton was a lone wolf, impatient of any vestige of red tape and normal service routine, but he was also in his own way a genius, and he soon saw that neither his own Lockheed nor the R.A.F. Blenheims were suitable for photographic reconnaissance work under wartime conditions. He decided that stripped-down, unarmed Spitfires were the only type of aircraft then available which could give results. Spitfires were, of course, in desperately short supply and every one was urgently needed by Fighter Command, but after many battles with the Establishment he managed to obtain a few of these machines. He also arranged for the photographs he took to be processed and interpreted by a small private company, the Aircraft Operating Company, of Wembley, which had specialized in aerial survey work for commercial firms before the war and possessed the only photogrammetric machine for studying and measuring the details of aerial photographs in the country.

Denning, who knew all about Cotton's activities, immediately realized that here was the only hope of securing photographic cover of the enemy's ports and gave the little organization all the support that he personally could supply and also secured for it the interest and backing of the Naval Staff. Unfortunately Cotton's successes vastly increased the demands which were made on him, and many of his inadequate resources had to be devoted to meeting the needs of the Army and the R.A.F. in France, needs which were just as pressing as those of the Navy. It was a considerable time before another set of pictures of Wilhelmshaven could be obtained, and just as there were too few aircraft, so were there too few interpreters. The principal expert in the Aircraft Operating Company was Michael Spender, a brother of the poet, Stephen, and of the artist, Humphrey. He welcomed any help which Denning could give him in identifying German naval ships and Denning himself soon became highly proficient at this new art. An interesting example of the experience and skill required in this field occurred early in 1940, when Bomber Command's own interpreters thought they had detected a concentration of U-boats in the port of Emden. Permission to attack this target had to be sought from the War Cabinet, and fortunately, before it was granted, the First Sea Lord asked for N.I.D.'s views, since Emden seemed a most unlikely base for U-boats. Denning was despatched post-haste to examine the photographs and was quickly able to establish that the alleged U-boats were in fact river barges and that what at first appeared to be their conning towers was nothing more than the crew's washing hanging out to dry.

It is fair to say that the establishment of Cotton's small unit and its subsequent growth into one of the most potent intelligence weapons of the war owed a very great deal to the support and encouragement of the Admiralty. The Air Staff were at first so reluctant to admit that their own methods were inadequate that they refused for many months to recognize the existence of the Aircraft Operating Company and the value of its techniques. It was only when Churchill, alerted by O.I.C. to the danger that the unit would collapse unless given official status, threatened to take the whole thing over for the Admiralty that it, too, was finally incorporated into the R.A.F. Although progress after this was steady, the shortages and difficulties which beset every organization at the beginning of the war were such that it was not until early 1941 that the Navy's needs for regular and extensive photographic reconnaissance could be met satisfactorily. Another incident from the beginning of 1940 illustrates the difficulties then being encountered. One of the earliest photographs of Wilhelmshaven showed the battlecruiser *Scharnhorst* in dock. Denning immediately informed Sir Charles Forbes, the C.-in-C. Home Fleet, who was much concerned about the lack of information of the whereabouts of the major German ships, that she had been located in Wilhelmshaven, but he did not say that she was in dock. Not long afterwards he had to accompany the D.N.I., Godfrey, to Scapa for a conference with Forbes about the paucity of information being supplied to him. During the course of the meeting Denning produced the photographs in question and was sternly rebuked by the Commander-in-Chief for not having previously told him that *Scharnhorst* was in dock and so out of action. Denning had to point out this was an isolated set of photographs: it could be seen that the dock was flooded but there was no means of determining whether the battlecruiser had just docked or, on the contrary, was on the point of undocking.

The very first photographs of the German Navy's other principal base, Kiel, were not secured until April 7, 1940. They showed the harbour full of shipping and the neighbouring airfields crowded with aircraft. What were revealed were, of course, the German preparations to invade Denmark and Norway, which they did only two days later, but without previous evidence with which to make a comparison it was impossible for the interpreters to say whether the situation was a normal or completely abnormal one.‡ To anticipate a little further it was not until July 1941, when P.R.U.* secured its first Mosquito, that any photographic reconnaissance of the eastern Baltic became possible. Only complete and frequent coverage of every enemy port could show whether all major units were accounted for in Home waters or whether one or more of them was missing and must be presumed to be at sea on operations.

Nor was it only P.R.U. which suffered from shortage of suitable planes. The Admiralty had from the outset been concerned about the possibility of the German pocket battleships escaping into the Atlantic. Provision had been made in the pre-war joint Admiralty/ Coastal Command plans for regular air patrols to be flown between Scotland and Norway. At the outbreak of war however the aircraft allocated to these duties had not the range to reach the Norwegian coast and an attempt had to be made to fill this gap with patrols by submarines. Even when longer-range planes did become available, it was soon obvious that the difficulties of locat-

‡ See Constance Babington Smith: *Evidence in Camera*. Chatto and Windus.
* Photographic Reconnaissance Unit.

ing ships or even of flying at all in the bad weather of the autumn and winter had been considerably under-estimated.

The first two German ships to reach the Atlantic were the pocket battleships *Graf Spee* and *Deutschland*. They did so undetected before war was declared, and because of British inability to carry out photographic reconnaissance (or indeed visual reconnaissance) of their home bases, the Admiralty remained ignorant of their presence on the sea lanes until October 1. Even then it took another three weeks before O.I.C. could be sure from their victim's distress messages and from reports from survivors that two rather than one raider were involved. The *Deutschland* was actually back home again for several weeks before this fact became known to O.I.C. In the case of the *Graf Spee*, O.I.C. was able to contribute practically nothing to her location and eventual destruction. The D/F organization, which at this time lacked any stations in the South Atlantic or Indian Ocean, failed to obtain fixes of the very few signals which she did make, and the only positive clues to her whereabouts were the occasional distress messages from some ships she attacked. The Royal Navy was practically back in the age of Nelson, when all the Admiralty could do was to station hunting squadrons in likely strategic areas and then leave it to the Commander-in-Chief or senior officer on the spot to form the right appreciation and act accordingly. It had not proved a bad system then, and naval officers had not lost all their intuitive skills in the intervening one hundred and forty years. Commodore Harwood accurately forecast Captain Langsdorff's moves and was waiting for him when he appeared off the River Plate on December 13, 1939.

Another sortie by the Germans, this time by the battlecruisers *Scharnhorst* and *Gneisenau* at the end of November of that year, had shown up further weaknesses in the British intelligence gathering system. The German intention was to attack the Northern Patrol of cruisers and armed merchant cruisers. No inkling of their presence at sea was obtained until they encountered the unfortunate A.M.C. *Rawalpindi* in the Denmark Strait. Despite a courageous resistance she was soon overwhelmed but not before she had managed to make an enemy report accurately identifying her opponent as a battlecruiser. Unfortunately she then corrected this to 'pocket battleship', which fitted in with O.I.C.'s faulty appreciation that this must be *Deutschland* attempting to return to Germany, an event which had, in fact, occurred eight days previously. *Rawalpindi*'s mistaken identification was understandable in view of the similarity of the silhouettes of the large German ships, but it greatly added to the confusion and hindered the attempts of the C.-in-C. of the Home Fleet to intercept the enemy. To make matters worse, the nearest British cruiser to *Rawalpindi*, *Newcastle*, had intercepted her signals and promptly closed her position. She sighted *Scharnhorst* while she was stopped and picking up survivors, but, no doubt influenced by *Rawalpindi*'s second signal, also reported her as a pocket battleship. She endeavoured to shadow the Germans as they hurriedly made off, but as no British ships were at that time fitted with radar, she lost them in a rain storm and in the event they successfully made their escape back to Germany without their true identities being established. The Director of Naval Intelligence later wrote: 'It was of vital importance to discover the name or at least the class of ship which had sunk her [*Rawalpindi*]. Our only sources were the survivors. The senior one—a Chief Petty Officer—was sent to the Admiralty and, after being questioned several times *en route*, was sent for by Admiral Pound, who asked a series of leading questions. By the time he reached N.I.D. the man was confused and, as an objective witness, useless. So many suggestions had been made to him in the meantime that the mental image of the shape and size of the German ship had become blurred.'† One may well ask why the First Sea Lord, with all his grave preoccupations, decided to take over a role which would have been much better performed by a junior member of the Intelligence Division. All in all, it was a very unsatisfactory performance from O.I.C.'s point of view. The departure of the German ships had not been detected, they had been wrongly identified twice, the shadowing cruiser had been unable to maintain contact, and then finally the last chance of correct identification had been thrown away by ham-fisted interrogation of a survivor.

While O.I.C. was floundering due to lack of reliable sources of information, Admiral Raeder was being well-served by his Intelligence Department. The German Air Force was not preoccupied, as it was soon to be, with a multiplicity of calls on its services. It

† See Godfrey: *Memoirs*. Typescript.

had a number of types of long-range reconnaissance aircraft well-suited to the task of keeping watch on the Home Fleet, while the R.A.F. were still finding it difficult to provide sufficient fighters to shoot them down or drive them off. Admiral Forbes complained bitterly that all his movements seemed to be faithfully reported to the enemy while he himself was almost completely in the dark. He had just cause for complaint, but it was not only the G.A.F. who were responsible. The German Navy had become very conscious in the inter-war years of the work of Room 40 and of the immense advantage which this had conferred on Jellicoe and Beatty. They had set up their own purely naval cryptanalysis service, the B.Dienst, which had made a determined attack on British naval codes and ciphers. In this task they were greatly aided by the Admiralty who, conservative as always, refused to accept proposals originated by Lord Louis Mountbatten that the Royal Navy should adopt a machine cipher as the Germans themselves had done and as the R.A.F. and the American Navy were in the process of doing.

Instead we clung to an outdated, cumbersome and, as was to be proved, insecure system of manual cipher tables. This in itself might not have been fatal, but at the time of the Abyssinian crisis elementary rules of signal security were ignored, and the B.Dienst was able to penetrate the Royal Navy's main operational and administrative ciphers. By the outbreak of war the Germans were decrypting a great many signals, but the actual process of doing this took time and could not always be completed quickly enough for operational use to be made of the results. Nevertheless the Germans were able to read a sufficient quantity of British naval W/T traffic to give them a clear picture of most movements in the North Sea and Northern Approaches until changes were made in August 1940. These changes then defeated them for a time, but, as we shall see, they had further successes which were of enormous benefit to them in the Battle of the Atlantic up to the middle of 1943. It should, however, be emphasized that cryptanalysis must be swift to be of real operational use and according to Dönitz only a fairly small proportion of the British signals reached the Germans sufficiently quickly for this purpose, although all of them added to their knowledge and understanding of British tactics and strategy. However, if, by the third year of

the war, the British were beginning to have a distinct advantage—
not only in the field of cryptanalysis but in all other areas of operational intelligence, it is certainly true that in 1940 the boot was
very much on the other foot, and O.I.C. was groping blindly,
while its opponents, for much of the time, had a pretty clear idea
of 'what was at the other side of the hill'.

At the same time, of course, that Admiral Forbes and the Admiralty were trying to grapple with the problems presented by the
German surface ships, another and potentially more serious threat
was developing, the U-boat war. At this time neither of the
Naval Staffs fully appreciated that Germany's greatest hope of
severing Britain's communications with the outside world and so
starving her into submission, lay, as it had done in the First
World War, with the submarine arm. The Flag Officer U-boats
[Befehlshaber der U.boote], Commodore, soon Rear-Admiral, Karl
Dönitz had no illusions, but his views had not prevailed with the
big ship enthusiasts like Raeder nor with Hitler, who was
enthralled by the prestige conferred by the possession of large battleships. Although the German Navy had only officially begun to
rebuild its U-boat fleet in 1935, they had, by 1939, almost reached
parity with the Royal Navy and had 56 boats in commission.
Dönitz, however, estimated that he needed 300 U-boats to achieve
his purpose: even the Z Plan only provided for 250. Nevertheless,
hoping that the war would only be a short one and that Britain
did not really mean business, Dönitz immediately made a big
effort and no fewer than 39 of his total strength of 56 were at sea
and waiting in the North Sea and the Atlantic on September 3,
1939. They began by reaping a rich harvest, largely from ships
which it had not yet been possible to gather into convoy, but the
initial effort could not be maintained, and by January 1940 the
number of operational boats had declined, due to sinkings and
training requirements, to 32. Of these 32 between one half and
one third would, at any one time, be in port between cruises. Of
those at sea a further proportion would be proceeding to or returning from patrol, so that no more than half a dozen to a
dozen, occasionally only a couple, would actually be in their designated operational areas. It was a pitifully small number and it was
a measure of British unpreparedness that they were able to
achieve as much success as they did.

Throughout this time the U-boats were operating in what was then considered to be the normal and conventional manner, that is to say independently of each other and in general attacking their victims submerged. The submarine in the first half of the 1940s did not greatly differ from its predecessors of 1918. When submerged it depended for propulsion on its electric batteries which gave it a maximum speed for a very short time of perhaps ten knots, and an economical speed of considerably less than this. On the surface its diesels would drive it along, and also recharge its batteries, at seventeen or in some cases twenty knots, but it was then at its most vulnerable to attacks from enemy warships, aircraft and even the single gun of defensively equipped merchant ships. The U-boats therefore required particularly precise information about the whereabouts of their prey if they were to be able to reach a suitable position for attack submerged. With so few boats at his disposal and with the additional limitations imposed on them by the long voyage from Germany round Scotland to the Atlantic and back, Dönitz started by confining his operations largely to the North Sea and the immediate approaches to the British Isles north west and south west of Ireland. In the latter areas air reconnaissance was difficult for the Germans and the B.Dienst were not, as yet, able to provide him with a large amount of information. There were, however, ample pickings in the early days from unescorted ships approaching or leaving the focal points, and in addition minelaying, both by U-boats, and then, when the new magnetic mine was ready, by the G.A.F., also caused Britain heavy losses.

The Submarine Tracking Room found the situation as difficult to deal with as their colleagues in the rest of O.I.C. concerned with surface ships. Because of their methods of operating, the U-boats did not have to indulge in excessive signalling and the opportunities of fixing their positions by D/F were few. Coastal Command was still starved of suitable aircraft, and one of the lessons of the previous campaign, namely that convoys given air escort were virtually immune from attack by U-boat, had not been appreciated because the records and statistical analyses dating from 1918 had not been studied by the Naval Staff. Coastal Command crews—and this was at least as much the fault of the Naval as of the Air Staff—had not been sufficiently trained in anti-submarine operations, nor were they provided with effective anti-submarine weapons. Successful attacks were few, and false reports, not only from aircrew but from merchant ships and coastwatchers, of the presence of a U-boat were frequent. Surface forces wasted energy on sweeps of empty sea and were unduly optimistic in their claims of 'kills'.

Nevertheless Thring had started the war with an almost accurate estimate of the Germans' total strength, and he had far too sceptical and shrewd a mind to allow himself to be misled for long by doubtful reports. His views carried much weight with the Assessment Committee which met to decide the claims of Britain's surface and air forces to have destroyed U-boats. This soon brought the Director of the Anti-Submarine Warfare Division, Captain Talbot, and the D.N.I., Godfrey, who were responsible for the findings of the Assessment Committee, into direct conflict with the First Lord, Winston Churchill. Churchill refused to accept their figures of U-boats sunk and broadcast his own highly optimistic version of our killings. Nor would he accept D.N.I.'s forecast of the future growth of the U-boat fleet. We now know that Godfrey and Talbot were right and that Churchill was wrong. Captain Talbot's abrupt posting to sea (which may in the end have been to his advantage) was certainly due in part to this disagreement and is an example of the fate that can befall those refusing to bow to a superior's wishful thinking. As for Godfrey, this was not the only brush he was to have with Winston, and may well have been one of the reasons for the astounding, not to say shameful, lack of any recognition of his immense services during the war, an omission which was, incidentally, deeply resented by every member of the Intelligence Division. Churchill went on to forbid the circulation of the reports of the Assessment Committee to anyone on the Naval Staff or in the fleet other than himself, the First Sea Lord and the Vice-Chief of Naval Staff, a perfectly incredible edict which Admiral Pound does not seem to have contested.‡

Thring, however, continued to base his calculations in the Tracking Room on what he considered to be the truth. With the scanty amount of information available and the nature and scale

‡ See McLachlan: *Room 39*. Weidenfeld & Nicolson, and Marder: *From the Dardanelles to Oran*. Oxford University Press.

of the U-boat operations at the time, he and his as yet inexperienced staff could do little more than record, and promulgate as necessary, events as they occurred. There was no attempt to forecast what the U-boats would do next, but at least it was possible to give a reasonable estimate of the weight of attack likely to be encountered in any given area.

Then, in April 1940, came the Norwegian campaign. Three factors should be borne in mind when considering Britain's failure to predict the German move. Firstly all attention was concentrated on her own plan to mine the Norwegian Leads, the inshore channels up the coast which were much used by German shipping carrying Swedish iron ore from Narvik to Germany. Moreover, insufficient thought seems to have been given to German reactions to this minelaying. In addition the Admiralty and the Home Fleet were preoccupied with the possibility of a breakout by the German battlecruisers or pocket battleships into the Atlantic, and any signs of activity on their part which were belatedly detected were associated in the Admiralty's mind with such a move, rather than with an operation which even Hitler's own professional advisers considered foolhardy in the extreme. Thirdly, throughout the winter there had been a spate of reports of imminent German attacks on the Low Countries or France, which had in the end all come to nothing. It was, therefore, not surprising if rumours of an invasion of Norway tended to be treated by all the Allied Intelligence agencies with a certain amount of scepticism. Above all, the inability until only two days before the attack was launched to secure any photographs of Kiel and the Western Baltic meant that O.I.C. was denied the one certain and irrefutable proof of what was afoot.

Despite all this some clues were available. Reports to the Secret Service and the Foreign Office did refer to an attack on Denmark and Norway, but inter-service co-ordination of intelligence was still extremely poor and no serious attention seems to have been given to them by any of the departments concerned. At B.P., a young Cambridge undergraduate who had recently joined the staff of the Naval Section, Harry Hinsley, had been studying German naval W/T patterns. He noticed that there was exceptionally heavy activity on the main Baltic frequency and also that an entirely new frequency had been brought into force. It did not occur to him that this presaged the invasion of Norway, but it did seem that something unusual was happening. He discussed this new situation with the B.P. liaison section in O.I.C. under Saunders, which also studied W/T intelligence, but no firm conclusions were drawn and the matter does not appear to have been taken any further. Had Hinsley's findings been considered in conjunction with the other reports, with the results of the photographic reconnaissance of Kiel and with the fact, which had just become known, that after an exceptionally hard winter the Belts were at last free of ice, it is possible that the right conclusions would have been drawn and that a general warning would have been issued.

It is true that on midday on April 7, the fleet was informed of the receipt of reports regarding German intentions, which were in fact accurate, but unfortunately this signal was qualified by the statement that 'all these reports are of doubtful value and may well be only a further move in the war of nerves.'* No special action was taken by the Naval Staff or the Home Fleet. It is less easy to understand why, in the light of this signal, O.I.C. failed to see the significance of the scene revealed by the Kiel photographs when these subsequently became available.

The truth of the matter is probably that O.I.C. could only accept the estimates of other organizations as to the probability of diplomatic and secret service reports, which it received. O.I.C. was not yet sufficiently sure of itself to form an independent judgement and sound a general alarm. It failed, but it was not alone in this failure. None of the allied Intelligence agencies predicted the German move with sufficient certainty to have the possibility accepted by the High Command, and the Norwegians themselves, with perhaps more tangible evidence of the moves being made against them, refused, in many cases even as German troops were landing on their territory, to believe what was happening.

The failure to get and give advance warning of the German invasion fleet gravely affected the whole campaign. It meant that the Home Fleet was not in a position to strike at the enemy when he was most vulnerable, while his ships were at sea full of troops and equipment or disembarking them in Norwegian ports without

---

* This report seems to have been handled by N.I.D. 1, the German Geographical section, not by O.I.C.

the benefit of fully organized air cover. Although improvements in the extent of and the speed with which intelligence was supplied to the Fleet were made during the next two months, Britain continued to suffer from O.I.C.'s inability to get warning of sorties by the German heavy ships and this contributed to a major disaster, the loss of the aircraft carrier *Glorious* which was evacuating R.A.F. fighter squadrons from Norway. The Germans unaware, for once, that the British were actually evacuating the whole of the country, had planned an attack on Harstad and the convoys running to it. Once again the *Scharnhorst* and *Gneisenau* succeeded in leaving Kiel without the Home Fleet being alerted. On this occasion, Hinsley's study of German W/T traffic had persuaded him that heavy ships were probably at sea. He spoke direct to Clayton and Denning, but his studies were still very tentative and his conclusions could not be confirmed from other sources. W/T intelligence on its own was no more than a straw in the wind. To alert the Home Fleet on this insubstantial and untested basis, and perhaps cause it to proceed in quite the wrong direction seemed to be running too great a risk, and in the end it was again decided to take no action. The *Glorious* had been given an escort of only two destroyers, a decision which is open to criticism. Once she was sighted by the battlecruisers her doom was sealed. Neighbouring troop convoys and the cruiser bringing the King of Norway to England were extremely lucky to escape a similar fate. Certainly, greater efforts to provide stronger protection for all these ships would have had to be made if it had been suspected that the German heavy units were at sea.

There were far too many mistakes made at all levels by those responsible for the conduct of the Allied campaign to lay all the blame for defeats on poor intelligence. Moreover, as already noted, sources of intelligence were lacking, co-ordination between different intelligence organizations was weak, and O.I.C. was not alone in failing to predict what was happening. Nevertheless if O.I.C. is to be accorded its due share of praise for its subsequent successes, it is only right that it should be criticized for an inadequate performance at this time.

By contrast, Raeder's daring and well-executed plans were very materially assisted by first class intelligence. German air reconnaissance functioned well, while the service given by the B.Dienst was superb. It was, declares one German historian, 'worth more to their side than a score of heroic deeds rewarded with high decorations'.† Again and again the B.Dienst supplied the German Naval Staff with accurate information about the movements and location of British forces, and undoubtedly saved the enemy more than once from disaster.

Well before the end of the Norwegian campaign the storm had broken on the Western Front and the Panzers were sweeping cross the Low Countries and France. The German Navy suffered such losses and damage off Norway that it was unable to play any effective part in what was almost entirely a land battle. Not only were all its major surface ships out of action and the greater part of its destroyer flotillas sunk, but its U-boats were virtually immobilized by the discovery that the magnetic firing mechanism of their torpedoes was defective. There was therefore a lull so far as German operations at sea were concerned, while Britain's attention was concentrated on Dunkirk, the evacuation of the French Atlantic ports, the entry of Italy into the war, the capitulation of France and, finally, on Operation Sea Lion, the German plan to invade Great Britain.

In some ways the intelligence problem became simpler. The distances involved were far shorter and more aircraft for reconnaissance purposes were available. Photographing the Dutch, Belgian and Northern French ports remained a highly dangerous operation, but at least it could be achieved with ten times the frequency of sorties over Wilhelmshaven or Kiel. (Coverage of these German ports was still so scanty that it was several weeks before we learned the true extent of the damage the German Navy had incurred.) On the other hand, the gradual collection of hundreds of tugs, barges and other small craft in every port from Ymuiden down to Le Havre could not be concealed and was faithfully recorded from day to day and week to week. A Joint Services Intelligence Committee, under the Chairmanship of Commander Colpoys, assisted by Denning, met in O.I.C. at eleven o'clock each morning to assess the state of the German preparations. This was a most welcome sign of improved inter-service co-operation. The

† See Caius Bekker: *Hitler's Naval War*. Macdonald.

Committee, in addition to photographic reconnaissance reports, the interpretation of which was now far more accurate, also had the benefit of information provided by a considerable volume of decrypted G.A.F. signals. The Germans' move to Belgian and French aerodromes had resulted in a great increase in W/T traffic and B.P. had been quick to take advantage of this.

By the end of September, very soon after Hitler had in fact taken his decision, the Committee was able to report to the Chiefs of Staff that the invasion was 'off', at least until next spring. The authorities however, seem to have been curiously reluctant to accept this view, and anti-invasion precautions, including in particular the retention in the Channel and on the East Coast of destroyers and cruisers desperately needed elsewhere, were maintained longer than would now seem to have been justified.

The reasons for O.I.C.'s comparative lack of success during the first twelve months of the war have been mentioned at the beginning of this chapter. Basically the three sources on which it should have been able to rely were, for various reasons, not able to produce 'the goods'; neither cryptanalysis nor air reconnaissance nor D/F was able to give the necessary information about German naval movements and intentions. Nevertheless, there were some encouraging features by the end of this period. O.I.C.'s staff were gaining experience and, in Denning's words, were establishing 'norms' against which any significant deviations could be assessed. The department was ready to shift into top gear as soon as more fuel in the shape of first class information could be fed into it. The Commanders-in-Chief and the Naval Staff in the Admiralty were becoming used to dealing with it and were realizing that, whatever its limitations, it was the best instrument to hand. More and more decisions were being taken by the operational authorities in the O.I.C. itself in the light of the information displayed on its plots and on the advice tendered by Clayton, Denning and Thring. Better liaison had been established with Coastal, Bomber and Fighter Commands of the R.A.F., with the Flag Officer Submarines, and with those Commanders-in-Chief responsible for anti-invasion operations. The expansion of the D/F organization was continuing and the need for better photographic coverage of German ports was now fully recognized even if it could not yet be entirely met. There was still a long way to go, but the benefits of Denning's pre-war planning were beginning to be felt.

3

October 1940–May 1941.
Signs of Improvement

THE ABANDONMENT of Operation Sea Lion was greeted by the German Naval Staff with much relief. They were now able to concentrate all their efforts on an attack on British sea communications. By the end of October 1940 they had six armed merchant raiders at sea; two in the Atlantic, two in the Indian Ocean and two in the Pacific. Although the heavy cruiser *Hipper* had attempted to break out into the Atlantic but had to return to Germany with engine defects, the pocket battleship *Scheer* was just passing through the Denmark Strait for a long raiding cruise. The battlecruisers *Scharnhorst* and *Gneisenau* had almost completed repairing the damage they had incurred off Norway, while the new battleship *Bismarck* and the *Hipper*'s sister ship *Prinz Eugen* were nearly ready to start working up in the Baltic. In the Channel and on the East Coast motor torpedo boats, or E-boats,* were attacking British convoys nightly. The U-boats, of which only 27 were operational at this time, although a further 37 were engaged on training or trials, were established in their new bases on the French Atlantic coast; this greatly reduced the time needed to proceed to and from patrol and so to some extent compensated for their small numbers. They were in the process of being reinforced

* 'Enemy boats', a misleading term whose use was vainly opposed by Denning who wished to adopt the German designation, S-boats, 'Schnell' or speed boats.

by 27 Italian U-boats, but these were to prove far less effective than their allies. The offensive by the U-boats and E-boats was also supplemented by the German Air Force, whose new long-range Focke-Wulf Condor bombers were based at Bordeaux and Stavanger whence they could reach out into the Atlantic, while their dive bombers from Northern France and the Low Countries concentrated on shipping in the English Channel and the North Sea. The G.A.F. also continued to mine British ports and bomb British harbours. It was not surprising that merchant shipping losses for the month amounted to no less than 103 ships totalling 443,000 tons.

On the British side, resources were severely stretched. Apart from losses and damage incurred in the Norwegian campaign and in evacuating the Army from France, flotilla vessels and aircraft urgently needed to escort convoys were still being retained on anti-invasion patrols, so that many ocean convoys had only a single destroyer as anti-submarine escort. Strong reinforcements of all classes of ships and of aircraft had to be sent to the Mediterranean to face an actively hostile Italy and a resentful, if neutral, France. Merchant shipping could no longer be routed through the Mediterranean but had to make the long haul round the Cape, as did the precious convoys of troops and war materials, destined for General Wavell in Egypt, which had to be given powerful escorts for their whole voyage. Troops also had to be escorted from India, Australia, New Zealand and Canada, and the threat, now becoming apparent, from the enemy's armed merchant raiders, not to mention the probability of a breakout by his heavy ships, meant that no area in the world could be considered safe. Coastal Command's still woefully limited resources were quite inadequate to give advance warning of invasion and at the same time to guard against break-outs between Scotland and the Denmark Strait and to escort convoys. It is true that the first of the new battleships and aircraft carriers, *King George* V and *Formidable* were about to join the fleet and that the old destroyers, received from the Americans in exchange for bases, were starting to come into service after re-equipping, as were some of the new anti-submarine corvettes, but it remained an unpleasant fact that there were neither sufficient ships, aircraft nor trained and experienced men for all the tasks which the Navy and Coastal Command were being called upon to perform. Could O.I.C. improve on its past performance and compensate at least in part for some of these deficiencies?

If we turn first to the armed merchant raiders, the problem was certainly not a simple one. The Germans had given considerable thought before the war to the question of the best type of merchant ship for conversion and the most efficient means of employing them. Unlike the British, who took up large passenger liners, the German ships were of medium size, fruit ships or cargo liners of some four to nine thousand tons, with a maximum speed of eighteen knots but a large radius of action. They were very well equipped, with modern guns (which could outrange the old weapons supplied to the British A.M.C.s) torpedo tubes, mines, one or two seaplanes and in some cases forty-foot motor torpedo boats. They were adept at disguising themselves as British, or more often Allied or neutral merchantmen, and although commanded by regular naval officers, usually had a number of reserve officers from the Merchant Marine well qualified to advise on merchant navy practice. Their instructions were to avoid action with warships, not to attack convoys, and to be content with small gains. They changed their areas of operations skilfully and frequently and relied for effect on the considerable disruption which their sudden appearance would cause to the regular flow of the large number of independently routed British and Allied ships in distant waters where, at that time, the U-boats could not penetrate. They maintained excellent wireless silence and, when occasionally they did report their successes to Germany, they immediately moved away many hundreds of miles. On some occasions they were content to lie virtually motionless in some remote part of the ocean, carrying out a self-refit, refuelling or just waiting for the heat to die down. They were supported by an efficient and well controlled organization of tankers and supply ships and were also able now and again to make use of the cargoes of their prizes. It was very much a reversion to the old days of privateers, and as in Nelson's time, Britain did not have sufficient cruisers to run them down. As was soon to become evident, and as had happened with some frigate actions against the Americans in 1812, the British A.M.C.s were no match for the German raiders on the few occasions when they did encounter them.†

† Two British A.M.C.s came off worst in encounters with raiders and one, *Voltaire*, was sunk.

The first raider to leave Germany had actually done so on March 31. She was followed by a second in April, another in May, and the fourth and fifth in June and July respectively. By the middle of May the discovery of mines off Cape Agulhas, in South Africa, disclosed to O.I.C. that at least one such ship was at sea. Although a number of merchant ships were either sunk or captured, not many of them were able to send a distress message, and we could not be entirely sure that some of the losses were not due either to stress of weather or to a U-boat. The failure of the merchant ships to make reports was not altogether surprising. They were not anticipating sudden attacks from apparently friendly vessels and were in any case loath to disclose their own positions to enemy D/F stations without good cause. The attack, when it came, was sudden and unexpected, and unless orders to stop and not to use the wireless were instantly obeyed, a hail of fire would be directed at the unfortunate vessel's bridge and W/T cabin. To make matters worse, on some occasions masters of ships attacked were unable to destroy their routing instructions, codes and other confidential papers, which proved of great value not only to their immediate captors but also to the B.Dienst back in Germany. For these reasons and also because of the strict wireless silence maintained by the raiders themselves, it was nearly the end of July before O.I.C. was sure that more than one raider was involved. But from then on the evidence began to accumulate.

At the end of July Denning created a new sub-section, to specialize on the subject.‡ The first approach could only be an historical one; the assumption that certain incidents were the work of the same ship, while others, because of the time and distance factor must be associated with a second or third raider. It was a slow and painful process, and until survivors were rescued, there was no means of knowing what types of ships were being used nor what their tactics or armament were. Gradually, however, O.I.C. began to build up a reasonably accurate picture. As the existence of each fresh raider was established she was given a distinguishing letter, for of course at this early stage their German designation was not known. The ship we called Raider A was not in fact the first to leave Germany but the second; the first to depart was the third to be identified and so was allocated the letter C. Later on we were

‡ This was almost the first duty given to the Author when he joined O.I.C.

able to establish that the Germans had allocated numbers to the Raiders, Ship 21 or 36 or 10, and that in addition they had names, *Atlantis* or *Orion* or *Thor*, but our alphabetical nomenclature was simple, avoided confusion and was maintained throughout. A weekly appreciation was prepared which summarized all the latest information and sometimes forecast the next likely areas of raider activity. After approval by the Assistant Chief of Naval Staff (Foreign), it was signalled to all Commanders-in-Chief so that they were kept as well informed as possible not only about events within their own commands but about the total situation.

By May 1941 it was possible to produce a supplement to the Weekly Intelligence Report, the confidential weekly newsletter issued to all ships and commands, dealing solely with armed merchant raiders. It listed seven raiders, A to G, the actual number in commission by that date, and after describing with considerable accuracy their general characteristics, methods of operation and tactics, gave details of each individual ship's size, speed, armament, captain, disguises, and a line drawing or in some cases a photograph showing her appearance, and finally a reconstruction of her cruise to date. Not all the details were complete or correct in this first edition, but it did contain all that was known in O.I.C. up to the time of publication and should have enabled any officer who cared to study it carefully to form a very clear idea of what he or the ships under his command were up against. Whether this was the best means of promulgating the available information now seems slightly in doubt. The Weekly Intelligence Report was chosen in order to gain the widest circulation; battleships and aircraft carriers had eight copies, cruisers three and all smaller vessels one, so that there could be no excuse that the information was so confidential or its distribution so restricted that few people could see it. Nevertheless it does seem to have been a fact that the conclusions which should have been drawn from its contents were not taken sufficiently to heart by the commanding officers of warships searching for the raiders, who continued, in many cases, to approach suspect vessels incautiously and too close. It was not, of course, an easy problem for those at sea to establish the true identity of an apparently harmless merchant ship until, later on, a system called Checkmate was introduced by which a warship could obtain rapid confirmation from a central plot in the Admiralty of the true whereabouts of any independently routed British or Allied merchantman. There would equally seem to have been some failure to bring home to all masters of merchant ships the dangers which the raiders presented, the necessity for vigilance even in the most remote areas of the ocean and the vital need for well thought out plans to destroy their confidential papers quickly in the event of an attack. Although there was a short prefix to a distress message, 'R.R.R.' to indicate attack by a surface ship, equivalent to 'S.O.S.' or 'S.S.S.' (attacked by submarine), it did not differentiate between regular warships and disguised merchant raiders and this led to some confusion, as often the victim had no time to add supplementary details. Eventually this was remedied by allocating 'Q.Q.Q.' for merchant as opposed to warship raiders.

However, a number of the raiders had somewhat lucky escapes and it was not until May 1941 that the British secured their first success, when the cruiser *Cornwall* intercepted a distress message from a tanker in the Indian Ocean which enabled her to find and sink one of the most successful of the raiders, Raider F, or Ship 33, *Pinguin. Pinguin* had been at sea for nearly a year and during that time had sunk or captured 17 ships and 11 small whalers totalling over 136,000 tons. In all the seven armed merchant raiders (the seventh, G had sailed in December 1940) operating between April 1940 and November 1941, together sank or captured 87 ships of more than 600,000 tons. This was only a fifth of the total tonnage which Britain lost from all causes during this period, but in addition to actual losses the raiders caused great disruption to the regular flow of trade in every ocean in the world.

There was, however, an even more serious threat, that from the pocket battleships, battlecruisers and cruisers. *Scheer* had reached the Atlantic, once again undetected by air or surface patrols, at the beginning of November 1940, and rapidly disclosed her presence there by attacking a homeward bound convoy from Halifax, HX.84, whose sole escort was the armed merchant cruiser *Jervis Bay*. Like *Rawalpindi* twelve months earlier, she had no chance against her much more powerful adversary, but she managed to get off an enemy report identifying her assailant and the gallant resistance which she put up gained sufficient time for the great majority of the convoy to disperse and escape. *Scheer* then

49

steamed south west towards Bermuda and sank another ship, which also managed to get off a distress message but without being able to say whether she was being attacked by a warship or, as might well have been the case, by a merchant raider. The report did not, therefore, help us to establish *Scheer*'s movements. She in fact proceeded to the South Atlantic and then in February 1941 into the Indian Ocean where her presence was eventually disclosed by reports from some of her victims, and by an aircraft from the cruiser *Glasgow*. Unfortunately, it was not possible to maintain contact and once again she disappeared to succeed, at the end of March, in returning to Germany without being detected. O.I.C. on the basis of B.P.'s study of W/T traffic, did inform the Home Fleet that there were indications of this happening, but they were two days too late, for by that time *Scheer* had reached the cover of the Norwegian coast.

At the end of November, *Hipper*, having repaired her faulty engines, was seen by air reconnaissance at Brunsbuttel, but it was not realized that she was about to make a sortie. Waiting until bad weather halted British air patrols, she managed to gain the Atlantic with the intention of attacking convoys. She had some difficulty in finding a target until on Christmas Eve she located and shadowed a troop convoy for the Middle East. It was however heavily escorted and she was driven off with slight damage which together with engine trouble was sufficient to make her put into Brest.

At the end of January 1941 *Scharnhorst* and *Gneisenau* under the command of Admiral Lütjens also sailed from Germany. On this occasion we correctly deduced from W/T traffic what was about to happen and Admiral Tovey, the new Commander-in-Chief of the Home Fleet, was warned and sailed cruisers to patrol the Iceland–Faeroes Passage. Three days later we received a reliable report from an agent that the two ships had passed northwards through the Great Belt and the Home Fleet itself put to sea and additional patrols were flown by Coastal Command. Luck was still against us because, although briefly sighted by a cruiser, the two German ships narrowly managed to evade the Home Fleet and reach the Atlantic.

A few days earlier, *Hipper*, on which Coastal Command had been keeping a careful watch in Brest, slipped out for a second cruise. After some success against unescorted ships her low endurance compelled her return to Brest, where she was heavily though unsuccessfully attacked by Bomber Command. The German Naval Staff wanted her back in Germany and she sailed again in the middle of March: thanks to bad weather and despite the fact that she herself sighted British patrolling cruisers, she was not seen and reached Germany at the end of the month.

In the meantime every effort had been made to deal with *Scharnhorst* and *Gneisenau* and the majority of the Atlantic convoys were being escorted by a battleship. The battlecruisers were under orders not to incur any risks and when they sighted, and were in turn sighted by, the old battleship, *Ramillies,* escorting HX.106, Lütjens hastily made off. *Ramillies,* by bad luck, had sighted and therefore reported only one enemy ship. She thought this might be *Hipper* which was, of course, at sea at this moment. It was therefore appreciated in O.I.C. that this ship might be attempting to break back to Germany and attention had to be concentrated for the time being on this possibility. The next news of *Scharnhorst* and *Gneisenau* came when they found ships recently dispersed from an outward bound convoy and sank five of them. Quickly shifting their area to the south east, the Germans came up against a homeward bound convoy escorted by the battleship *Malaya.* Once again the Germans sheered off and, returning back to the route of the Halifax convoys, again encountered ships recently dispersed and on this occasion sank sixteen of them. They were however sighted soon afterwards by the more modern but slow battleship *Rodney.* It was again appreciated that a break back to Germany might be under way and suitable dispositions were made accordingly. Lütjens was in fact already on his way to France, but by the time this had been established by a sighting by an aircraft from *Ark Royal* and then by a Hudson of Coastal Command, it was too late for any further action to be taken, and on March 22 his squadron anchored safely in Brest.

Admiral Raeder and the protagonists of surface attack on British sea communications had, at first sight, good cause for satisfaction. The battlecruisers had cruised for two whole months without once being brought to action. The supply organization had worked superbly and not a German tanker had been lost. Twenty-two ships of over 115,000 tons had been sunk and in addition the whole British convoy cycle had been seriously disrupted. In conjunction with the armed merchant raiders and *Scheer* and *Hipper*, they had forced on us an enormous dispersal of effort. Lütjens' ships were safe back in Brest and appeared to be ideally poised for a fresh sortie as soon as they were ready. Raeder did not know it, but he was very shortly to be sadly disillusioned.

From the British point of view the results had been very disappointing. That *Scheer* had proved extremely elusive was perhaps only to be expected, but that both she and *Hipper* had succeeded in leaving and returning to Germany without O.I.C. being positively aware of the fact suggested that we still could not entirely rely on obtaining the advance warning that was essential if raiders were to be intercepted other than by pure chance. Neither air nor surface patrols had been able to detect their passage. As regards the battlecruisers it was even more disappointing that, although clearly sighted on several occasions, it had never been possible to bring them to action. Nevertheless, as with the armed merchant raiders, O.I.C.'s performance had improved month by month. The battlecruisers' departure had been accurately forecast in ample time and it was largely ill-luck that the Home Fleet had so narrowly missed them at the outset. Air reconnaissance had increased and was continuing to do so. The first effective radar sets were now being fitted in some British cruisers, and far from *Scharnhorst* and *Gneisenau* being well placed for further sorties they very soon discovered that they had become prime targets for attack by the bombers and torpedo bombers of the R.A.F.

We must now leave the large German surface ships and consider their small sisters, the E-boats. It must be remembered that, although the German Navy was greatly outnumbered, and had far fewer units available to it than it would have wished, it had nevertheless, during this period of the war, the initiative, the ability to choose when and where it would strike at Britain's long and very vulnerable communications. Certainly in 1940 and early 1941 the Germans were able, with only a dozen or so E-boats at their disposal, to inflict heavy losses on British coastal convoys. As always, advance warning of an enemy attack was what was needed, and in this instance it was provided with commendable speed. During the summer's fighting in France, the R.A.F. 'Y' Service had observed that the Germans were using V.H.F.* wireless for plain

---

* Very High Frequency.

language tactical messages between their tanks and aircraft and it was found that this traffic could be read and monitored in Britain. It was realized in O.I.C., when the E-boats started to operate in the Channel from August onwards, that they were using a similar procedure. Commander Sandwith's section, D.S.D./N.I.D.9, responsible for the control and administration of the Navy's 'Y' and D/F stations, very quickly set up a small 'Y' station on the North Foreland manned by the Civilian Wireless Service and members of the Women's Royal Naval Service (W.R.N.S.). Before long it was at least possible to give convoy escorts some warning of an impending attack, but it took longer before the right type of escort could be provided and even longer before the war could be carried into the enemy's own waters.

The special section of O.I.C., which handled air intelligence, was now working closely with R.A.F. Intelligence, and with B.P. who had begun to decrypt a large volume of German Air Force W/T traffic. The German Air Force seems to have made much greater use of W/T than either the German Army or Navy, both of whom preferred to rely whenever possible on land lines. This was an immense boon to us, and the fierce dive-bombing attacks on convoys and the mining of British-swept channels were more easily pinpointed by O.I.C.'s air and mining specialists as a result. Moreover, it was sometimes possible to gain some insight into likely German Naval intentions by deductions from G.A.F. moves and plans.

Grievous as the losses were which Britain was suffering on the east and south coasts from the combination of E-boats, aircraft and mines, and in more distant waters from the depredations of the surface ships, it was Dönitz's few U-boats who were in fact inflicting the greatest damage. We have already noted that ocean convoys could not be provided with anti-submarine escort further than fifteen degrees west. Even then the escort often only consisted of one or at the most two destroyers, with perhaps some trawlers and the occasional corvette. There were also still far too many merchant ships leaving and approaching British shores proceeding independently. Many of these were neutrals, others were stragglers or rompers from convoys, yet others were those ships with a speed in excess of fifteen knots which it was felt better not to include in convoys. All this great mass of shipping now had to be routed via the North Channel, since the South Western Approaches and the English Channel had, with the occupation of France, become too dangerous. Convoys and independents bound to and from Gibraltar and Africa had also to be routed perilously close to the French and Spanish coasts. There was no lack of targets for Dönitz's young men.

Dönitz and other post-war German writers have complained bitterly and with good cause about the inability of the German Navy to establish its own Air Arm and of the gross lack of co-operation on the part of the German Air Force. This criticism does not, however, entirely hold good for this period of the war. The long distance G.A.F. Focke-Wulf Condors could cover the whole route from Gibraltar to Britain and reach out several hundreds of miles into the North Western Approaches. They reported both independents and convoys for the U-boats, and themselves carried out many successful bombing attacks, particularly on isolated ships. Dönitz remained very dissatisfied with the service he was getting until at the beginning of 1941 he secured, for the time being, a measure of operational control over the Air Group in question. Even then he found, as Coastal Command did, that navigational errors were frequent. This was overcome by any aircraft sighting a convoy transmitting beacon signals on which the U-boats took bearings. The aircraft 'homed on' the U-boats, a process which we could detect in time to warn the convoy concerned.

Despite the fact that major changes were introduced in British operational ciphers in August 1940, (these largely deprived the Germans of their insight into the movements of the Home Fleet which had been such a boon to them in the Norwegian campaign), the B.Dienst was succeeding in deciphering a number of signals relating to British convoy routing. Dönitz writes in his *Memoirs*: 'I received further information about enemy convoys from the highly efficient section at Naval High Command. Most signals contained instructions with regard to the rendezvous for convoys and their escorts, but their timely deciphering was, largely, a matter of luck. Between June and September 1940 I made several attempts to use these signals as the basis for a joint operation by a number of boats. . . . In September the cryptographic section picked up a signal in ample time, four days before a homeward bound convoy was due to meet its escort'. The success of the B.Dienst was particularly valuable at a time when the number of U-boats actually at sea on operations was so restricted. Later on when their numbers increased, much more extensive reconnaissance could be carried out by the U-boats themselves, but from 1940 up to the middle of 1943 the contribution made by the B.Dienst to Dönitz's success in the Battle of the Atlantic must have been equal to at least an additional fifty U-boats. It is, however, interesting to note the stress he laid on the 'timely' decrypting of signals. Even at the beginning of 1943, when the B.Dienst was working at the peak of its efficiency, only a small proportion of the signals could be decrypted in time for operational use to be made of them.

We noted earlier that the U-boats had hitherto been operating in the conventional manner, independently of one another and making their attacks, for the most part, submerged and by day. These methods were uneconomical. The U-boat's slow underwater speed often meant that it could not gain a suitable position from which to fire its torpedoes and there was no concentration of effort against convoys. Dönitz was well aware of these difficulties. Before the war he had conducted numerous exercises in the Baltic, the North Sea and in the Atlantic with U-boats attacking on the surface and at night. The U-boat's surface speed of some seventeen knots meant that it could overtake the seven- to ten-knot convoys and even many of the somewhat faster independents, while the combination of darkness and the U-boat's very small silhouette rendered it almost invisible both to its victims and their escorts. In addition, experiments had been made to see whether a number of U-boats could not operate together, like a division of destroyers, which is in fact what they then became, except that they retained the important advantage of being able to submerge when they wished to do so. The maximum strength was thereby concentrated at the vital point. A further benefit of these Wolf Pack tactics, as they came to be called by the British, was that it was possible to spread a number of U-boats out on a patrol line with intervals of ten or fifteen miles between each boat so that, depending on the number of boats involved, a considerable area of sea could be covered for reconnaissance purposes. These patrol lines would be positioned across the supposed route of a convoy and would sweep slowly backwards and forwards along its assumed line of advance. The first U-boat to make a sighting would not immediately attack but would report at once to U-boat Command and then make beacon signals and report any change of course until the rest of the Pack could also gain contact. Initially an attempt was made to control these attacks by a senior officer in one of the U-boats concerned, but it very soon became apparent that this was neither necessary nor desirable, and from then onwards operational control was firmly exercised by the Befehlshaber der U-boote (B.d.U.) from his headquarters in Lorient. This of course involved a considerable amount of signalling, and Dönitz had to weigh up the advantages of this system against the disadvantages of presenting his enemy's D/F organization with the opportunity of obtaining a large number of fixes. He came to the conclusion that the risks involved were well worth accepting, but he continued, at least for a time, to keep careful watch on the situation and to analyse the results achieved by both sides. He was not, at first, impressed with the effectiveness of the British D/F system. Fixes did not appear to be accurate to more than sixty or eighty miles at the best, and although he detected evidence that some convoys were routed away from areas from which there had been German W/T traffic, others appeared to steam straight on, oblivious of what lay ahead of them. There were probably two reasons for this. Firstly, although the D/F organization was being expanded as rapidly as possible, the loss of the French stations had been a setback and the establishment of stations overseas, necessary if good 'cuts' were to be obtained between Britain and Gibraltar or seven hundred or a thousand miles west of Ireland, took time. Our fixes towards the end of 1940 were probably not much more accurate than Dönitz supposed. This situation, however, was gradually remedied as the D/F organization's expansion began to gather pace, and Dönitz seems to have been slow to realize the change when it did begin to occur. Perhaps of even greater importance was the fact that the low endurance of the escorts and the necessity of meeting inward-bound convoys made radical changes of route extremely difficult. It was but rarely attempted at this period and indeed for some time convoys tended to be routed along 'tram lines' on which British hunting forces were concentrated.

Dönitz had not felt able to introduce Wolf Pack tactics in the first year of the war, firstly because of the small number of boats which could be concentrated in any one area, and then because of the demands of the Norwegian campaign. Even in the autumn of 1940 his numbers remained small and the difficulties of finding convoys considerable. The majority of successful attacks were still being made on independent ships and there were targets in plenty. This was what the U-boat commanders called *Die glückliche Zeit* (The Happy Time), when the aces, Prien, Schepke, Kretschmer and others established their reputations. By the New Year, however, more U-boats were beginning to be available and the pattern of British convoy traffic was becoming known. Fewer ships were travelling independently: even the neutrals thought it safer in convoy. Pack attacks then became the norm.

It is surprising now that the British seem to have been taken so much by surprise. U-boats had attacked on the surface in 1917 and Dönitz himself had published a book in January 1939 giving some of his ideas on the advantages of such tactics. It must be admitted that insufficient attention had been paid to the problems of U-boat warfare, and because the Royal Navy had not supposed that U-boats would operate on the surface, it had not been realized that the Asdic, on which British hopes were confidently pinned, would be rendered largely ineffective. The British were certainly caught on the wrong foot, and in the Submarine Tracking Room, Thring was as sceptical as all the other experts when the first reports began to be received from those at sea with bitter personal experience of the new methods. Thring had done a marvellous job in establishing the Section's reputation for integrity and accuracy, in inculcating in his inexperienced staff his own analytical and disciplined approach to evidence presented to him. But he was over sixty and was not receptive to new ideas. He did not get on too easily with the regular officers from other Divisions who, although junior to him in years, were now his seniors in rank. He remembered what and how things had been done in the last war. He was disinclined to accept that both the Germans and the British might develop different methods. Above all he refused to accept that there was any possibility of predicting what the U-boats might do next. To reconstruct a U-boat's cruise by working backwards from one incident to the previous one, yes that was possible, but to attempt to go forward and try to guess its future movements was not only impossible but either useless or, if any attention were to be paid to such romancing, positively dangerous.

These views were not altogether shared by some of the senior officers who were by now increasingly using the Tracking Room to inform themselves of the latest U-boat situation, amongst them Captain Creasy, the Director of the Anti-Submarine Warfare Division, and Captain Edwards, the Director of the Operations Division (Home). They were much struck by the ability of Thring's civilian assistant, Rodger Winn. Winn, at this time aged thirty-seven, had been a successful barrister in civil life and had volunteered his services before the war as an interrogator of prisoners of war. He would no doubt have been an excellent one, but fortunately he had, for some reason, been directed to the Tracking Room, where he had been serving since August 1939. He had been prevented by an acute attack of polio when a small boy from realizing his first ambition to join the Royal Navy, and had been left with a twisted back and a limp. It was a tremendous triumph of willpower that he had largely overcome these disabilities, but he still suffered a good deal of discomfort if he had to stand for any length of time, and to counteract this had formed the habit of taking some of his weight by resting his hands on a table or chair in front of him. Of medium height, he was broad with very powerful shoulders. He had a good sense of humour and an unlimited fund of entertaining stories concerning his experiences as a barrister. His work in the Tracking Room was eventually to earn him promotion to the rank of Captain R.N.V.R., an O.B.E., a C.B., and the American Legion of Merit. Returning to the Bar after the war, he was, at the time of his death in 1972, a Lord Justice of Appeal.

Winn was far from convinced that it was impossible ever to try to forecast the future movements of U-boats. By now, certain patterns of behaviour had been established. Certain types of U-boat signals were being associated with certain situations; the short signals which might be sighting or weather reports, the much longer ones which might indicate damage or the intention to return to base at the end of a patrol. It was all very tentative, but Winn believed it was worth while to 'have a go'. If, as he subsequently said, one beat the law of average and was right only fifty-one per cent of the time, that one per cent, in terms of lives and ships saved, or U-boats sunk, was surely worth the effort. There is a story, the truth of which is now somewhat hard to vouch for as the principal characters involved are dead, that at about this time Captain Edwards came down to the Tracking Room and observed on the plot that there were two valuable tankers homeward bound and in close proximity to each other. Some distance ahead of them on the plot was a tab indicating the position, deduced from a D/F fix, of a U-boat. Edwards asked Winn whether he had any ideas as to the U-boat's future movements and whether it would endanger the tankers. Winn's view was that, in view of the length of the signal the U-boat had just made, it was probable that it was about to start its return to base, and that if his theory was correct, it might well intercept one or both of the tankers. Edwards decided to make an experiment, and obtained Trade Division's somewhat reluctant agreement; one tanker was diverted to a route that in Winn's opinion would take her clear of the probable path of the U-boat; the other tanker, in accordance with Trade Division's wishes, was left on its original direct Great Circle† course to her destination. Next morning Winn's guess, for it was no more, was proved right. The tanker which had been diverted was unmolested but her unlucky sister was sunk.

Whether it was due to this episode or not, the decision was taken towards the end of 1940 that Paymaster Captain Thring must be moved to less onerous duties and that Winn should be commissioned in the R.N.V.R. and appointed in his place. When Clayton and Colpoys put this proposal forward to the D.N.I., it was a revolutionary one. To appoint a civilian to head such a vital department was unprecedented. Godfrey was never much impressed by precedents and had already formed his own view of Winn's abilities. Nevertheless, such was the importance now being attached to the work of the Tracking Room that any change in its head was not a matter for D.N.I. alone, but something that would have to be discussed with the Vice-Chief of Naval Staff and the First Sea Lord himself. Thanks to the enthusiastic support of Creasy and Edwards, D.N.I.'s proposal was

† The shortest distance between any two points on the earth's surface is on a great circle.

accepted and Winn was duly appointed as a Temporary Commander R.N.V.R. (Special Branch). As with Denning's appointment three and a half years earlier, it was a stroke of singular good fortune that someone so ideally suited to the job in hand was available and was selected.

The Staff of the Tracking Room at this time consisted, apart from Winn, of two retired Lieutenant-Commanders R.N., one of whom, Derek Crosse, was later to serve with much distinction on the staff of the C.-in-C. Western Approaches as Staff Officer (Convoys), and three civilians, one of whom had served in Room 40. A close relationship was being built up with the Operations and Anti-Submarine Warfare Divisions, but the extraordinarily intimate co-operation with the Movements Section of the Trade Division, which was later to prove one of the keys to the Tracking Room's success, had not yet been established. Peter Kemp's D/F plotters were still located in another room because up to that time their work had seemed more vital to Denning's watch on the surface ships than to the U-boat section. Nevertheless the first tentative attempts at forecasting as opposed to merely recording events as they happened were now being made, and the idea that ships and convoys might be routed on the basis of such 'guestimates' was beginning to gain acceptance. The Tracking Room was still feeling its way, and it cannot be said that it achieved any spectacular results. If it was now fit and trained to go, the real race was still to be run.

By the end of April 1941 the Germans had lost from all causes 39 U-boats. They had 32 operational, seven fewer than the figure with which they started the war,‡ but their total strength had doubled, and 47 new boats had been commissioned in the previous three months. They had, in twenty months, with some help from the Italians, sunk 729 British, Allied and neutral ships of nearly three and a half million tons, and the average monthly sinkings were now nudging and would soon pass the quarter of a million mark. There could be no doubt where the worst threat lay.

‡ Roskill gives 49 operational on September 3, 1939. Of these, ten were in the Baltic operating against the Poles. They included a number of school boats which returned to training duties as soon as the Polish campaign was over.

We have already posed the question whether O.I.C. would improve its performance and do something to compensate for some of our grave shortages and difficulties. So far as actual results during this period were concerned, the answer certainly cannot be an unequivocal yes. Nevertheless further progress had been made; O.I.C.'s relationship with B.P. was now on a firmer and closer basis, the Naval Staff were coming to rely on its appreciations and forecasts, as were the Commanders-in-Chief at home and overseas and the Air Officer Commander-in-Chief Coastal Command and his Group Commanders. The flow of information into O.I.C. was improving from almost all sources, and Coastal Command patrols and photographic reconnaissance flights were increasing in frequency and effectiveness.

In addition a major improvement had been effected in O.I.C.'s physical environment. The quarters in the sub-basement, although far more satisfactory and better equipped than the six rooms and the passage on the first floor of the Admiralty occupied up to the outbreak of war, were nevertheless extremely cramped and uncomfortable. The ceiling was low and festooned with white-painted pipes of one sort or another, the air conditioning primitive and the lighting poor and hard on the eyes. The staff, all of whom were working very long hours with infrequent rest days, many of them sleeping in the building at night, were suffering badly from 'flu and other ailments which if not serious in themselves certainly did not contribute to maximum efficiency. Although all the windows were bricked up, the complex was far from bomb proof, and in the autumn of 1940 work had been started, at the height of the Blitz, on the enormous block, to be known as the Citadel,* at the north-west corner of the Admiralty. It was partially completed in six months and O.I.C., together with the Operations and Trade Main Plots and War Registry at once moved down into its bowels. The accommodation was not palatial, but it was more spacious, quiet and comfortable than the old quarters had been. There was in particular a much larger room for Winn's Submarine Section, and the opportunity was taken to move the D/F plot in there, since their work would obviously be increasingly bound up with the battle against the U-boats.

* or Lenin's Tomb by some unkind critics.

One last big step forward was required, the ability to rival the work of the B.Dienst, the ability to look into the enemy's mind which only successful cryptanalysis of his naval W/T traffic could give us. In May and June, this was at last to be achieved.

4

German Naval Ciphers and B.P.

THIS BOOK is not a treatise on cryptology, nor is it a history of Bletchley Park, greatly though O.I.C. was indebted to that organization and close as were their links. The work of B.P. during the war was subject to maximum security restrictions and the staff of O.I.C., although well aware of B.P.'s work, which for four years was to constitute their most priceless source of enemy intelligence, were not encouraged to probe too closely into the cryptanalysts' methods or difficulties. It was sufficient that from the end of May 1941 onwards not a day passed without the receipt by O.I.C., sometimes in small quantities, sometimes in a large mass, of tele-printed English translations of decrypts of German W/T signals of one variety or another. We were warned when our own particular tap was likely to be turned off and we heaved a sigh of relief when we learned that it was going to be turned on again, but we had neither the opportunity, the time nor the inclination to bother ourselves too much about the reasons. Unlike the staff of Room 40 we were not cryptanalysts, we were Operational Intelligence Officers.

Nevertheless, if the reader is to understand the true value and also the limitations, for there were considerable limitations, of cryptanalysis, some explanation must be given of the methods and ramifications of the German Naval ciphering system and, so far as is possible, having regard to the continuing security restrictions, of B.P.'s organization. For the former the author is largely indebted to Professor Jürgen Rohwer, Germany's leading historian of the Battle of the Atlantic and the Wireless War which accompanied it. As to the latter, the account which follows can only be partial and incomplete until such time as the publication of the Official History of Wartime Intelligence, now being prepared by Professor F. H. Hinsley, is authorized.

As far back as 1928 the German Army had adopted a machine cipher, an adaptation of a commercial machine called Enigma G. The general principles of this type of machine were fairly widely known and more than one make was on the market in Europe and America. Though a number of improvements were introduced in successive models in the interest of security, the basic machine had a typewriter-like keyboard, was about the size of an office typewriter, was powered by electric batteries and contained in a wooden box. The enciphering mechanism consisted of a number of rotatable drums or rotors about half an inch wide, around the circumference of which were engraved the letters of the alphabet. These rotors were mechanically geared together so that, when one was moved by depressing a typewriter key, the movements of the others were irregular. Electric impulses, passing through the rotors successively and reflected back from the end one through different mazes determined by the relative positions of the rotors, effected the encipherment of each individual letter and the result was indicated by a lamp lighting up the appropriate letter. The cipher key for a particular period, say twenty-four hours, was determined by the starting position of each of the rotors and was of course easily changed. More drastic changes could be introduced by the replacement of one or more rotors. While the machine in this form was not particularly speedy, as the results of encipherment or decipherment of each letter had to be observed, read off and written down, many thousands of letters could be enciphered on each key before the machine began to repeat itself; this obviously posed a major challenge to cryptanalysts.

It seems to have been the Polish Intelligence Service who first realized what the Germans were doing, and by sometime in the late twenties or very early thirties they had reconstructed the German Army machine and may have been decrypting at least some of the Wehrmacht's W/T traffic. The French too, with the help of an agent employed for a time in the German General Staff's Cryptographic Department, had made some progress. How far, if at all, the British had progressed is not known, but there seems to be little doubt that their first real step forward occurred when Commander Alistair Denniston, the Head of the G.C. & C.S. and his French opposite number, Colonel Braquenie, met the chief Polish cryptanalyst Colonel Langer in Warsaw on July 24–25, 1939. From this meeting they brought back, in the very nick of time, two of the Polish Enigma machines, a gift quite as valuable as the *Magdeburg*'s signal book had been in 1914, and one for which Britain owes the Poles an immense debt of gratitude. If Chamberlain's guarantee to Poland did little for that unfortunate country, it certainly produced a priceless asset for Great Britain. Possession of the machine did not, of course, mean that the British or the French were immediately able to read German W/T signals. In order to do that they had to know the current keys or settings, and these were changed at increasingly frequent intervals. Nor was there, in peace time, a sufficient volume of traffic for the cryptanalysts to work on. However, after the collapse of Poland in September 1939, some of the Polish cryptanalysts escaped to France and by the end of October they and the French had made a partial break-in, and were decrypting, though often with a considerable time lag, a certain amount of German Air Force traffic. The German Air Force, who used the same machine, although with different settings, made much greater use of W/T than did the Army and generally seem to have been rather less conscious of the rules of signal security. During the campaign in France, however, the Army's rapid advance and the need for close tactical co-operation with the G.A.F. led to a considerable increase in the amount of traffic, and according to the French second-in-command of their Cryptanalytic Service, Colonel Bertrand, an increasing number of signals both from the Army and the Air Force were being decrypted in time for operational use to be made of them, although there seems to have been some distrust on the part of the French High Command of this source of information.* Presumably B.P. was participating in this work. At any rate, according

* See Rohwer: *Geleitzug-Schlachten im März 1943*. Motorbuch Verlag, Munich.

to Group Captain Winterbotham in his book *The Ultra Secret*, G.A.F. traffic was being read in Britain in small quantities as early as April 1940. It would seem to have taken some months before current reading in sufficient volume to be of great importance was achieved, but, again according to Winterbotham, the decrypts played a vital part in the Battle of Britain.

Why, then, did the German Naval Ciphers remain inviolate until the middle of the following summer? The answer lies in the fact that although the German Navy had also adopted machine ciphering and had in fact procured its machine from the same source, their cryptographic experts had succeeded in introducing a number of technical modifications into the machine, which greatly increased its security and the problem for an enemy crypt-analyst.† In addition, and contrary to the practice of the G.A.F., almost all administrative traffic was sent by landline until the enormous extent of the German conquests in 1940 and 1941 compelled the Navy equally to make some use of W/T in communicating with new and distant bases and naval commands. Even then, teleprinter or land cable communication was established whenever possible, Norway and France being cases in point. There is little doubt that the German Navy was the most security conscious of the three services.

A further difficulty was placed in the way of B.P. The same settings or even ciphers were not used for all purposes, any more than there was only a single cipher in use in the Royal Navy. Not all of them were in use from the beginning to the end of the war but most of the more important ones were. Thanks to the versatility of the Enigma M machine, it was able for several years to handle all these different ciphers. Only in 1943 was a significant modification, in effect a new machine although still working on the same basic principle, introduced for the operational U-boats.

† Professor Rohwer, in a paper at the Third Naval History Symposium at Annapolis in October 1977, stated that the M-3 naval Enigma machine had four different settings, three of which were changed daily and one of which was changed with each message. Five spare rotors were carried, giving a total of eight, from which three could be chosen. This permitted 336 different combinations of rotor sequences. Each rotor had 26 positions giving 17,576 ring positions. In addition there were 1,547 possible plug connections and the operator could set each rotor to 26 different positions, giving 17,576 possibilities. The theoretical possible total of all these permutations was in the region of 160 trillion!

The result was that the volume of traffic, so vital to successful cryptanalysis, remained in many cases small. After a time, although not always simultaneously, the various ciphers were given code names and it will be convenient to refer to them by these names even though none of them had been introduced as early as May 1941 when the British achieved their first break-ins. The following is a list of the principal ciphers used:

1. H Y D R A. This cipher was used for all surface ships in the Baltic and North Sea and then for ships operating from or off the occupied territories; it was, in consequence, the cipher used for minesweepers and anti-submarine and patrol craft in Norway and France. It was also, initially, the cipher used by all operational U-boats.

2. T R I T O N. This cipher was eventually used for the operational U-boats in the Atlantic under the direct control of B.d.U. as opposed to those boats placed under the command of Gruppe Nord, the Naval Command in Norway, or those transferred to the Mediterranean or engaged in training in the Baltic.

3. T E T I S. This cipher was the one used for training U-boats in the Baltic.

4. M E D U S A. This cipher was used for all U-boats in the Mediterranean.

5. A E G I R. This cipher was used for all surface warships likely to remain for any length of time outside the Baltic or North Sea, for example the *Graf Spee* or *Scheer* on their extended commerce raiding cruises.

6. N E P T U N. This cipher was used only for the heavy ships of the main fleet when they were on specific operations, as, for example, the first and last sortie of *Bismarck,* or the dash through the Channel of *Scharnhorst* and *Gneisenau*. Its use was, therefore, comparatively rare.

7. S U D. This was the cipher used for surface ships in the Mediterranean and the Black Sea.

8. S P E C I A L C I P H E R 1 0 0 was used for disguised merchant raiders and supply ships in overseas waters. There was in ad-

dition a special cipher which could be allocated to single ships for their individual use.

9. TIBET was a cipher used by those supply ships overseas, for example tankers, which had taken refuge in a neutral port at the outbreak of war and had only been supplied with the earliest type of cipher machine.

10. POTSDAM. This was the cipher used for operations against the Russians in the Baltic.

11. FREYA. This cipher was used for communication between O.K.M., the Oberkommando der Marine or German Admiralty, and naval shore commands when the use of landline was impossible or, for some reason, undesirable. Messages sent by landline used a different cipher system altogether.

12. SLEIPNER was the cipher used by vessels engaged in torpedo-firing practice in the Baltic.

13. BERTOK was used for communication between the Naval Attaché in Tokyo and O.K.M.

It will be seen therefore that there was a considerable range of ciphers, some of which were only used intermittently and others only to a limited extent. Major changes were made monthly in all ciphers, except Aegir and Special Cipher 100 which remained valid for one year. Ships were issued with the appropriate monthly tables in advance and in accordance with the maximum length of time they would be away from base. Thus in 1941 most operational U-boats, whose cruises did not then generally exceed eight weeks, would be issued with the necessary instructions and material for, say, three months. In addition to the major monthly changes, lesser changes in the cipher settings took place every twenty-four hours. At first these changes took effect at midnight, but later in the war, the new setting came into force at noon. Throughout the range it was possible, by means of a double or treble encipherment, to send signals for the eyes of 'Officer only' or for 'Commanding Officer only'. Yet another refinement were the so called 'Short' signals. These were standardized messages whose length was greatly reduced by means of a simple code which was itself enciphered in the normal way but which, for recognition

A wartime view of the Citadel (commonly referred to by the irreverent as Lenin's Tomb) constructed at the north-west corner of the Admiralty, 1940–1941. O.I.C.'s quarters were below ground level. *Imperial War Museum, London*

Gross-Admiral Eric Raeder, Commander-in-Chief of the German Navy 1928–1943. *Imperial War Museum, London*

"Ned" Denning, taken in 1958, when as a Rear-Admiral he had been appointed Director of Naval Intelligence. *With kind permission of M.O.D.*

Gross-Admiral Karl Dönitz, Flag Officer U-boats 1935–1943, Commander-in-Chief of the German Navy 1943–1945. *Imperial War Museum, London*

purposes, was prefaced by a letter of the Greek alphabet. Thus Alpha Alpha was used in Neptun, Beta Beta in Triton. Sighting reports were prefaced Epsilon Epsilon while Weather Reports reverted to the Roman alphabet with WW. The objective was speed and simplicity for sender and receiver, and to make it more difficult for accurate D/F fixes to be obtained.

There can be little doubt that the German Navy's system was superior to those of its sister services, and also to that of the Royal Navy. The fact is, however, that no service in any of the belligerent powers during the Second World War succeeded in keeping every cipher it used secure. Every power, including some of the neutrals like the Swedes, managed, at one time or another, to decrypt some of the signals of other nations. Rommel benefited greatly, not only from reading British Army tactical traffic, but also from the fact that Berlin was for long able to decrypt the reports to Washington from the American Military Attaché in Cairo. The Italians read British and Yugo-Slav signals, the Americans and the British the Japanese, the Russians almost certainly read the Germans and the Germans the Russians.‡ There should have been some very red faces in every cryptographic and signal security department in the world. What is even more surprising is the apparently almost universal lack of liaison between these departments and their respective cryptanalysts. While each nation accepted the fact that its own cryptanalysts could read at least some of their enemy's ciphers, they were curiously blind to the fact that they themselves were being subjected to exactly the same form of eavesdropping. The German Navy seems to have been quite as guilty of this sin as most. Lieutenant-Commander Barrow-Green, in O.I.C.'s Mediterranean Section, had a good laugh in 1942, when, after a successful attack on an Axis convoy, he read a German Naval signal complaining bitterly, but quite wrongly, that the convoy's movements must have been betrayed by lax Ital-

‡ According to Capitaine de Vaisseau C. Huan, the Russians raised U.250 after she was sunk in the Gulf of Finland on July 30, 1944, and recovered her Enigma machine. Huan also points out that Admiral Golovko, the Russian Commander-in-Chief in the Arctic, wrote in his memoirs in 1960 that he was aware that Admiral Fraser knew in advance of the German intentions to send *Scharnhorst* to sea at the end of December 1943 (see Chapter 13). It is most improbable that the British passed any Special Intelligence to the Russians (or vice-versa), which raises the interesting question of how Golovko came by this knowledge.

ian security. Even as recently as 1973, Dönitz, in an interview with Ludovic Kennedy, was apparently still loath to accept that most of his ciphers had been consistently and thoroughly penetrated for four years of the war.

To be fair, the German Navy had some cause for their confidence in the perfection of their ciphering arrangements. It was considered by their experts that the use of the machine cipher, with its changes of settings and almost infinitely variable range, would present cryptanalysts using the then current methods of mathematical analysis and manual calculations with literally years of work. It was, of course, recognized that if the enemy captured a machine with all its accompanying material and instructions, a limited period of reading would be possible, but once the period covered by those instructions had expired, the introduction of the new settings which would then become valid would put the enemy back to square one. The instructions were, moreover, printed on soluble paper, so that their timely destruction in the event of the capture of the ship or U-boat carrying them seemed reasonably, or more than reasonably assured. In short, the Germans were satisfied that their system would defy the enemy's cryptanalysts, that their provisions for the destruction of the valid settings and instructions were more than adequate, and that even if this did not prove to be so, the resulting damage could be of only limited duration.

The British Government Code and Cipher School had, like N.I.D., seen the need for expansion at the time of Munich. Its head, Commander Alistair Denniston, had visited the Oxford and Cambridge colleges that summer and had recruited a number of dons from these and other Universities. They returned to academic life when the crisis was over, but were recalled again in the following August. Among them was a don from Kings, Frank Birch, who had been a member of Room 40 in 1918. He was a brilliant and eccentric individual who was reputed to spend every Christmas vacation playing the 'Dame' in provincial pantomime. He became the Head of the Naval Section at B.P.

Although cryptanalysis was to a great extent centralized, special liaison sections to deal with Army, Air and Naval decrypts were established. After the successes with the German Air Force, and then later that of the German Army traffic, B.P.'s Army and Air liaison sections were amalgamated and assumed responsibility for the safe distribution of those decrypted signals of operational value. This may or may not have been the best system, so far as Army and Air Force intelligence was concerned, but it was not suitable for or acceptable to the Admiralty. The Admiralty's objections were not due, as has sometimes been alleged, to any wish on the part of the Senior Service to emphasize its lofty superiority and its disdain of the Army and Air Force, but to sound practical reasons. The Admiralty, unlike the War Office and the Air Ministry, was an operational Headquarters. It exercised a general operational control of Britain's maritime forces everywhere and reserved the right, which it invoked on many occasions (too many, some might think), to take even tactical control into its own hands. This was certainly essential in some cases, as for example in the moves made when *Scharnhorst* and *Gneisenau* were raiding in the Atlantic or when *Bismarck* broke out. Only the Admiralty could determine which commands and which ships required specific information, and only the Admiralty was in a position to pass that information to ships at sea and to naval overseas commands by means of Whitehall W/T. Secondly, as we have already noted in connection with Room 40, it was essential that the results of cryptanalysis should be co-ordinated with all other forms of intelligence before operational use could be made of them, and this fact had been clearly recognized before the war by Denning and agreed by Denniston and Troup. Thirdly, there was the requirement for an Intelligence Centre to have knowledge of British plans and dispositions, and this B.P. could not have to the same detailed and intimate extent that was possible for O.I.C. Finally, although the security of B.P.'s non-naval decrypts seems to have been admirably preserved, the best means of ensuring this for naval messages was certainly by filtering them all through O.I.C., who were called upon to strike the correct balance between the desire to obtain the maximum operational advantage from the knowledge which cryptanalysis was to impart, and the importance of not arousing German suspicions that their ciphers had been compromised.

On the other hand it was vital that there should be close liaison between the Admiralty, as represented by O.I.C., and B.P. The flow of information could not be allowed to be in one direction only. The cryptanalysts must be helped over purely naval questions and be kept informed of naval priorities. The attempt to achieve this by leaving Saunder's small section in O.I.C., when G.C. & C.S. moved to Bletchley Park, had not, for one reason or another, proved to be the right answer, and it had gone back to B.P. in December, 1940.

For these reasons, although the Army and Air liaison sections were amalgamated, Birch's Naval Section retained its separate identity throughout the war. Naval Section was to play a key part in O.I.C.'s success, not only in suggesting to both Denning and Winn possible solutions to baffling problems, but in maintaining, primarily for the benefit of the cryptanalysts, extensive and admirably cross-indexed records, which on occasions however also provided important background information for O.I.C.

As well as those dons whom he had recruited in 1938, Denniston paid another visit to Oxford and Cambridge just after the outbreak of war and this time selected about a dozen undergraduates. Among them was a third-year man from St. John's, Cambridge, Harry Hinsley, who joined the Naval Section and whose studies of W/T traffic we have already noted. Hinsley worked more closely with Denning and Winn than anyone else except Birch himself. He had a brilliant and fertile mind and it is no surprise that he is now President of his old college, and the reigning University Professor of the History of International Relations. Others in the Naval Section were the brothers Walter and Ernest Ettinghausen, the first of whom later on, under his new name of Eytan, was to become Israeli Ambassador to France, and Permanent Secretary of the Israeli Foreign Office.

By the end of the war, B.P. had grown into an organization employing some 10,000 people.* Considerable use was made of Hollerith machinery, and quite early on, a mechanical precursor of the modern electronic computer had been constructed by Alan Turing, to speed up the mathematical calculations which the Germans had correctly assumed would take our cryptanalysts many months of work to perform manually. In the end there were dozens of these ponderous machines, some at B.P., others as far

---

* According to *The Times* of March 17, 1977, there are now '1,856 officials engaged in code-breaking at the Government Communications H.Q. in Cheltenham'.

afield as Eastcote and Stanmore. Some 1,200 W.R.N.S. tended the monsters. Why only W.R.N.S. were chosen for this monotonous work is not clear. It was a soul-destroying job and very like being in prison, except there was no remission for good conduct. Quite the reverse: once detailed, that remained the lot of these devoted and highly intelligent girls for the duration. There were few chances of promotion, no contact with the rest of the Navy, and, due to the very necessary security restrictions, little social life when off duty. Mechanical servicing of the 'Bombes', as they were known, was the responsibility of a small band of R.A.F. technicians, whose life was no more glamorous or interesting than that of the W.R.N.S. Almost the only recognition that this dedicated band of men and women received was a typical message, greatly appreciated, from Winston Churchill, commending them for the fact that, 'The chickens were laying so well without clucking!'

We have, however, anticipated future events. At the beginning of 1941 the German Naval ciphers were still defying all B.P.'s efforts and it was realized that only a 'pinch', the capture of a naval Enigma machine with current settings and accompanying material, would give us the necessary start.

The first capture was, to some extent, an accident. During the raid on the Lofoten Islands on February 23, 1941, the German armed trawler *Krebs* was disabled, her commanding officer killed before he could complete the destruction of his secret papers, and the ship abandoned by the survivors. A British boarding party discovered spare rotors for the cipher machine, but the machine itself and the rest of the cipher material had been thrown overboard.†

This 'pinch' prompted the thought that a special operation might be mounted specifically to capture cipher material. O.I.C. had observed and plotted from D/F fixes the presence of two German trawlers which were sending regular weather reports from the area between Iceland and Jan Mayen. Three cruisers, in one of which was the O.I.C./B.P. signals expert, Captain Jasper

† The release to The Public Record Office, London, in October 1977 of the first series of actual decrypts shows that a break into Hydra was achieved in March 1941, presumably as a result of material captured from *Krebs*. The traffic decrypted was, however, old, a limited period of February signals, and was of very little operational value. A second, and equally limited break for some March traffic was made in April.

Haines, R.N., were despatched to carry out a search and, on May 7, found and captured one of the trawlers, *München*. Although, once again, the Enigma machine had been disposed of, ancillary material relating to the settings of the cipher used by the trawlers was secured. Valuable though it was, it was not enough, and another operation was planned to catch the second trawler. This took a little time, but on June 25, cruisers and destroyers, again carrying an O.I.C./B.P. specialist, Lieutenant Allan Bacon, R.N.V.R., surprised and captured *Lauenberg* with documents and cipher material which the Admiralty subsequently described as being of 'inestimable value'.

Before this, however, in fact on the day after *München* had been captured, an even more important 'pinch' had been made. On May 8, U.110, commanded by one of Dönitz's aces, Kapitän Leutnant Julius Lemp, had attacked an outward bound convoy, OB.318, south of Greenland, but had been heavily counter-attacked and blown to the surface by the Senior Officer of the 3rd Escort Group. Captain Baker Cresswell saw the chance of securing not only a prize but also cipher material, of whose vital importance he was very conscious. He had no O.I.C. expert with him, but a boarding party under Sub-Lieutenant David Balme, R.N., reached U.110 and not only managed to prevent the U-boat from sinking but recovered, intact and undamaged, its cipher machine with all its accompanying material and many other secret documents. Baker Cresswell took great pains to prevent his prisoners from seeing what was happening, and the capture of U.110 was successfully kept a secret not only throughout the war but right up to 1958. The fact that the U-boat eventually sank before she could be towed to Iceland, although a disappointment at the time, may well have contributed to the maintenance of the secret.

The tremendous importance of this capture cannot be overemphasized, for U.110's cipher material was valid at least until the end of June and permitted B.P. to start reading. Nor was the German confidence that, once the validity of the current settings had expired our cryptanalysts would be again defeated, justified; we continued to read Hydra, albeit with varying time lags when periodically new settings had to be cracked, throughout the war. The penetration of this cipher, just when all our other sources of information were also beginning to produce greatly improved results, at last enabled O.I.C. to function as it had always been hoped that it would. It was equivalent to a major victory in itself, but in addition led B.P. on to successes with other ciphers, such as Neptun, the operational cipher for the heavy ships, and Sud and Medusa in the Mediterranean. The Intelligence scales, which had hitherto been heavily weighted in the favour of the Germans, were beginning to swing more to our side.

5

The Sinking of the *Bismarck*

AND SO, at last, Bletchley Park would be able to provide the Royal Navy with the same sort of help which it had already been giving to the R.A.F. and the Army, and which the B.Dienst had been supplying so successfully to Admirals Raeder and Dönitz. However, before we can examine the practical results which were to flow from this invaluable asset, we must consider a highly dramatic operation in which knowledge gained from cryptanalysis played a very minor part. This episode is particularly interesting from the Intelligence point of view because it marks a watershed in O.I.C.'s history. Up to this time our conventional sources of information, after an ineffective start, had been gradually and consistently improving. The pursuit of *Bismarck* was to demonstrate that at their best, and without significant help from B.P., they could provide the sort of intelligence which the Commander-in-Chief of the Home Fleet had for so long been demanding.

Scharnhorst and *Gneisenau* were still safely in Brest after a highly successful cruise of commerce destruction. Raeder now planned an even more devastating attack, using the two battle-cruisers in combination with two new warships which were at last ready for operations, the battleship *Bismarck* and the heavy cruiser *Prinz Eugen*. Both ships greatly exceeded pre-war treaty limitations on size and outclassed their British equivalents. Although the Admiralty were not, at the time, fully aware of this, it was clear enough that if the Germans should send out a squadron comprising a modern battleship, two battlecruisers (more strictly fast battleships, and regarded as such by the Germans), with a heavy cruiser, the destruction which it could inflict in the Atlantic would be appalling. The Home Fleet at this time consisted of Tovey's flagship, *King George* V and her sister ship, the very newly commissioned *Prince of Wales*, the battlecruiser *Hood*, which despite her size, speed and beauty, had been designed before Jutland and was now obsolete, the equally obsolete and even less powerful *Repulse*, and the new aircraft carrier *Victorious* whose aircrews were still inexperienced. At Gibraltar there was Force H, consisting of another old battlecruiser, *Renown*, and the famous carrier *Ark Royal*. Other battleships, mostly First War veterans, were available for convoy work, but all in all it was a far from reassuring picture.

Fortunately, the Germans found that *Scharnhorst* would require engine repairs which would take several months to complete, and then on April 6, one of four torpedo bombers of Coastal Command managed, before it was shot down, to hit and severely damage *Gneisenau*. Flying Officer Kenneth Campbell received a posthumous V.C. for this extraordinarily gallant attack, which almost certainly contributed to warding off a major disaster.

The inability to employ either of the two battlecruisers was a setback for the Germans. After some debate as to whether it would not now be better to postpone *Bismarck*'s departure until she could be accompanied by her sister ship, *Tirpitz*, still in the process of working up, Raeder decided that he must not forego the opportunity to strike a further blow at British sea communications, and the decision was taken to send out *Bismarck* and *Prinz Eugen* on their own. They sailed from Gdynia on May 18, under the command of Admiral Lütjens, who had commanded the sortie of *Scharnhorst* and *Gneisenau*.

The Admiralty had long been anxious to learn when *Bismarck* would be ready for operations. She had been commissioned at the end of August 1940, but, unlike the British, who were compelled to press every ship into service at the earliest possible moment, the Germans insisted on a long and thorough period of working up before they would commit a warship to actual operations. Denning, in O.I.C., had followed her move from Hamburg to Kiel, back to Hamburg and then back again to Kiel, thanks to the greater frequency of photographic reconnaissance which was now becoming possible, but when she moved to the eastern Baltic in March 1941 he had to be content with such information as could be obtained from agents. This, however, included one report from Gdynia that she was being issued with fresh portfolios of charts* and another from France that moorings for a battleship were being prepared in Brest. It was obvious by April not only that she was ready for operations but that an Atlantic sortie was being planned, and the Home Fleet was alerted.

The next sign, during the second week in May, was a very considerable increase in German air reconnaissance over Scapa Flow and up towards the Denmark Strait. Some of the evidence for this came from the decrypting of low-grade German Air Force signals. It was obvious that, barring postponements, a breakout attempt was now imminent. Admiral Tovey therefore strengthened his cruiser patrols in the Iceland-Faeroes passage and in the Denmark Strait where he stationed *Norfolk* and *Suffolk*. The latter ship was one of the first to be fitted with an efficient radar set, a fact that was to prove of great importance. The scene was being set, but Tovey's problem was similar to that of his immediate predecessor, Admiral Forbes, and of Jellicoe in the First War. When should he put to sea with the main strength of the Home Fleet? If he sailed too early, he might have to return to refuel at a critical moment; if he delayed too long, the enemy might already have gained the safety of the vast expanses of the Atlantic. He must have precise information of the movements of the German squadron before he could make a move.

The next act in the drama was played in neutral Stockholm. Sweden was in a difficult position. Since the fall of Denmark and Norway she had virtually been cut off from the West and could,

* Denning believes that this information was in fact derived from a decrypt. If this is correct, it is possible that a limited break into some administrative traffic permitting the reading of some out-of-date signals was achieved earlier than hitherto supposed, perhaps as a result of material recovered from *Krebs*. See Chapter 4. It is, however, more probable that if a decrypt was available it was of a German Air Force signal. See footnote on page 6. Signals concerning charts for prize crews and other matters, dating back to April but making quite clear that the object of the forthcoming mission was a commerce raiding cruise in the Atlantic, were decrypted on May 21, that is when the two ships had already reached Bergen.

on her own, put up little effective opposition if the Germans should decide to attack her. Some of her military and political leaders, if not positively pro-German, were at least convinced that Germany was bound to win. Britain, it must be remembered, still stood completely alone. It was no wonder that Sweden's neutrality was strictly enforced so far as Britain was concerned and benevolent, to say the least, vis-à-vis Germany. There were, however, certain Swedes who were passionately sympathetic to their conquered cousins, the Norwegians, and to the British. One such was a Major Törnberg, Chief of Staff to the head of the Swedish Secret Service. He was friendly with the Norwegian Military Attaché, Colonel Roscher Lund and with the British Naval Attaché, Captain Henry Denham, who since his arrival in Stockholm in the previous year had worked hard at making friends and influencing people.

On the afternoon of May 20, Lütjens had his first piece of bad luck. When north of Gothenburg and just after altering course to the north-west for the southern coast of Norway, he was sighted by the Swedish cruiser, *Gotland*, which as a matter of routine, reported the composition and course of the German squadron to Stockholm. Törnberg saw this signal and at once took steps to ensure that the substance of it reached Roscher Lund, without apparently specifying the original source, presumably to maintain his own security. Roscher Lund hurried to Denham who by nine o'clock that evening had sent the following Most Immediate signal to the D.N.I. in London: 'Kattegat to-day 20th May. At 1500 two large warships escorted by three destroyers, five escort vessels ten or twelve aircraft passed Marstrand course north-west. B.3.' 'B.3.' represented Denham's grading of the reliability of the information he was passing. It was a system devised in N.I.D., and subsequently adopted by the other services, to indicate its assessment of the reliability of information received: A to E, for the source and 1 to 5 for the contents of the report. Thus Denham's grading showed that his source was good and the information, in his opinion, possibly, but not certainly, correct.

When, soon after midnight, Denning, who as usual was sleeping in O.I.C., received Denham's signal he was not of course surprised and mentally upgraded it to B.2. He soon received further confirmation in the shape of a report from Christiansand, at the southern tip of Norway, where members of the local Resistance had also sighted the German ships and had, at great risk to themselves, immediately signalled the fact to London. Denning promptly informed the Naval Staff and Admiral Tovey and by 3:30 A.M. on May 21, had arranged for Coastal Command to start to search the Norwegian coast at first light until *Bismarck* and *Prinz Eugen* were again located. They had in fact put into Korsfjord, the entrance to Bergen, so that *Prinz Eugen*, but not for some inexplicable reason *Bismarck*, could top up with fuel. There they were sighted and photographed at 1:15 P.M. by a P.R.U. Spitfire from Wick piloted by Flying Officer Michael Suckling. So important was it to be sure of the true identity of the ships seen that the photographs, after examination at Wick, were flown down to London, where Wick's interpretation was confirmed.

Now that Lütjens' ships had been located and positively identified, Tovey was able to take further steps and therefore sailed *Hood* and *Prince of Wales* to join *Norfolk* and *Suffolk* in the Denmark Strait. He could not, however, leave Scapa Flow himself with the rest of the Home Fleet until he was sure that the Germans had left Korsfjord. To his dismay the weather closed in and Coastal Command had to cancel all reconnaissance patrols until further notice. It looked as if no information would be available for at least twenty-four hours, and this might well be too late. Clayton, Deputy Director Intelligence Centre, despatched Denning and Kemp post-haste to B.P. to impress on the Naval Section the vital importance of securing further information about the Germans' intentions. Unfortunately B.P. were unable, at that moment, to give any help.

In fact *Bismarck* and *Prinz Eugen* had sailed the previous evening as soon as the latter ship had completed her fuelling and they were now steaming north, thankful for the continuing bad weather promised by their meteorologists. However, at the naval air station at Hatson, the commanding officer, Captain Fancourt, R.N., realized the vital importance of obtaining confirmation of the Germans' departure, and his second-in-command, Commander Geoffrey Rotherham, volunteered, despite the dreadful conditions, to try to reconnoitre Bergen in one of his old twin-engined Marylands, used for target towing. Thanks to his brilliant navigation and the skill of his pilot he succeeded, and by that evening was able to assure Tovey that there were no heavy ships in Bergen or any of the surrounding fjords. The C.-in-C. took *King George* V, *Repulse* and *Victorious* to sea that night, heading south of Iceland.

Lütjens, by contrast, was being badly served by his Intelligence Department. Considerable precautions had been taken to try and keep his departure secret, including the issue for the first time of the big ships' operational cipher, Neptun, and the banning of all merchant shipping movements in the Great Belt for twenty-four hours. Despite this he had been detected, a fact which he suspected and which was rapidly confirmed to Raeder by Admiral Canaris, chief of the German Secret Service, probably as a result of decrypting Denham's signal. The G.A.F.'s reconnaissance of Scapa Flow had been sufficiently intense to alert the British that something was in the wind, but was proving in the event inefficient and unreliable. It had failed to report the strengthening of the cruiser patrols in the Denmark Strait, and above all was unable on several days to achieve more than visual reconnaissance of the Home Fleet's anchorage. Even when photographs were obtained, their first phase interpretation was inaccurate and left Lütjens gravely misinformed about the composition and movements of the Home Fleet, an error that was compounded by the usually perspicacious B.Dienst, who reported that there were no signs from W/T traffic of any unusual activity. Finally German Naval Intelligence had not appreciated the advances made in British radar. When, late on May 23, *Bismarck* and *Prinz Eugen* encountered *Norfolk* and *Suffolk* in the Denmark Strait, the Germans were surprised and disconcerted by the ease with which their shadowers maintained contact with them throughout the night. But for these failures, in such contrast to the situation during the Norwegian campaign, Lütjens would almost certainly have delayed his passage through the Denmark Strait, and once sighted there might well have turned back. His orders, after all, were to avoid battle if possible and to concentrate on commerce destruction.

Back in the Admiralty hopes were high. The German ships had been found: they were being successfully shadowed and reported by the two cruisers; *Hood* and *Prince of Wales* were on an intercepting course and by early on the next day, the 24th, it would surely be all over. The author well remembers going off duty that night, happily confident that when he returned *Bismarck* and *Prinz Eugen* would have been disposed of. Like very many others he could not at first believe the news next morning that, within a few minutes of action being joined at 6 A.M., *Hood* had been hit by salvoes from both the German ships and had blown up leaving only three survivors. *Prince of Wales*, with some of her main armament out of order (she still had civilian technicians on board trying to put right teething troubles in her 14-inch guns), was also hit and forced to withdraw out of range. She had, it is true, herself hit *Bismarck* causing an oil leak which, in conjunction with Lütjen's failure to top up at Bergen, was to have a profound effect on the situation, but of this we had no precise knowledge.

However, there was still Admiral Tovey in *King George* V, with *Repulse* and *Victorious*, steaming up fast south of Iceland. *Prince of Wales* and the cruisers were shadowing the Germans and, as the reports came in and were plotted on Denning's chart, it seemed certain that retribution could not be long delayed. At midnight on the 24th *Victorious* was within range and launched an air attack. One hit was secured, but it did not seem to be serious. We were unaware that Lütjens had already decided that shortage of fuel would compel him to make for France and that he had signalled this intention to Kiel, nor that he had managed to detach *Prinz Eugen* unobserved so that she could operate independently. The shadowing reports continued to arrive regularly and we felt sure that next morning the Home Fleet would make contact.

Then at 3 A.M. on the 25th, *Suffolk*, on the outer leg of a zigzag, lost contact. For a time we hoped she would regain it, but as the hours passed and as the searches by ships and aircraft failed to discover any trace of the Germans, depression and anxiety deepened again. Had *Bismarck* turned back for Germany or was she to escape into the Atlantic as *Scheer*, *Hipper*, *Scharnhorst* and *Gneisenau* had done before her? Once truly lost it would require quite exceptional luck to find her again, and nothing short of a miracle to do so with a force capable of destroying her.

But it was Lütjen's luck that was out: ours was in. Just before 7 A.M. the telephone from Scarborough, the controlling D/F station, rang on the D/F plotters' desk in O.I.C., and Peter Kemp began to take down the bearings of a German signal on the big ship frequency. Just under one hour later a further long signal was intercepted. The German Admiral cannot have realized that he had at long last shaken off his pursuers, and thinking that his position, course and speed must be known to his opponents, decided he would report details of the engagement with *Hood*, the successful detachment of *Prinz Eugen*, his now critical shortage of oil and his determination to make straight for France. None of this, of course, could be known to us. To Denning and Kemp, who had returned by now to the Admiralty, it was inexplicable. What emergency could be causing the Germans to reveal their position in this way? Surely they must realize that we had lost them and had no idea in which direction they were moving? However, when Kemp began to lay off the bearings on the special Gnomonic chart† required for this purpose, he became less cheerful. *Bismarck* was, at this time, some 1,200 miles due west of Edinburgh, and as the bearings from the United Kingdom stations were pencilled onto the chart it was obvious that they were not going to produce a neat 'cocked hat', or clear cut fix. They were good for latitude but poor for longitude: they ran almost parallel, giving several very acute intersections. For some reason nothing had been received from Iceland or Gibraltar, so to the laymen it appeared that there were three or four possible positions spread over several hundred miles. It could be that *Bismarck* was now doubling back on her tracks, returning again through the Denmark Strait, or perhaps through the Iceland-Faeroes passage, to Norway. However, after twenty months of war the D/F plotters had become highly skilled, and the more Kemp looked at the bearings the more sure he was that they indicated exactly the contrary. He gradually became certain that *Bismarck* was now well to the south-east of her last reported position and that this must mean that she was proceeding to France. He discussed the question fully with Denning who agreed, as did Clayton when they reported the situation to him.

The normal procedure for signalling D/F fixes was simply to give O.I.C.'s estimate of the position of the transmitting unit, and had this been done on this occasion the signal would have read more or less as follows:

† Charts following the Great Circle lines of the earth as opposed to those with Mercator's projection used for navigation.

'From Admiralty.   Most Immediate.   Secret.
To . . . C.-in-C. Home Fleet, Force H., *Rodney*, *Ramillies*.
Repeated AIG 47.
Inconclusive D/F bearings on ——kc/s. at 07.49 indicate
enemy surface ship within 100 miles of 55N 34W.
COMMENT. Admiralty appreciate *Bismarck* proceeding
south-east probably to Biscay.'

However, when Denning and Kemp proposed this to Clayton
he reminded them that Tovey, before the start of the operation,
had specifically requested that he be supplied with the actual bearings only and left to draw his own conclusions as to the position
indicated by them. His reason was that two of his destroyers had
recently been fitted with H/F D/F sets from which he hoped to
receive bearings which, when added to those signalled to him by
O.I.C., would give first class cuts. In the event neither of the destroyers was with him at the time, but even if they had been,
there seems no reason why he should not have received O.I.C.'s
estimate of the fix to compare with that shown on his own plot.

At the time of the transmissions the Home Fleet was some distance to the south-west of *Bismarck* which was already on a south-
easterly course for France. Tovey was of course ignorant of this
fact and was quite rightly concerned with the other two possibilities, namely that she was either proceeding to the west or
south-west to carry on her raiding cruise, or that she had turned
back to the north-east for Norway. As long as the Home Fleet
continued to search on the basis that either of these assumptions
was correct it was allowing *Bismarck* to draw further and further
away from it, and with no great margin of speed available the
chances of overtaking her, once the other possibilities had been
exhausted, became more and more remote. It was the night after
Jutland all over again.

The poor quality of the bearings received in O.I.C. had resulted
in some time elapsing before study of them was completed and
the question of whether to signal a fix or only the bearings was
finally decided. It was not until after ten o'clock that they were received in the flagship, three hours after the transmission had been
made, during which time *Bismarck* had made good another sev-
enty miles away from the Home Fleet. This was bad enough, but

there then followed an error on board the flagship which very nearly resulted in the *Bismarck*'s escape. For some reason which has still not been conclusively settled, Tovey's staff decided that the bearings showed a position not south-east but north-east of *Bismarck*'s last known position, suggesting that she was returning to Norway. For several precious hours the Home Fleet steamed to the north-east, thus widening still further the gap between it and its adversary. Both Denning and Kemp remain convinced to this day that the reason for this mistake was because the flagship was not carrying the special gnomonic charts essential for plotting D/F bearings.‡ Unless these had been specially supplied before she put to sea for the chase, there was no reason why she should have been. Kemp subsequently laid off the bearings on an ordinary Mercator's navigational chart and, sure enough, the best apparent fix thus revealed was several degrees further north than the similar fix on his own chart. Denning has a distinct recollection of an 'inquest' into the whole matter when the operation was over, after which he had to arrange for gnomonic charts to be issued to *King George* V. This is strong evidence, but Captain Frank Lloyd, Master of the Fleet and responsible for its navigation, who after all was on the spot at the time, indignantly denies this suggestion. It may be that it was simply the far greater experience of Kemp and his team which enabled them to make the right choice from what everyone agrees was a very inconclusive set of bearings. The procedure was certainly not repeated, and on the infrequent occasions in the future when bearings were signalled to ships at sea, they were always accompanied by O.I.C.'s estimate of the fix.

Be that as it may, in O.I.C., where the Operations Staff had gathered, there was growing anxiety. Tovey had signalled his position at 10:47 and unless he had better information than O.I.C., which of course had to be accepted at the time as possible, he was moving in the wrong direction.

By this time a number of measures had already been taken. Force H had been instructed to leave Gibraltar in case *Bismarck* was heading south-east, the battleship *Rodney*, on her way to America for a much needed refit, had reversed course, and the Jutland veteran *Ramillies* had been ordered to leave the convoy she

‡ Captain Roskill now states in a letter to the author that he has 'formal evidence' that this was the cause of the error.

was escorting and also join in the hunt. Cruisers, destroyers and aircraft were all alerted and diverted from their existing tasks to try and draw the net tighter. But precisely which course should they assume *Bismarck* was on?

Denning and Kemp begged to be allowed to send out their estimate of the fix, but for once there was considerable disinclination to interfere with the man on the spot just because the Intelligence experts held a contrary view to his. However, the Directors of the Plans and Operations Divisions were each instructed to consider the situation and both came back with appreciations supporting the O.I.C. view. Finally between 10:23 and 11:08 signals were despatched to Tovey and the other ships and authorities concerned informing them that the Admiralty considered *Bismarck* was making for France. This theory was strengthened when at 10:54 another and slightly more conclusive fix was obtained, and this time O.I.C.'s plotted position was passed to Tovey, who did not, however, receive it until 2 P.M. An hour and a quarter later he altered course to the south-east but by this time the gap had widened even further. Another fix had been obtained at 1:20 but the transmission was on the U-boat, not the surface ship, frequency. Despite the fact that the Germans had never adopted such a procedure in the past it was assumed that this signal emanated from *Bismarck* and that she must be communicating direct with U-boats. The transmission in fact came from a U-boat reporting the position of *Victorious*. The bearings were again poor but showed an apparent fix close to *Bismarck*'s actual position. This position was passed to Tovey as further evidence of the direction in which *Bismarck* was proceeding. It was a more fortunate mistake than that made earlier.

During the afternoon, and after Tovey had altered to the southeast, the Admiralty instructed *Rodney*, who at that time was ahead of *Bismarck* but right across her future track, not to steer for France but north for the Iceland-Faeroes gap, the direction in which Tovey had so recently been searching. Why this signal was sent remains a mystery. One theory is that it was originated by Winston Churchill, who always had difficulty in resisting the temptation to take charge at such moments. Alternatively it may have been designed to ensure that *Rodney* joined forces with *King*

George V, now on her own as *Repulse* and *Victorious* had been detached to fuel. If so it was poorly worded, and perhaps unintentionally confused intelligence with operational matters. Fortunately it made little difference so far as *Rodney*'s movements were concerned, but it baffled Tovey who assumed that the Admiralty was now of the opinion after all that *Bismarck* was heading for the Iceland-Faeroes passage, not for France. He altered to a compromise course, which he hoped would cover both contingencies but which nevertheless still further delayed his pursuit. Increasingly puzzled, he could contain himself no longer and at 4:30 inquired from the Admiralty if they really thought *Bismarck* was heading for the Iceland-Faeroes passage. The reply, inevitably, was slow in coming and by the time that it did reach him, he had already decided for himself that Lütjens was going for France not Norway. He was by now a long way astern of his quarry.

Whatever the doubts in Tovey's mind, there were none in those of the officers of O.I.C. Active preparations were in fact being made for *Bismarck*'s reception in Brest and operational control had passed from Gruppe Nord in Kiel to Gruppe West in France. The consequent change in the pattern of W/T traffic had not gone unnoticed. We were also beginning to get decrypted G.A.F. messages consistent with preparations to give her air cover as soon as she came within range. There could be no question about the enemy's general destination. The only hope now lay with Force H coming up from Gibraltar. *Renown* was even less fitted to take on *Bismarck* single-handed than *Hood* had been, but if *Ark Royal*'s aircraft could at least slow down the German battleship, *King George* V and *Rodney* might still join up and catch her. What was needed, as always, was accurate information about her position, course and speed.

Plans were therefore discussed with Coastal Command for box searches by flying-boats at first light next morning. The Flag Officer Submarines was instructed to sail six submarines to the Bay of Biscay, and various cruisers and destroyers were diverted from their current tasks to steer on intercepting courses. All now depended on finding *Bismarck* and on being able to direct *Ark Royal*'s aircraft on to her and, despite the odds, on their then being able to carry out a successful attack. At 7 P.M. final and positive confirmation of the battleship's precise destination reached O.I.C. It did not affect the situation greatly, because all possible steps were already being taken, but it was a relief to Clayton, Denning and Kemp to have proof of the correctness of the views which they had been expressing for the past twelve hours.

Bismarck's victory over *Hood* had very naturally been triumphantly broadcast to the German people and the world, but many listeners must have wondered to themselves whether she would still be able to escape from or defeat the large number of British ships which must now be seeking her. Amongst them was, apparently, a high-ranking G.A.F. officer, either stationed in or visiting Athens, who, according to some accounts, had a midshipman son on board the battleship. At any rate, in response to some enquiry, a signal in what B.P. called the 'red' G.A.F. cipher was sent to Athens* stating that *Bismarck* was making for Brest. It may even have given some imprecise indication of her position, but this is less certain. After some delays, due to corrupt groups in the original German message, B.P. managed to unbutton it and telex it around 6:30 P.M. to O.I.C. It was an interesting example of the need to restrict knowledge of an important operational nature solely to those with an incontrovertible need to know, and also of how a scrap of otherwise useless information from one service might be of great value to another. As it happened, the damage, from the German point of view, had already been done, but it might have been O.I.C.'s and the Admiralty's only clue to *Bismarck*'s movements.

Up to the last, the outcome of the whole operation remained in doubt. The Catalina flying boat, which finally sighted *Bismarck* some 700 miles west of Brest at 10:30 A.M. on the 26th, was on an additional patrol personally suggested by Sir Frederick Bowhill, the Air Officer Commander-in-Chief of Coastal Command. But for his shrewd guess as to the precise course *Bismarck* would take, she might still have escaped detection. But it was not to be. By that evening Force H was near enough to launch *Ark Royal*'s aircraft. The weather conditions were appalling but our only hope

---

* The officer concerned may have been General Jeschonnek or possibly General Milch. In any case it seems more probable that the cipher used was a G.A.F. not a diplomatic one.

lay with the carrier's slow and outmoded Swordfish. Tovey and *Rodney* were too far behind to catch *Bismarck* before she was under the protection of the G.A.F. and Dönitz's U-boats, unless she could be drastically slowed down. The Swordfish did even better than that. Amongst the torpedo hits they secured was one on her stern which crippled her rudders and damaged her propellers. She could only steam in circles. She no longer had any hope of escape.

King George V and *Rodney*, with destroyers and cruisers from other hunting forces, came up during the night. Tovey attacked next morning, and soon reduced *Bismarck* to a battered and burning hulk. At 10:36 A.M. on May 27, with her colours still flying, she sank, scuttled by her survivors.†

Like Waterloo, 'it had been a damned nice thing—the nearest run thing you ever saw in your life'. Most of Tovey's ships, including his flagship, had barely enough fuel to get home. A few more miles and *Bismarck* would have been under the cover of the G.A.F. A U-boat had actually sighted Force H before *Ark Royal's* attack but had already fired all its torpedoes. In the very last hours of the operation B.P. had started to decrypt cipher Hydra, and O.I.C. knew and warned Tovey that U-boats were being ordered to make for the scene to take off *Bismarck's* War Diary and attack her opponents. If *Ark Royal's* aircraft had not secured a hit in the one place that could cripple her she might still have eluded us. But luck had been with the Germans on all their previous sorties. Perhaps they had no right to count on it again.

It was not, however, just good luck which led to the final British victory. For the first but not the last time, accurate and rapid intelligence had enabled the Admiralty and the Commander-in-Chief to concentrate overwhelming force at the decisive point. Tovey was generous in his praise and wrote in his Report of Proceedings, 'The accuracy of the information supplied by the Admiralty and the speed with which it was passed were remarkable; and the balance struck between information and instruction passed to the forces out of visual touch with me was ideal.'

† See Ludovic Kennedy: *Pursuit*. Collins. There seems little doubt that scuttling charges were fired but whether they actually caused *Bismarck* to sink is doubtful. It would have been a remarkable coincidence if they had taken effect at exactly the same moment as *Dorsetshire's* torpedoes.

O.I.C. could feel well-satisfied that, at last, its efforts had contributed to a resounding success. Early warning had been given of *Bismarck*'s imminent departure, she had been detected before she ever reached the North Sea, found again in Korsfjord, and intercepted and shadowed in the Denmark Strait. The story should have ended there, but after *Bismarck* had sunk *Hood* and then shaken off her pursuers, it was O.I.C.'s skilled interpretation of the D/F bearings of her long signals which, at the eleventh hour, provided the clue which led to her second interception and destruction.

Some recent accounts‡ give all the credit to cryptanalysis, but in truth it played only a minor part. Evidence from G.A.F. wireless traffic certainly helped to point to the Denmark Strait as *Bismarck*'s probable outward route, but the decrypts suggesting G.A.F. activities in the Bay of Biscay on the 26th, the Athens message and the instructions to U-boats were all received too late to influence events. They were no more than added confirmation of the correctness of the appreciation made by O.I.C. at seventhirty on the morning of the 25th, to which effect was given in a variety of signals and instructions issued before noon on that day. Suggestions that signals to and from *Bismarck* were decrypted at this time are certainly without foundation.* B.P.'s enormous contribution to the war at sea was still to be made.

Another valuable source also supplied highly accurate information which arrived too late. A French naval officer, Lieutenant Phillipon, working in the dockyard at Brest, and a member of the Resistance, learned early on May 25 that preparations were being made for *Bismarck*'s reception there. He had already sent us reports concerning *Scharnhorst* and *Gneisenau*, including one about Flying Officer Campbell's successful attack which reached us within forty-eight hours of the event. Although he despatched his message about *Bismarck* at once, when Denning and Kemp were anxiously considering the D/F bearings and when Tovey and the Home Fleet were searching in the wrong direction, it did not

‡ See Winterbotham: *The Ultra Secret.* Weidenfeld & Nicolson, and Cave-Brown: *The Bodyguard of Lies.* W. H. Allen.

* Recent releases confirm that, although most if not all the signals to and from *Bismarck* during the course of the operation were decrypted, none was in fact read until nearly twenty-four hours after she had been sunk.

reach O.I.C., and probably never could have done, in time for operational use to be made of it: an illustration of the difficulties faced by the bravest and best-informed agents in supplying really urgent operational information.

6

June–December 1941.
Special Intelligence at Last

IF CRYPTANALYSIS had played no significant part in the sinking of *Bismarck*, it certainly enabled the Admiralty to deliver a shattering blow against her supply ship organization, which virtually ruled out any further long distance cruises by the remaining heavy units and also prevented a planned extension of the U-boat war to South African waters.

By the middle of May, the hoard of material captured from U.110 had reached B.P. and had been put to speedy use.* A flood of decrypted and translated signals concerning the operational U-boats began to pour into O.I.C. Some of these signals were current ones—that is to say, they were completely up-to-date and were read by B.P. as soon as they were transmitted and as quickly as by the intended recipients. Others were older ones dating back as far as the beginning of February. Together they made it possible, for the first time, for Winn in the Submarine Tracking Room to build up a comprehensive and accurate picture of the whole operational U-boat fleet including the dispositions and movements of those boats actually at sea in the North Sea and Atlantic. We will return to this later, because the decrypts gave other information which in the short run was at least of equal importance.

Bismarck's supply fleet had consisted of six tankers and one sup-

---

* Current reading was not achieved until June 1.

ply ship. Two of the tankers were stationed in the area between the north coast of South America and the west coast of Africa and the remainder in the North Atlantic. Their duties were not only to supply the big ships but also U-boats, and for this reason, as well as to avoid the possibility of their being mistaken for British or Allied ships and sunk by their own side, their positions were notified to all U-boats likely to encounter them.† As soon as this knowledge became available to O.I.C., steps were taken to organize hunting groups of cruisers and aircraft carriers to round them up. Had *Prinz Eugen* remained at sea as planned, her location would also have been revealed in the same way and she would almost certainly have suffered the same fate as *Bismarck*. Fortunately for her, she had developed engine defects soon after parting company from the battleship and had put into Brest on June 1 for an overhaul. The supply ships however were not to benefit from such inverted luck. The first to be intercepted was the tanker *Belchen* on June 3, south-west of Greenland. On the next day it was the turn of the two southernmost tankers, *Esso Hamburg* and *Egerland* and the tanker *Gedania* and the supply ship *Gonzenheim* between seven hundred and nine hundred miles west of Brest. The last two tankers, the *Friedrich Breme* and the *Lothringen*, were caught in mid-Atlantic on June 12 and 15 respectively. It was a clean sweep but it was not the end of the story, because two supply ships for armed merchant raiders, *Babitonga* and *Alstertor*, were also intercepted, the first just north of the equator on June 21, and the second a couple of hundred miles off the Spanish coast on the 23rd. It was a classic example of what could be accomplished with first-class intelligence if ships were available to act on it.

Only two ships were captured. The rest were either sunk or scuttled themselves. It has been suggested that documents taken from the captured ships played a part in our success in finding the others, but this seems improbable.‡ It is true that a great deal of valuable information was secured from *Gedania*, but British cruisers, unlike many German ships, did not carry special 'Y' parties trained to make immediate use of captured material, unless, as

† It is now clear that all signals to the supply ships themselves were read currently and so gave O.I.C. a clear idea of their dispositions and movements. One ship, *Spichern*, managed to escape and reach France.

‡ See footnote on preceding page.

was the case with the weather reporting trawlers, the whole object of the operation was to make a 'pinch'. Nothing generally could be done with captured papers until they were handed over to the experts in N.I.D. and B.P., and this inevitably took time.

O.I.C.'s elation at these successes was rapidly tempered by the realization that they might have compromised our new-found source of knowledge. The Germans would surely ask themselves how it had been possible for their enemies to discover the whereabouts of every single ship in the supply fleet and might well come to the conclusion that this could only have happened as the result of the penetration of their ciphers. If they did so, then they would certainly introduce changes as quickly as possible and we should again be 'blind'. These fears were well founded and the German Naval Staff did indeed carry out a searching inquiry not only into the loss of the supply ships but also into the question of whether there had been any breach of security in connection with the *Bismarck* operation. As regards the latter some facts were easily explainable: the unfortunate sighting by *Gotland*, for instance, or reports from Christiansand and Brest, where the Gestapo were certain that agents were active. Other facts could also be attributed to spies and agents, all the more readily because the Germans had what amounted to a phobia about the British Secret Service, 'so famed for its efficiency' as the report remarked. *Bismarck*'s long signal was quite reasonably assumed to have resulted in an accurate fix of her position and to have sealed her fate. It was not, therefore, surprising that the conclusion was that 'the possibility of the enemy's being able to read signals by deciphering them has been unanimously discounted by all the experts'.

The elimination of the supply ships and the weather reporting trawlers was, however, rather more difficult to explain away. The first inquiry again dismissed the possibility of the ciphers having been compromised, but doubts seem to have lingered, because when nearly a year later some incautious remarks were made by some British prisoners of war, a second inquiry was held, but once again it was considered that 'it is not necessary to put the blame on a breach of security as regards the code and cipher tables'. Once more the Secret Service was held responsible, plus bad luck and the possibility that some operational instructions had been captured from the two tankers. Experts—and the inquiry was headed by a signalman—are notoriously reluctant to admit that their own arrangements can be anything less than foolproof.

O.I.C. and B.P. were, of course, ignorant of these findings and were much relieved when it gradually became apparent that the gaff had not been blown, and that no major changes in ciphering procedures were being introduced. Nevertheless the lesson was taken to heart, and thereafter every effort was made to associate any operational activity which was in fact based on cryptanalysis, with some less precious source of intelligence such as D/F fixes or photographic reconnaissance, in the hopes that the enemy would also come to this conclusion if he conducted an inquiry. Only rarely and only after careful consideration was there any departure from this rule, which had the additional advantage of preventing the knowledge or even suspicion that we were decrypting German signals becoming widespread in the fleet and so in some way reaching the enemy.

To conclude the story of the surface raiders and their supply ships at this period, two further successes and one serious failure must now be mentioned. One of the most successful of the armed merchant raiders, Raider C, *Atlantis*, the first such ship to leave Germany back in March 1940, after operating in the Atlantic, then in the Indian Ocean and finally in the Pacific, had returned by November 1941 to the South Atlantic on her way home. She was instructed to meet and refuel U.126 south of the Equator so that the U-boat could continue further south to Cape Town. The instructions to U.126, although not those to *Atlantis* herself, were duly decrypted by B.P. and the cruiser *Devonshire* was ordered to carry out a general search for raiders and supply ships in the area concerned. She was warned that U-boats might well be encountered and so was not surprised when, her aircraft having sighted *Atlantis*, reported that a U-boat was apparently also present. On this occasion rapid confirmation was obtained from C.-in-C. South Atlantic that no British or Allied merchant ship could be in the vicinity so *Devonshire* opened fire from long range and sank the raider. With a U-boat present she could do nothing for the survivors, who were however picked up by U.126 as soon as *Devonshire* had departed. They were far too numerous to be accommodated for long in a single submarine, so two other U-boats were ordered to give assistance and then to rendezvous with a supply ship, *Python*, some 1,700 miles away from the position in which *Atlantis* had been sunk. Dönitz somewhat sadly remarks in his *Memoirs*, 'this meeting point, too, was located by the enemy', and *Python* was sunk by *Devonshire*'s sister ship, *Dorsetshire*. Over four hundred survivors were rescued by the U-boats, eventually transferred to Italian submarines summoned to the scene, and finally brought safely back to France, a considerable achievement. It was however clear to Dönitz that 'we could no longer hope to be able to maintain our U-boats in the Atlantic by means of surface supply ships and tankers. Their task was shortly to be taken over by the submarine tankers, the building of which had been put in hand at the beginning of the war'. It was equally clear to the German Naval Staff that surface raiders would have much more difficulty in the future, at least in the Atlantic, in securing supplies of fuel and provisions.

The losses, though, were not all on the German side. A few days before the sinking of *Python*, the Australian cruiser *Sydney* had encountered Raider G, *Komoran*, off the coast of Western Australia. Unable to establish the other ship's identity, *Sydney* had rashly approached to within 2,000 yards, when *Komoran* suddenly opened fire and torpedoed her. The damage was mortal but, before she herself sank, *Sydney* set her opponent on fire so that in the end she had to be abandoned. Although most of the raider's crew survived, *Sydney* was lost with all hands and without having been able to get off a single signal. It was a terrible example of the dangers of approaching an unidentified merchant ship too closely and without proper precautions.

By the end of 1941, however, three raiders out of the original seven had been sunk and the remainder had returned either to German- or Japanese-controlled ports. None was at sea. In 1942 a fresh wave was sent out, but they did not achieve the same measure of success as their predecessors.

Decrypts had certainly played a decisive part in all this. One of the raiders and eight supply ships owed their destruction to the betrayal of their positions by this source. Up to June 1941, no supply ship except *Altmarck* had been intercepted although many had been at sea in support of *Graf Spee, Deutschland, Scharnhorst* and *Gneisenau* and *Hipper*. Without cryptanalysis it is highly improbable that we should have had much better luck than we had experienced in earlier periods. Some of *Bismarck's* supply ships might have been found, but the majority would surely have escaped us and certainly neither *Devonshire* nor *Dorsetshire* could have been directed so precisely to such remote areas of the South Atlantic. It was a severe blow to German plans and one from which their surface ship operations on the broad oceans never fully recovered.

The Admiralty's worries about the heavy ships were not, on the other hand, greatly diminished. *Bismarck's* sister ship, *Tirpitz*, was now actively working up in the Baltic, and *Scharnhorst*, *Gneisenau* and *Prinz Eugen* seemed ideally poised for sudden short sorties against the Freetown-Gibraltar-U.K. route and the extremely valuable W.S. troop convoys to the Middle East. In consequence they were promptly subjected to heavy attacks by Bomber Command, and within five days of being hit by Flying Officer Campbell's torpedo *Gneisenau* suffered further severe damage from bomb hits so that repairs took nearly eight months to complete. When *Scharnhorst's* engine overhaul was finished, she was moved south to La Pallice, to try and avoid Bomber Command's attentions and to carry out exercises to regain her operational efficiency. Her new hideaway was quickly discovered and she was bombed, damaged and compelled to return again to Brest for further repairs. Nor did *Prinz Eugen* escape her share of damage, so that for a considerable period all three ships were immobilized although not unfortunately put permanently out of action.

The exact amount of damage suffered could not always be immediately detected by photographic reconnaissance, but the task of Denning's section in maintaining surveillance of the enemy squadron was certainly simpler than would have been the case had the three ships been in a German port. Photographic reconnaissance was still a difficult and dangerous task, but it was now being carried out with much greater efficiency and regularity than had previously been possible, and despite the Germans' efforts with smoke screens, camouflage and anti-aircraft defences, it was possible to follow the process of repairs, the preparations to dock or undock and the occasional exercises in coastal waters on a fairly consistent basis. Phillipon, who had informed us about the preparations made to receive *Bismarck*, continued to send detailed and accurate reports which were supplemented by others from two workmen actually employed in the dockyard: even more than with P.R.U., this was something we could not have hoped to obtain if the German ships had been in Kiel or Wilhelmshaven. Last but not least, Hydra, the cipher used by patrol craft and minesweepers in French waters, was now being decrypted continuously, although there were occasional delays. From this traffic it was often possible to obtain some clue as to an intended movement by the big ships. Communications between the various shore authorities, Gruppe West in Paris or O.K.M. in Berlin, remained, of course, beyond our reach, but the combination of photographic reconnaissance, agents' reports and a limited amount of information from decrypts of the small vessels' W/T traffic was sufficient to give Denning a pretty clear picture of the situation. When, early in 1942, after essential repairs had been completed, the German Naval Staff decided that the three ships must be brought back to Germany, Denning was able to inform the Admiralty and the R.A.F. that such a move was imminent.

It is now time to consider the results which the sudden and most welcome flow of decrypted signals had on the work of the Submarine Tracking Room. Dönitz had carefully weighed up the pros and cons of his U-boats maintaining strict wireless silence when on operations. In his *Memoirs* he writes as follows: 'It was of course obvious that as time went on the British would expand their D/F network and would achieve better results. . . . We had therefore to assume that the enemy would pick up every radio signal made by a U-boat and would be able to locate the boat's position. Every radio signal made, therefore, put us at a disadvantage. But these signals were equally of very great value to U-boat Command and what we had to do was to decide whether radio should or should not be used by U-boats. In any case it was obviously essential that the use of radio should be restricted to a minimum. But it was equally obvious that radio could not be dispensed with entirely. The signals from the U-boats contained information upon which was based the planning and control of those combined attacks which alone held the promise of really great success against the concentrated shipping of any enemy convoy. By means of intensive training and instruction U-boat Command did its best to pick its way along the narrow path between the pros and cons of radio transmission. An order on the subject gave the following instructions to commanders as a general guide:

'*In the actual operational area:* radio to be used only for the transmission of tactically important information, or when ordered to do so by U-boat Command or when the position of the transmitter is in any case already known to the enemy.

'*En route to or from the patrol area:* As above. Signals of lesser importance may be sent, but only very occasionally; in this connection care must be taken that the transmission does not compromise the area for other U-boats either already in the area or on their way to it.

'*Technical:* Frequent changes of wavelength, additional wavebands and wireless discipline to add to the enemy's difficulties with D/F.'

Given the fact that Wolf Pack tactics required a good deal of signalling, these were admirable instructions to counter the effects of our D/F system, as we had indeed already found to our cost. Even when an accurate fix was obtained, it was not easy to decide whether it came from a U-boat operating independently or in a pack, whether it was proceeding to or from patrol or whether its message was of an immediate or of a long-term character. As Dönitz had perceived, some successful diversions of convoys were made, but in other cases imprecise D/F fixes or faulty deductions from them resulted in failures to avoid dangers. Cryptanalysis soon changed all that. We rapidly learned the exact number of U-boats at sea, and not only the contents of their own signals but, even more important, the instructions constantly being pumped out to them by Dönitz from his headquarters in Lorient. As already emphasized, cryptanalysis must be swift if it is to have any value for operational purposes. The settings for the German cipher machines were changed daily, but so long as the instructions for the changes from U.110 remained valid there was no problem, and B.P. had no more difficulty in reading all signals transmitted than did the German recipients. These instructions ran out in July but the German confidence that, if such circumstances should ever occur our cryptanalysts would then be defeated, proved in the event to be misplaced. Some delays did begin to occur, but they were rarely of more than forty-eight hours' duration and throughout this period much traffic continued to be decrypted currently.

Of course as little as twenty-four hours' delay might mean that it was too late to take action, and even current reading could not provide us with knowledge of instructions given to U-boat commanders before sailing. We did however receive some help from the standing instructions for outward-bound U-boats to report their position when safely past a certain point, usually after crossing 15 degrees west if sailing from a French port or when through the Iceland-Faeroes passage if coming from Germany or Norway. In the case of the Biscay boats, whose ports of departure were known, this would usually show whether they were bound in a southerly or south-westerly direction or whether they were heading for the North-Western Approaches. U-boats destined for distant operations, such as U.126 bound for the South Atlantic, would probably get no further instructions until they had reached their designated operational area, but those intended for operations against North Atlantic convoys would, after their short position report, be given a fresh point for which to steer and then a few days later more precise orders based on the U-boat Command's latest appreciation of British convoy and escort dispositions. In such cases a twenty-four or even a forty-eight hour delay in reading the signals concerned would not necessarily be fatal.

Although the number of operational U-boats was still limited, it was beginning to increase alarmingly: sixty-five in July, eighty in October and ninety-one by January 1942. Of course only a proportion of them could be in their patrol areas at any one time, not often more than a third of the total number. It was also fortunate that despite bitter complaints on his part, Dönitz was compelled by O.K.M. to divert too much of his still modest strength to what he considered subsidiary and less vital tasks, to the Baltic and to Norway to operate against the Russians and to the Mediterranean to help Rommel and the Italians in their struggle in the Western Desert. By December no fewer than eighteen U-boats had passed through the Straits of Gibraltar, and this theatre of war was to remain for Dönitz a running sore in the same way that the Spanish Peninsula had been for Napoleon.

By this time, too, British resources were increasing both in quality and quantity, and for all these reasons it is not easy to assess exactly the effect of the Tracking Room's new source of knowledge. In May and June the monthly shipping losses from all causes in the Atlantic had exceeded 300,000 tons. In July and August, by which time Winn had got into his stride, they fell to under 100,000 tons. They rose again in September and October, when the U-boats were operating against the Gibraltar convoys with the benefit of good reconnaissance by the German Air Force and consequently fewer opportunities on our part for successful diversions, to over 150,000 tons, but in November and December they were down to only 50,000 tons. In January 1942 the losses soared again to 276,000 tons, but this was due mainly to the opening of the campaign in the coastal waters of the U.S.A. where, following America's entry into the war, the U-boats were to enjoy for many months to come a second 'glückliche Zeit'. Certainly the Tracking Room's contribution must have been one of the factors leading to increased British success in the Battle of the Atlantic during the second half of 1941.

Within O.I.C. itself various changes were introduced to cope with the flow of decrypted information which was now pouring in. A number of O.I.C.'s original staff had been transferred to other duties, and as far back as September 1940 Denning had realized that he must have additional men. An application had been made to the Paymaster Director General's Department for three Paymaster Lieutenants of 'above average intelligence'. The Director General replied ominously that O.I.C. would get the first three officers available, but in the event was better than his word and supplied Paymaster Lieutenants Clements, Fenley and Harrison who were to prove a tower of strength to Denning for the next two and a half years. They became the experts on the German-swept channels and any movements along them, Harrison being responsible for the Norwegian coast, Clements for the Baltic, Kattegat and Skagerrak, and Fenley for the Heligoland Bight, Channel and Bay of Biscay. It required much patient and detailed research to establish the exact position of these swept channels, but documents captured from the *Gedania* and U.110 proved to contain a wealth of information, and the three officers were also greatly assisted by analyses carried out by Naval Section at B.P. where the pressure from current operations was less intense. As a result of the close co-operation between the two organizations, from 1941 onwards the British records of swept channels and the location and movements of patrol craft, convoys and major warships along them was almost as accurate and as up-to-date as those maintained by the Germans. This was information of inestimable value in planning attacks on coastal convoys, on which the Germans depended heavily for the supply of their troops in the occupied countries, and Coastal and Bomber Commands as well as the Royal Navy relied largely on Denning and his staff. The accuracy of their information was also of great use to the minelaying campaign increasingly waged by the R.A.F. and the Navy, which not only sank many German ships but also caused them to divert an ever-increasing effort to minesweeping. This in turn provided us with a further source of intelligence when the signals made by and to the minesweepers were decrypted.

In the Tracking Room the staff position was less happy. Winn still had fewer than half a dozen assistants. They had to maintain an Atlantic plot on which were shown not only the latest estimated positions of all U-boats but also the positions and routes of British warships, convoys and independently routed vessels. This was of course on top of their task of dealing with the minute to minute and hour to hour flow of incoming signals concerning attacks, sightings, D/F fixes, and the queries from the Operations, Plans and Trade Divisions in the Admiralty, from Coastal Command and from headquarters in Ottawa, Newfoundland, Iceland, Freetown, Gibraltar and Cape Town. The situation was beginning to resemble that in Room 40 in 1916 when only the most urgent matters could receive attention. When the flow of decrypts began, Winn, partly for security reasons and partly because of shortage of staff, had to handle and file them all himself. He had no shorthand typist, not even a confidential filing clerk. In February 1941 as the importance and complexity of the work of the Room increased, it had been felt essential to transfer someone who was fully conversant with its methods and background to the Staff of the Commander-in-Chief Western Approaches. The choice had fallen on Lieutenant Commander Derek Crosse, who was appointed Staff Officer (Convoys) at Liverpool. Although this meant that the Tracking Room had in effect a fully trained and experienced representative on the C.-in-C.'s staff, it was a serious depletion of Winn's already over-stretched resources. He received no replacement until December 1941 when the author was transferred from Denning's Raider Section, where he was replaced by a very talented young officer, Sub-Lieutenant Hutchinson, R.N.V.R. Not long afterwards another experienced man, Lieutenant Foster, R.N.V.R., also one of the originals and one who had served in Room 40 in 1918, had to be sent out to Freetown to set up a miniature Tracking Room there. The staffing position was to remain very difficult for another six months.

The supply of decrypted information had raised other problems to which immediate solutions had to be found: how to ensure that everyone with a need to know, but no one for whom the knowledge was not essential, should be made aware of the information that was now available. The first decision was that there should be no circulation of the texts of decrypted signals outside O.I.C. The German signals, once decrypted and translated into English at B.P. were sent exactly as received on the direct teleprinter line to O.I.C.'s special teleprinter room, manned night and day by a devoted band of 'Teleprincesses'. There they were scrutinized by one of Denning's watchkeepers, extra copies typed if required, and distributed by hand of 'Secret Lady' to the appropriate section or sections, whose responsibility it then became to assess their significance and take whatever further action seemed necessary. This might well involve informing members of the Naval Staff or Commanders-in-Chief at home or overseas or the A.O.C.s-in-C. of Coastal, Bomber or Fighter Commands. A very carefully restricted list of individuals 'in the know' was compiled, starting, of course, with the First Sea Lord, Sir Dudley Pound. The First Lord of the Admiralty, A. V. Alexander, presumably with the Prime Minister's concurrence, was not one of the chosen few and he had no access to O.I.C. or to its secrets. Indeed many of O.I.C.'s papers were stamped 'Not to be shown to 1st Lord' and when he did occasionally visit the Lower War Room, the main Plot was suitably camouflaged for his benefit.* Winston had of course been well aware of our earliest break into the G.A.F.

* On one such day, when accompanying a Canadian V.I.P., he eluded his escort and found his way into the office in which Denning's assistant Fenley was working. Alexander began to cross-examine him about the exact nature of the work he was doing. Fenley, in accordance with his instructions, protested that he was not at liberty to reply, which somewhat naturally infuriated Alexander who insisted that he be given an answer. Despite increasingly anguished pleas from Fenley that 'he would really rather not say, Sir', the situation was only saved when the Canadian exploded 'Well, if this is Naval Intelligence I take my hat off to it!' and stalked out of the office.

traffic and had apparently insisted on being shown the raw intercepts personally. However, although he had been a frequent visitor to O.I.C. when he himself was First Lord, he never came there as Prime Minister, and the sheer volume and complexity of the German Naval signals was such that they were not intelligible and often not even interesting except in the context of all the other information which was only displayed on O.I.C.'s secret plots. He was, of course, kept properly informed of anything of major importance by the First Sea Lord and would sometimes ring up the Duty Captain at night to know what was going on. Fortunately, however, O.I.C. was not called upon to supply him with the spicy tit-bits of gossip and hot news which he was accustomed to receive from the Army and Air Force.

In the Admiralty, the Vice-Chief and Assistant Chiefs (Home, Foreign and Trade) of the Naval Staff and the Directors and Deputy Directors of the Operations, Plans, Trade, Anti-submarine Warfare and Torpedo and Mining Divisions were on the list, as were the Duty Captain and Duty Commander and the officer in charge of Trade Movements Plot and his deputy, but none of their subordinate staff. It was a much larger number of people than those privy to Room 40's secrets, but it was still a tiny proportion of the total Admiralty staff. In addition, of course, there were the Commanders-in-Chief at home and overseas (but only those whose areas were affected by the intelligence available), their Chiefs of Staff and perhaps two or, at the most, three of their other staff officers, and the same procedure was applied to the A.O.C.s-in-C. of Coastal, Bomber and Fighter Commands and their immediate subordinates.

Obviously the most secure means possible had to be found to transmit this very special intelligence by signal and the one-time pad system was used.† The normal procedure was to quote a full but paraphrased version of the original decrypt and then, under the heading 'Comment', give the deductions drawn by O.I.C. from the German message. This clearly distinguished facts from opinions and left it open to the recipient, who might sometimes possess local information not available to O.I.C., to come to a

---

† As its name implies, this system involved the use of a cipher for a single message only. The cipher table was then destroyed, thus presenting enemy cryptanalysts with an impossible task.

different conclusion if this seemed justified. These signals were given the top security classification, 'Hush. Most Secret', but it was soon realized that something more was needed to ensure that signals containing or based on information from decrypts were seen only by the strictly limited number of officers in the know. Commander Colpoys, of O.I.C. suggested that they be given the designation Ultra, about the only Latin he could remember, and this was then adopted. The word Ultra has now come to be used in a generic sense for all information available to the British in the last war derived from cryptanalysis, whatever the nation or service of origin and whatever form it took.‡ This usage is incorrect and in the Navy, at least, it was only applied to outgoing signals and documents as a security grading and the actual information itself was always referred to as 'Special Intelligence' or 'Z', because this letter was used as a prefix in the telex messages from B.P.

One side-effect of these arrangements was that the great majority of important operational decisions were not taken in the main Operations Rooms in the Admiralty and other commands, whose plots could not show the enemy dispositions in detail. They were taken instead in Denning's or Winn's rooms in the O.I.C., or in small side offices at Western Approaches or Coastal Command, or on special charts in flag officer's ships at sea, where whatever Special Intelligence was currently available could be safely displayed to the few senior officers with access to it.

Because of the need to protect the source and also because of the impossibility of constructing and distributing sufficient one-time pads, Special Intelligence could never be passed to the captains of private ships or the senior officers of convoy escort groups. Instructions to them had to appear to be based on conventional types of intelligence such as D/F fixes or photographic reconnaissance or in extremes just to an 'Admiralty appreciation'. There were however occasions when an officer who had been admitted to O.I.C.'s secrets while serving in the Admiralty and had then returned to sea, could read between the lines of such an apparently innocuous signal and know that it was in fact based on Special Intelligence.

In spite of the disasters in the Far East and Britain's desperate

‡ See F. W. Winterbotham: *The Ultra Secret*. Weidenfeld & Nicolson.

struggle in the Mediterranean, 1941 closed on a much happier note for O.I.C. than 1940 had done. All our conventional sources of intelligence were now functioning with great speed and efficiency. The *Bismarck* operation had demonstrated that. Special Intelligence was now beginning to give us an almost complete insight into the German Navy's routines and procedures in the Baltic, North Sea, Arctic, Mediterranean and Atlantic. It was no longer possible for weeks to elapse before we became aware that a major enemy ship had left Germany or that U-boats were proceeding to new and hitherto safe areas. If not always completely up-to-date, our information was now never completely stale, and if one source could not for the moment produce the answer, then another one or a combination of several almost always would. No longer need the Commander-in-Chief of the Home Fleet complain that the enemy knew all his moves while he remained in total ignorance of theirs. The Intelligence scene, at least, seemed set fair, whatever the operational difficulties might be. Unfortunately 1942 was to demonstrate that all O.I.C.'s problems were not yet over and that there were still unpleasant setbacks to be faced and awkward obstacles to be overcome.

7

January–July 1942.
Operation Paukenschlag
and the Great Black-out

DÖNITZ HAD always chafed under the ban on attacks within the American 'Neutrality Zone' imposed on him by Hitler. Two days after Pearl Harbor, he was informed that all restrictions had been lifted and he immediately started to plan the strongest possible attack against shipping off the eastern seaboard of the United States, where he correctly anticipated that the anti-submarine defences would be ill-prepared and inexperienced. To reach the convoy assembly ports of Halifax, and Sydney, Cape Breton Island would involve Biscay-based U-boats in round trips of some four and a half thousand miles, but the distance to and from New York was as much as six thousand and areas still further south even greater. As the first of the U-boat tankers would not be ready for operations for some months and refuelling from surface ships was now out of the question in the North Atlantic, only the larger 740-ton U-boats had the necessary endurance. Initially Dönitz could not obtain permission from O.K.M. for the release from their current tasks of more than six such boats for this mission, but preparations, with the code name Paukenschlag (Drumbeat) were promptly put in hand, and five boats actually left their French bases before the end of December. Their area of operations was to be from the St. Lawrence down to Cape Hatteras and, to ensure complete surprise, they were instructed to attack nothing except really large ships while on passage, to avoid detection when approaching the North American coast, and to wait for a signal from U-boat Command before going into action in order that they should all act simultaneously and thus create the greatest possible effect. On January 7 they were informed that the 13th of the month was to be the day for the first roll on the drum. Far from content with this, Dönitz managed also to secure permission to divert seven 500-tonners, which were operating near or proceeding to the Azores, to the Newfoundland-Nova Scotia area where he calculated they could remain for two or three weeks. By mid-January another wave of four 740-tonners would be ready, and these boats were destined for the Aruba-Curaçao-Trinidad area and its immensely valuable concentration of tanker traffic. To prevent British and American suspicions being aroused by the substantial reduction of activity in other areas of the Atlantic which would inevitably result from these moves, one U-boat was ordered to simulate the presence of many more by making a large number of dummy W/T signals in the North-Western Approaches. Considering Dönitz's limited resources, it was a well thought out scheme.

How far, in the event, did he manage to achieve the surprise which he sought? As early as December 29, Winn warned the Naval Staff in the regular weekly appreciations which he had just started to write, that 'there are indications of an inconclusive character that several U-boats may be moving to the Western Atlantic, possibly to operate in the Caribbean or off Halifax'. A week later he was able to state that the W/T deception measures observed in the North Western Approaches were probably intended to conceal the movements of (a) six U-boats to Cape Race, Argentina and St. Johns, Newfoundland, (b) seven U-boats round the Azores operating against the U.K.-Gibraltar-West African convoys, which had been diverted, (c) four U-boats in the North Western Approaches thought to be bound for the Mediterranean. He added that there was no conclusive evidence of any activity in the South Atlantic, but two 740-tonners had not been satisfactorily located. In his report for the week ending January 12, he was able to report that 'The general situation is now much clearer and the most striking feature is the heavy concentration off the North American seaboard from New York to Cape Race. Two groups have so far been formed. One of six boats is already in position off Cape Race and St. Johns and a second of five is approaching the American coast between New York and Portland. It is known that these five boats will reach their attacking areas by January 13. Five other U-boats are between 30 degrees and 50 degrees west proceeding towards one or other of the above areas, and may later be reinforced by yet another five westbound U-boats making a total of twenty-one boats. It was presumably with the intention of concealing this concentration that the W/T ruse in the North Western Approaches was carried out as described last week. The U-boat concerned is now returning to a Biscay port. Three of seven U-boats recently stationed in the Azores area have now proceeded to the Cape Race area'.

By the time of the next report on January 19, the attack had of course opened, but the approximate numbers involved and their areas of operations had now been established. Winn estimated that there were ten between Newfoundland and Nova Scotia and seven between Nova Scotia and Norfolk, Virginia. 'It does not appear,' he wrote, 'that these numbers are likely to be exceeded, but the U-boats already there have been instructed to remain until they are down to the bare minimum of fuel necessary for their return passage. One U-boat has been ordered to proceed to Bermuda . . . her final destination appears to be the coast of Florida. Three other U-boats may also be bound for the same general area'. On January 26 he warned, 'It is apparently intended that the far western campaign should be extended for at least two or three weeks. This plan may have been inspired by the not inconsiderable success achieved, notably off Cape Hatteras and Hampton Roads. Only bad weather appears to have hampered the activity of the U-boats'. At the beginning of February he stated that 'the tonnage lost in January will be found to amount to an ugly figure in the neighbourhood of 200,000 tons. No offensive countermeasures have been employed'. Finally, summing up the opening stages of the campaign, he remarked on February 9, 'So far as can be judged, the enemy will thus maintain for at least a further month some fifteen U-boats in the coastal area of Nova Scotia and the U.S.A., prolonging the present weight of attack whilst defensive counter-measures are still in the stage of preparation. Nothing has yet been done to harry the U-boats in the far west. Most of the first batch have now regained their bases no doubt with increased confidence and efficiency. Shipping losses have continued at a costly rate and the U-boat C.O.'s have discriminated in picking out tankers and big ships, continuing to leave escorted convoys well alone.'

It will be seen, therefore, that Paukenschlag came as no surprise to the British Admiralty. Nor can it have been entirely unexpected by the American Navy Department. Some such attack should in any case have been anticipated as an obvious result of Germany's declaration of war, but with the information available in O.I.C., the gist of which was passed to Washington, it seems inconceivable now that the Americans could have been so completely and totally unprepared as was in fact the case.

According to Dönitz, this was what the five commanders of the Paukenschlag group found on their arrival: 'Conditions there were almost exactly those of normal peace-time. The coast was not blacked-out, the towns were a blaze of bright lights. The lights, both in lighthouses and on buoys, shone forth, though perhaps a little less brightly than usual. Shipping followed the normal peace-time routes and carried the normal lights. Although five weeks had passed since the declaration of war, very few anti-submarine measures appeared to have been introduced. There were, admittedly, anti-submarine patrols, but they were wholly lacking in experience. Single destroyers, for example, sailed up and down the traffic lanes with such regularity that the U-boats were quickly able to work out the time table they followed. They knew exactly when the destroyers would return, and their knowledge only added to their sense of security during the intervening period. A few attacks with depth charges were delivered by American patrol vessels; but the attackers did not display the requisite perseverance, and the attacks were abandoned too quickly, although quite often, thanks to shallow water, they stood a good chance of succeeding. The aircraft crews employed on anti-submarine work were also untrained.

'The merchantmen used their radios without any restrictions. They frequently signalled their positions, with the result that the U-boats were able to form a very useful picture of the shipping in their vicinity. The merchant service captains, obviously, had received no instructions with regard to the various forms of attack the U-boats might employ, and the possibility of night attacks appeared to have been completely overlooked.'

This situation was all the more unfortunate because in the north-eastern Atlantic, off Gibraltar and in the Mediterranean, the Germans were now finding the going much tougher. Targets were harder to find, convoys more heavily escorted and the escorts themselves, both surface and air, more experienced and better equipped. Above all, the gradual introduction of short wave 10cm radar was at last giving the surface escorts the ability to detect surfaced U-boats at a distance and in bad visibility or in the dark. The rate of 'killing' was improving. Dönitz therefore concentrated on the weak spots, off West Africa or Brazil, but above all on the American coast and in the Caribbean and the Gulf of Mexico. Shipping losses in these latter areas soared, and were mainly responsible for the increase in the total North Atlantic sinkings from the 50,000 tons of December 1941 to over half a million tons in March 1942. It was all the more galling because this holocaust could have been largely avoided if only the U. S. Navy had been prepared to learn from the bitter experience of the British and Canadians, gained in nearly two and a half years of war and freely and fully imparted to them since 1940. The Navy Department, however, preferred to make its own mistakes and learn in its own fashion. There seemed to be a feeling that 'we've got the ships, we've got the men, we've got the money too, and we don't need a bunch of Limeys to teach us how to run our war'. Unfortunately, many of the ships being sunk were British and in any case all tonnage, whatever its flag, was serving a common cause. It was to be many months before the situation was to improve.

One of the many weaknesses in the American anti-submarine defences was the absence of a central operational intelligence department comparable to O.I.C. The Navy Department, unlike the Admiralty, was not an operational headquarters and in this respect was more akin to the British War Office or Air Ministry. Control of actual operations was left strictly to the various Commanders-in-Chief, and although it can perhaps be argued that this was a better system than the Admiralty's, it had meant that there had been no demand for a central source of intelligence on which day-to-day or hour-to-hour operational decisions could be based. Nor was there a naval intelligence tradition such as Hall had

bequeathed to the Royal Navy. The U. S. Navy did not partici-
pate in the First World War until 1917 and then mostly by the
attachment of its forces to British Commands on whom they
depended for plans and intelligence. If a proper study of the
strength and weaknesses of Hall's organization had not been made
in Britain after the war and if Room 40 had been closed down, it
was perhaps scarcely surprising that even less thought had been
given to the subject of the fleet's requirements for intelligence on
the other side of the Atlantic. If it had been, Pearl Harbor might
well have been avoided.

. There was, of course, the Office of Naval Information. This,
within limits, was an efficient and well-organized department, but
it was no more geared to the needs of the shooting war than the
British N.I.D. had been in 1936. It was distrusted not to say
despised by Admiral E. J. King, the Commander-in-Chief of the
Atlantic Fleet, whom Roosevelt promoted to be Chief of Naval
Operations and Commander-in-Chief of the Navy shortly after
Pearl Harbor. King was a very forceful character, devoted to his
Service and determined that it should not again play second fiddle
to the Royal Navy. If not actually anti-British (as his biographer
has argued), he was certainly not over-receptive to ideas and suggestions from the Admiralty. Of course, immediately after Pearl
Harbor, American attention was concentrated on the Pacific, but
it still seems strange that long before this someone had not seen
the necessity for an Operational Intelligence Centre, at least for
the Atlantic theatre, since the American Mission in London had,
since the autumn of 1940, had full access to the O.I.C. and must
have been well aware of the key role it was playing in the Battle
of the Atlantic. As it was, Cinclant, the C.-in-C. Atlantic Fleet,
and the Commanders of the Sea Frontiers and their sub-com-
mands had intelligence officers on their staffs, in the same way as
the British C.-in-C. Home Fleet and other commands had Staff
Officers (Intelligence). However they were individuals, each working in his own watertight compartment without the benefit of an
exchange of information with one another, let alone of a central
body to feed them with every scrap of intelligence which it had
collected, sifted and analysed from every possible source, including the wealth of information available in O.I.C. Naturally, appreciations of the current situation varied in each command, there

was no correlation, nothing on which an overall plan could be based, no central plot where all dispositions could be displayed and decisions taken.

As the weeks went by and the shipping losses mounted without any signs of successful offensive or even defensive measures being employed, concern mounted in the British Admiralty. The British had of course been through all this themselves in 1939 and 1940, but the Americans had had more than two years to prepare, and it seemed incredible that their genius for speedy and efficient organization was still showing no signs of producing results. Admiral Godfrey had visited Washington at the end of 1941 and had made suggestions which had resulted in the establishment of a Joint Intelligence Committee and a Joint Intelligence Staff on the British model. His personal assistant, Ian Fleming, who accompanied him, had drafted plans which led to the creation of the Office of Strategic Services, the wartime forerunner of the C.I.A.* Godfrey saw that another visit was essential, but that this time it required a specialist with wide practical experience of the problems to be discussed and also with exceptional powers of advocacy. There could be but one choice, Winn. Not only did he meet the first two requirements but he had spent two years, after leaving Cambridge, first at Yale and then at Harvard. He knew the Americans and knew how to get on with them.

Godfrey had no difficulty in obtaining the enthusiastic support of the First Sea Lord and the Vice-Chief of Naval Staff for his proposal, and they additionally instructed Winn to do all in his power to hasten the introduction of coastal convoys. It was a formidable task to entrust to a temporary Commander of the R.N.V.R.: Winn would almost certainly have to deal with the redoubtable Ernie King himself and at this time the U. S. Navy was in general more rank-conscious and far less tolerant to its reserve officers than the Royal Navy had become.†

* See McLachlan: *Room 39*. Weidenfeld & Nicolson.
† The Royal Navy, at least in those days, was still very sure of itself and appeared to feel, perhaps with reason, that anyone representing the majesty of the British Admiralty had no need of a large number of stripes on his sleeve. When, a year later, it was proposed to send the author on a visit to Ottawa and Washington, Winn suggested that he be given the acting rank of Lieutenant Commander. The recommendation was rejected on the grounds that any Lieutenant in His Majesty's Navy who was incapable of keeping his end up with American Admirals, Canadian Air Marshals or indeed anyone in the whole wide world, was quite unfit to hold the rank of Lieutenant.

When Winn arrived he had two problems: firstly to persuade the Americans that an O.I.C. was necessary at all, and secondly to suggest how it should be inserted into the existing command structure. He very quickly realized that he would get nowhere by proposing that the new unit should form, as seemed logical and as it did in the Admiralty, part of the Office of Naval Information. The atmosphere of trust and confidence between Intelligence and Operations, so carefully fostered by Godfrey, Clayton and Denning over the previous three years, just did not exist in Washington. The only hope lay in persuading Admiral King and his Assistant Chief of Staff, Rear-Admiral R. E. Edwards, that some such section, but forming part of the Commander-in-Chief's own staff and under his direct and personal control, would materially assist him in the overall direction of the Navy and would be an essential weapon in the war against the U-boats.

COMINCH‡ already had an information room, under the 'able and forceful' Commander Dyer, but it was concerned more with strategic than operational intelligence, and it took Winn three days of hard argument to persuade Dyer that it was not only practicable to attempt to forecast the movements of U-boats, but that it was sensible to base the dispositions of anti-submarine forces and the routing of merchant shipping on these forecasts. Dyer was finally converted but pointed out that the idea would have to be sold to Admirals King and Edwards, before it stood any chance of being accepted by the semi-autonomous Commander-in-Chief of the Atlantic Fleet, Admiral R. E. Ingersoll, and the Commander of the Eastern Sea Frontier, which ran from the St. Lawrence down to North Carolina, Vice-Admiral Adolphus Andrews.

Winn therefore approached Edwards. He was another tough character, who also started by denying that it was possible to forecast U-boat's movements and therefore useless to try and route shipping on such a basis. After much argument he began to weaken, but went on to say that the Americans wished to learn their own lessons and that they had plenty of ships with which to do so. Winn felt that Edwards, like so many Americans, would

‡ Commander-in-Chief U. S. Fleet. The previous abbreviation CINCUS was changed after Pearl Harbor.

react well to plain speaking, so taking his courage in both hands, he retorted with calculated heat, 'The trouble is, Admiral, it's not only your bloody ships you are losing: a lot of them are ours!' Edwards was taken aback for a moment but then gave a laugh. 'Well, maybe you've got a point there. Perhaps there's something in what you say. You had better see Admiral King.' He must have been more impressed than he appeared, because, when Winn did see King, the ground seemed to have been well prepared. The Commander-in-Chief gave Winn a friendly hearing and instructed Edwards to set about the creation of a tracking room forthwith.

Once convinced, the Americans moved with a speed and efficiency that was surprising to anyone accustomed to the ways of the Admiralty. Before Winn left Washington for New York where, at Edwards' request, he was to sell the idea to Admiral Andrews, the necessary accommodation had been found and the additional staff required were being selected. The officer chosen to head the new 'Atlantic Section, Operational Intelligence, COMINCH' was Commander K. A. Knowles, a regular who had retired from the Navy in 1936 with minor eye trouble. He took up his duties in June and was to prove the perfect counterpart to Winn. In July he flew to London to meet Winn and pick his brain. The co-operation between Op 20 (later F.21) and O.I.C. that grew up during the next two and three-quarter years was probably closer than between any other British and American organizations in any Service and in any theatre. The American Tracking Room was to have a profound influence on the success of American anti-submarine operations, perhaps in some ways greater than that of the British Tracking Room because, in 1943 and 1944, the nature of those operations was somewhat different from those conducted by the British and Canadians. Winn certainly accomplished the primary purpose of his mission with complete success. Such was the impression which he had created that when, later on, Op 20 experienced difficulties in obtaining the full co-operation of the Convoys and Routing Division, under its Anglophobe chief, Rear-Admiral M. K. Metcalf, a very high-level request was made for Winn to pay Washington another visit.

Of course, even with traditional American hustle, it took some time for Knowles to establish his new Atlantic section and even longer to accustom the Eastern, Caribbean and Gulf Sea Frontiers to the idea of accepting and working on his forecasts. His task would have been easier if he had been receiving the constant flow of Special Intelligence on which Winn had been able to rely for so long, but this had abruptly ceased some months earlier. On the first of February the Germans had introduced an entirely new cipher, Triton, for the Atlantic U-boats, which completely defeated B.P. until almost the end of the year. Suddenly the benefit which we had enjoyed of seeing at least something of what was happening at Dönitz's 'side of the hill' was taken from us. It was a major set-back and we almost reverted to the position in which we had been before June 1941. Almost, but not quite.

In the first place our conventional sources of intelligence, D/F fixes, photographic reconnaissance, reports from our air and surface forces and so on, were functioning with much greater efficiency and frequency. The D/F system had been greatly extended with stations in Iceland, Newfoundland, Bermuda, Freetown, Ascension, Cape Town, and now all along the U.S. coast. A separate communication network had been set up to permit the rapid transmission of overseas bearings to Kemp's team in the Tracking Room. The plotters, Fitzgerald, Vaughan and Caddy, were even more experienced and were being reinforced by girls from the universities so that each watch could be double-banked. The period of decrypting the Atlantic traffic had permitted a comparison of estimated fixes with the actual positions revealed by cryptanalysis, and some of the idiosyncrasies and weaknesses of individual stations could be allowed for. There was a considerable improvement in the general accuracy of the fixes being obtained.

Photographic reconnaissance, too, was far more effective. Not only Germany's western ports but the whole of the Baltic was being covered on a fairly consistent basis. The U-boat building yards were regularly photographed. Each new U-boat was spotted and recorded within a week or two of first being laid down, its size and type determined and its progress followed to final launching and commissioning. The whole U-boat building programme was revealed, and highly accurate forecasts of its results produced; but this brought us small comfort because it showed clearly that new construction still far exceeded current sinkings. So far as Allied merchant shipping was concerned the exact reverse was the case, but at least we knew the worst.

Another incalculable benefit of having been able to read Hydra for so long was the insight which it had given us into the way the U-boat war was being conducted, and perhaps even into the way that Dönitz's mind worked. We knew the U-boats' methods, the average speed of advance when proceeding to or from patrol, the endurance of the various types of U-boat and characteristics of many of their commanding officers, the types of patrol lines favoured and the exact meaning of the short signals used for making sighting, weather or position reports. All this was something that would have taken much longer to discover, if it could have been achieved at all, if we had not had the benefit of Special Intelligence.

Perhaps most important of all was the fact that the change was only introduced for the operational U-boats in the Atlantic. It is true that these were our most dangerous enemies, under the direct operational control of Dönitz, but there was other information which affected them to be culled from Tetis, the cipher for boats training in the Baltic, while the boats allocated to the Admiral commanding Norway and all minesweepers and patrol craft continued to use Hydra. These two ciphers remained unaltered and we continued to decrypt them with the same consistency, if also with the same occasional time lags, as before.

Tetis enabled us to follow the history of each U-boat from the moment it was first commissioned, through its months of working-up and training, until it finally left the Baltic for its first operational cruise to a Norwegian or French port. We could, in consequence, calculate not only the rate of building but the exact number of boats which, for months ahead, would be added to the operational fleet.

Thanks to the extensive British sea and air mining programme, and also in some areas to the risk of attack from British aircraft and submarines, each U-boat leaving or entering port had to be escorted along the whole length of the appropriate swept channel by minesweepers and patrol craft. Dönitz records that in 1942, over a thousand such U-boat escort operations were carried out from the Biscay ports alone. As an escort dropped an outward-bound U-boat or picked up an inward-bound one, she reported the fact to her local shore command by W/T in cipher Hydra. These reports, of course, also reached the Tracking Room and as a result we could follow the first operational sortie of every U-boat up the Belts and out into the North Sea. No further positive identification could then be made until, with its cruise completed, it was reported by a fresh escort as inward-bound off a Norwegian or French port. By this means we continued to learn when a U-boat left for operations, and when and if it returned. Despite German suspicions to the contrary, no agent could have hoped to provide us with such precise, accurate and timely information day in, day out, for four years of war.

Besides knowing when a U-boat left for operations and when, and if, it returned, we knew the exact strength of the U-boat fleet and where each boat was based. We were able to make belated checks on the claims of kills from our own forces where there was no conclusive evidence from wreckage or survivors, although it might of course take some weeks before we could establish that a particular boat was overdue. Our estimates of the total number of boats at sea at any one time therefore remained remarkably accurate. This was a great benefit, but it was a long way removed from the complete picture which had been displayed on the Tracking Room plot up to the beginning of February.

Winn had to ask himself whether in these circumstances there was any point in continuing to try and estimate the movements of individual U-boats on their nine- or ten-week cruises which might take them many hundreds of miles away into the North Atlantic or right across the ocean to America or the west coast of Africa. He decided that the attempt must be made and that, as before, even if we only just beat the law of average, such small success would still be valuable. He also had to convince his superiors, the Assistant Chief of Staff (U-boats and Trade), the Directors of the Trade and Operations Divisions, and the Commanders-in-Chief Western Approaches and Coastal Command, who had by now become accustomed to seeing a clear and comprehensive picture based on Special Intelligence. They might have concluded that U-boat tracking under these new, or more strictly, old conditions was just sheer fantasy and a complete and dangerous waste of his and their time. However, Winn's reputation stood high and they readily accepted what he described as a 'Working Fiction', namely that the Tracking Room's estimates, its best and most considered guesses, should be treated as facts and acted on accordingly until such time as they were proved wrong.

How, then, did we set about our task? Of course we started in February with a precise knowledge of which U-boats were at sea and a reasonably good knowledge of their whereabouts and intentions. It was not difficult to plot on outward-bound boats whose destinations were already known or those whose fuel state obviously required a return to base. We also knew which U-boats were in port and how long they had been there and when they set out again. But from then on, intelligent guesswork had to take over. Should this short position report, D/F'd on the hundred fathom line in the Bay of Biscay, be associated with the U-boat that had recently sailed from St. Nazaire or with that other one which had left about the same time from Lorient? A brief sighting by a Coastal Command patrol some days later might, if associated with one boat, indicate a Great Circle course for the Caribbean, while an attack on an independently routed ship south-west of Iceland might suggest a movement into the North-Western Approaches. Every U-boat was given a pin with two letters, AA, BB, etc., representing its true identity. When a boat sailed, its pin was taken from the appropriate port board, placed on the end of the swept channel and plotted on every twenty-four hours with due allowance for weather conditions or the presence of strong air patrols, which might necessitate a slower than average speed of advance. Thereafter each and every incident, sighting, attack or D/F fix, had to be related to a particular U-boat. The incidents themselves were pencilled in on the chart so that, when something unexpected occurred that did not fit in with previous ideas, the whole process could be started afresh and the incidents formerly associated with one U-boat now allocated to another or others. It was, of course, very much a hit-or-miss process and adjustments were continually having to be made, but Winn insisted on complete honesty and, no matter how involved and painstaking the process of re-estimating, fresh pins could not be added to the plot to account for awkward events, or old ones removed just because there had been no recent evidence to support that particular U-boat's presence where we were showing it. Despite all its errors and imperfections the plot did bear some relation to reality, with approximately the right number of U-boats on patrol or on outward or homeward passage.

It was obvious that Dönitz was continually probing for weak spots but, naturally enough, it was not always possible to anticipate exactly which one he would choose next. Winn was, however, sure that he would not abandon the American seaboard and Caribbean until a complete convoy system had been introduced and the efficiency of the anti-submarine forces greatly increased. His weekly reports for the first half of the year continued to draw attention to the lack of effective counter-measures, the appalling toll of losses (over six hundred thousand tons in June), and the comparatively modest number of U-boats responsible for this devastation. At the same time he remained constantly on the alert for any signs of a real resumption of the battles on the North Atlantic convoy routes, and for the extension of the U-boat war into the South Atlantic or even the Indian Ocean.

The campaign in the far west was being aided by the long-awaited emergence of tanker U-boats, or 'Milch Cows' as the Germans called them. We had in fact spotted the first of them from an aerial photograph just before she left Kiel in April 1942, but her precise function was not established and it was thought for a time that her size and broad beam might indicate that she was a minelayer. By early May she had in fact refuelled fifteen U-boats five hundred miles north-west of Bermuda, an operation of which we could only have been made precisely aware by Special Intelligence. Winn nevertheless suspected that something unusual had happened and on June 1, he reported that 'Though there is no confirmation that U-boats are being supplied at sea either by surface vessels or by other U-boats, there are several indications that such supplying may, in fact, be taking place. It is possible that hitherto it has taken the form of one U-boat handing over sufficient fuel to enable another to return to France'. It was another two months before he was able positively to confirm that Milch Cows were operating. These supply operations greatly increased the time that even the 500-tonners could spend in distant waters, and were therefore the equivalent of a significant increase in the total number of operational U-boats. By May nearly thirty U-boats were operating from Nova Scotia down to Florida, in the Caribbean, the Gulf of Mexico and off Trinidad. On the other hand the American defences, reinforced by some British air and surface forces, were at last beginning to improve. On April 14, the U.S.S. *Roper* had achieved the first kill in American waters and a month later the first coastal convoy began to run, although it took a good deal longer before the system could be extended to cover the whole area. Dönitz realized that this second 'glückliche Zeit' would not last for ever and began to consider deploying at least some of his forces in other areas, in the South Atlantic off Brazil and still further afield off Cape Town and even in the Indian Ocean. In particular, he saw the need to transfer a greater weight of attack back to the North Atlantic convoy routes which, for six months, had been subjected only to sporadic attention from boats on passage to other areas. He was encouraged in this by the growth in the size of the operational U-boat fleet, which reached 140 in July, and by his success in persuading O.K.M. to moderate their demands for diversions to other theatres.

He realized, however, that the British defences had improved both in numbers and effectiveness, and that successes would not be achieved as cheaply or as easily as they had been during the past six months off the United States seaboard. The German press had recently given a good deal of publicity to a message from Raeder congratulating the U-boat commanders on their 'victories' against the Americans. Dönitz felt that this euphoria was misplaced and dangerous, and on July 27 issued a public warning that the results had only been achieved by incredible exertions and that harder times lay ahead. Winn immediately realized the significance of this statement, and on the same day it was issued he circulated the following comment: 'A possible interpretation is that we are at the end of a phase in the U-boat war. References have been made in other German broadcasts to the increased effectiveness of U.S. anti-submarine measures. Losses sustained thereby and the recent decrease in sinkings in the American zone may have decided the Germans to change their strategy. Such a change may be gradual and is unlikely to involve a complete withdrawal from American waters, but it is already apparent that the comparative immunity recently enjoyed by the trans-Atlantic and U.K.–African convoys is a thing of the past. It is probable that the Germans now feel compelled to accept a higher rate of U-boat losses involved by a return to attacks on convoys.' He did not have long to wait for confirmation of this theory, since nine days later

Convoy SC.94 was attacked 450 miles south of Greenland. The battle lasted from the 5th to the 13th August. Eleven merchant ships were lost, but of the eighteen U-boats involved two were sunk and four damaged. Although, despite increasingly successful counter-measures, diversionary attacks in American waters, and even further afield in the South Atlantic and Indian Oceans, were maintained, the SC.94 operation was to set the pattern for the next ten months until the battle of the Atlantic reached its climax in May 1943.

8

The Channel Dash and PQ.17

IN THE first half of 1942 Britain suffered two defeats, despite the fact that in both cases O.I.C. managed to predict German intentions with considerable accuracy. Hitler had convinced himself that the British were planning to invade Norway, and to Raeder's and Dönitz's dismay insisted, towards the end of 1941, that all the German Navy's large ships and also a sizeable force of U-boats be concentrated there to meet this imagined threat. *Tirpitz* was now ready for operations and she was the first of the large ships to move north. *Scharnhorst, Gneisenau* and *Prinz Eugen,* however, were still in Brest, their repairs almost completed but liable, at any time, to suffer further damage at the hands of Bomber Command. Despite this danger, Raeder wished to retain them there because he felt that, with *Tirpitz* posing a threat to the British northern convoy routes, the Home Fleet would be hard put to give the necessary protection to the southern ones against sudden short forays from France. Hitler, on the other hand, insisted that the Brest squadron should return to the North Sea; he could see more clearly than Raeder that, sooner or later, the three ships were bound to be put out of action again, perhaps permanently, if they remained where they were. He compared them to a cancer patient. An operation, though dangerous, might save him; if nothing was done, death was inevitable. The only alternative he offered Raeder was to dismantle the ships where they lay and transfer their crews and armament to other tasks. This Raeder could not stomach, and so planning for the operation was started in January. The question was which route to choose: out into the Atlantic and north-about Scotland, or up the English Channel. Both routes seemed dangerous. Raeder favoured the former, but Hitler, whose famous intuition was not always wrong, proclaimed that a sudden dash up the Channel would be so unexpected that it stood a better chance of success. He was supported by Vice-Admiral Ciliax, who was to be in charge of the operation and this was the plan that was finally adopted. It was given the code name Cerberus. Hitler was proved right by events, but it was not because the choice of the Channel had not been foreseen in the Admiralty. It had, but whereas all the British plans misfired badly, those of the Germans ran smoothly and with great efficiency.

The possibility of an immediate return to Germany through the Channel had been considered by the Admiralty as soon as the German ships had first reached Brest in March 1941. The heavy commitments of the Home Fleet in watching the northern exit to the Atlantic and in safeguarding British troop convoys to the Middle East meant that the main responsibility for dealing with such an eventuality had to rest with the R.A.F. This was fully accepted by the Air Ministry, who were confident that any movement through the Channel would present a 'unique opportunity' for concentrated attacks by bomber and torpedo aircraft under the protection of Fighter Command. Plans were drawn up and issued under the code name Fuller. As the months went by, with the German ships penned in Brest, the likelihood of Fuller being implemented receded until, towards the end of January 1942, Denning, who had never relaxed his vigilance, issued warnings that all three ships were again seaworthy and that some major operation must be reckoned probable.

There was plenty of evidence to support this view. Phillipon and the two dockyard workmen had reported that repairs had been completed, and the former went so far as to suggest that the Germans would force their way through the Channel, leaving Brest in darkness and running the gauntlet of the Straits of Dover in daylight. Another pointer was that the destroyers which had escorted *Tirpitz* from Germany to Trondheim, instead of remaining there with her, were immediately transferred south to Brest. Signs of additional minesweeping activity along the swept channels were apparent, from Special Intelligence, despite attempts to conceal them by working at night and in a carefully controlled manner. Movements of E-boats and German fighter squadrons were also consistent with plans for a sortie. Paymaster Lieutenant Clements, one of Denning's experts on the swept channels and the movements of German small craft, remembers studying these clues when on watch one night and coming to the conclusion that they could only mean a break up Channel. He could hardly wait to tell Denning his theory when the latter came on duty next morning. All Denning did was to open a drawer of his desk and hand Clements a memorandum he had written for the First Sea Lord a week before expressing exactly this view.

There were of course other possibilities. Although the German ships were repaired they had not had time to carry out proper sea trials, or bring their crews back to their full state of efficiency. The squadron might therefore remain where it was, despite the risks, until these weaknesses had been remedied. Again, it was possible that it might make a run for the Mediterranean and an Italian dockyard. Perhaps, after all, it would be sent out on another commerce raiding cruise or combine this with a return to Germany north-about.

Denning had considered all these possibilities and had enumerated them in his paper to Admiral Pound, but, for the very reasons which persuaded Hitler, and eventually the German Naval Staff, to plump for the Channel, he also came to the conclusion that this must be what they would attempt. The question of exactly when the operation would take place depended on a number of factors which were as apparent to the British as to the Germans. A flooding spring tide which would speed them on their way and, at its height, help them over any uncleared minefields was one of them. A long night with no moon was another. Such conditions would apply on February 12. Ten days before that, the Admiralty issued an appreciation which was in fact largely Denning's work and which is worth quoting at some length.

It stated: 'The Brest ships cannot be fully efficient yet; although they have led a charmed life the Germans must be anxious to get them away to a safer harbour. Only if we can anticipate the plan of their departure can our chances of destroying them be good.

'There are three, possibly five, large and five small destroyers at Brest, all of which have recently arrived. Minesweeping operations in the approaches to Brest have recently been observed. There has been no distinctive shape detected in any of the air reconnaissances flown by the Germans in the vicinity of Brest. There are indications of movement but no indications of its direction.

'The short cut for the German ships is via the English Channel. It is 240 miles from Brest to Cherbourg and another 120 miles from Cherbourg to the Dover Straits. While ships could make the passage from Brest to Cherbourg or from Cherbourg to the Dover Straits in the same dark period, they could not make the complete passage from Brest to the Dover Straits in one dark period.

'At first sight this passage up the Channel seems hazardous for the Germans. It is probable, however, that as their heavy ships are not fully efficient, they would prefer such a passage, relying for their security on the destroyers and aircraft which are efficient, and knowing full well that we have no heavy ships to oppose them in the Channel.

'We might well therefore find the battle-cruisers and the heavy 8-inch cruiser with five large and five small destroyers, also say, twenty fighters constantly overhead (with reinforcements within call) proceeding up the Channel. To meet this sortie, we have about six MTBs at Dover, but no destroyers with torpedo armament.

'Our bombers have shown that we cannot place much reliance on them to damage the enemy, whilst our Coastal Command torpedo-bomber aircraft will not muster more than nine.

'Taking all factors into consideration, it appears that the Germans can pass east up the Channel with much less risk than they will incur if they attempt an ocean passage.'

Six days later the A.O.C.-in-C. Coastal Command issued his own appreciation, which was of course based equally on intelligence supplied by Denning, and came to the same conclusion. He added that the 'attempt to force the Channel' might take place 'any time after Tuesday, February 10', only two days ahead.

The element of surprise, therefore, on which the Germans had been counting so heavily, no longer existed. Unfortunately, having up to this point accurately listed the options open to the enemy and correctly assessed the one which they would choose, the British then made a mistake which greatly added to their eventual difficulties. Contrary to Phillipon's prescient forecast that the Germans would leave Brest in darkness and pass Dover in daylight, all the British authorities, the Admiralty, the Air Ministry, Coastal, Bomber and Fighter Commands and Vice-Admiral Dover, considered that the Germans would wish to have the cover of darkness for the most dangerous part of their journey and that they would in consequence leave Brest in daylight.

Despite this view, precautions were taken to detect departure at any hour of the day or night. Denning suggested to Admiral Horton, Flag Officer Submarines, that he should station his only available modern submarine, *Sealion*, close in off Brest. Horton was at first most reluctant to do so, but was eventually persuaded by Denning that O.I.C.'s knowledge of the position of the German minefields was sufficiently accurate to reduce the dangers involved to reasonable proportions. Two additional old submarines were to patrol further out to sea. They would all, of course, have to withdraw each night to charge their batteries. To ensure early warning of any night-time departure and so permit the concentration of Bomber and Coastal Commands' forces, three night patrols by radar-equipped aircraft were arranged, a western one off Brest, a central one off Ushant and an eastern one in the Le Havre–Boulogne area. Early morning sweeps were to be made by Spitfires in the eastern Channel.

British offensive measures were also strengthened. Extensive mining by air and naval forces was carried out all along the Germans' probable route from Cape Barfleur to the Frisian Islands in areas suggested by O.I.C. Coastal Command's few Beaufort torpedo bombers were reinforced by six naval Swordfish and six destroyers with torpedo armament were stationed at Harwich. Bomber Command placed three hundred aircraft at two hours' notice.

Despite the mistaken view that the Germans would wish to leave Brest in daylight and pass Dover at night, it did seem that the plans covered all contingencies, and Denning certainly had no reason to feel anything but satisfied with the part that O.I.C. had played in alerting both the naval and air authorities to the probable course of coming events. Provided adequate warning of the German squadron's departure could be obtained—and there seemed no reason why it should not be—it appeared highly unlikely that it would succeed in getting through without, at the very least, suffering serious losses.

British plans did, however, require some hours to come into operation, particularly if the attacks by all the different forces were to be properly co-ordinated, and this in turn was completely dependent on adequate advance warning. In the event, an almost incredible sequence of failures and misjudgements resulted in the German squadron being able to approach within a few miles of Dover before any of the British authorities were aware of what was happening. The Germans' departure on the night of February 11 was delayed by an air raid, and when they did sail, shortly before midnight, *Sealion* had just withdrawn to charge her batteries. Two of the three Coastal Command patrols suffered radar failure and the third was called home early, in each case just when the enemy was passing through their areas and when he would otherwise have certainly been detected. The fact that these gaps had occurred in the patrols was never reported to Dover. The fighter sweeps at first failed to spot any activity which they considered unusual, and when at 10:42 A.M., they did finally see the German ships off the mouth of the Somme they mistakenly did not break W/T silence to report the fact. Well before this, they should have been detected by the British shore radar stations, but most of these were effectively jammed by the Germans, and the significance of this was not appreciated, while the reports of those that were not jammed were disbelieved for too long. It was not until 11:25 A.M. that Admiral Ramsay, Vice-Admiral Dover, was informed that Admiral Ciliax's ships were almost off Calais. By this time it was far too late for effective and co-ordinated action to be taken against them. One after another the M.T.B.'s, Swordfish, Beauforts and destroyers made gallant attacks, but they were all driven off or shot down by the powerful sea and air escort which the Germans had organized. Bomber Command's mass attack was delayed, partly because, on his sole authority, the A.O.C.-in-C., had withdrawn 200 of the 300 aircraft allocated for a raid on Germany, and had placed the remainder at longer notice for readiness.

In the end 242 aircraft were despatched but the weather conditions had deteriorated, and they too achieved nothing.

Ciliax had had immense luck. Not only had he entirely escaped detection for eleven hours, and then successfully driven off all the attacks which had been made on him, but some of the many minefields which the British had laid had been discovered and swept, one of them only just before the squadron had to pass through it. Others had been avoided, more by luck than anything else. However, at half-past two *Scharnhorst* struck one of Bomber Command's mines and was temporarily brought to a stop. But the damage was not too serious and she soon got under way again and began to overhaul the other ships which had continued their passage. Once again luck was with Ciliax, as it was shortly after this that the British destroyer and bomber attacks were launched. They might have had greater success against a ship stopped dead in the water. Neither she nor *Gneisenau* were, however, safe. During the evening both ships exploded magnetic mines. The *Gneisenau* suffered only minor damage and with the *Prinz Eugen* reached Brunsbuttel early the following morning, the 13th. The *Scharnhorst* was more severely damaged and it was nearly an hour before she was able to start to creep into Wilhelmshaven, where she finally arrived at ten o'clock, also on the 13th.

It was a tremendous disappointment. *The Times* declared that 'Vice-Admiral Ciliax has succeeded where the Duke of Medina Sidonia failed. . . . Nothing more mortifying to the pride of sea-power has happened in home waters since the Seventeenth Century'. The Germans appeared to have escaped completely unscathed, since the mine damage which the two battlecruisers had incurred, which was known to O.I.C. from Special Intelligence, could not for that very reason be revealed to the general public. Be that as it may, repairs to *Scharnhorst* kept her out of action for several months, while no sooner was *Gneisenau* docked to deal with her less severe damage and to fit her with a more powerful armament than she was hit and very severely damaged by Bomber Command. She took no further part in the war.

Denning, however, had no cause to reproach himself. He had correctly forecast the sortie and the route the Germans would take. The only damage which they suffered had been from mines laid in positions which he had proposed. He had in fact suggested further aerial minelaying immediately he learned that Ciliax was approaching Dover, but in the event only thirteen could be dropped and it appears that the damage was caused by some of the earlier ones. Whatever the causes of the British failure, they could not be laid at the door of O.I.C.

The Germans had certainly achieved a striking tactical victory. It was, on the other hand, a serious strategic reverse. Amongst other things, it resulted in a substantial reduction in the strength of the forces which they had hoped to concentrate both for the defence of Norway and for attacks on the convoys, which were carrying an increasingly important volume of supplies to Murmansk and Archangel to sustain the Russians.

From August 1941 to May 1945, 42 convoys totalling 813 ships set out for North Russia from Iceland or Great Britain. Thirty-three ships returned without completing the voyage due to stress of weather or other causes. Of the remaining 780, 60 were sunk by the enemy, but 720 arrived safely at their destinations. The 36 returning convoys lost 27 ships. Yet, of all these 78 convoys the only one, perhaps the only convoy in any theatre in the war now remembered, except by those who sailed in them, is PQ.17.

The British, as is well known, prefer to dwell on their defeats rather than their much more numerous victories, but PQ.17 was by no means the worst disaster which we suffered in the war at sea. It does however, have the unenviable distinction of being the only British convoy to be abandoned by its escort in the face of a predictable and devastating attack by the enemy. How did it come about that thirty-four British and Allied merchantmen and three rescue ships were left defenceless against the onslaughts of Dönitz's U-boats and Göring's bombers, despite the Royal Navy's centuries-old tradition of sacrificing its ships and men to ensure 'the safe and timely arrival' of vessels entrusted to their care? The reason was that the convoy was ordered to scatter, which inevitably meant that its well-drilled and efficient escort could do nothing to protect its charges. This decision was taken by the professional head of the Navy, the First Sea Lord, Admiral Sir Dudley Pound, himself. It was a decision taken in extremely difficult circumstances when alternative courses of action seemed, at least to some, likely to produce even more disastrous results, but it was taken against the advice of two of the most experienced and capable officers in O.I.C., and, with the benefit of hindsight, it can now be seen to have been totally and fatally mistaken. The story has in it most of the elements of a Greek tragedy and it is perhaps this that causes it to retain its dreadful fascination.

The decision to send supplies to Russia by the Northern route was a political one, dictated by Stalin's unwillingness to allow any extension of British influence in North Persia, which he feared would be the result if this longer but, as was eventually proved, far easier and more efficient route had been used from the outset. The sea route to Murmansk and Archangel in North Russia was, from a naval point of view, completely unsound. Climatically the conditions were appalling, quite the worst to be endured at any time by any regular succession of convoys anywhere: ferocious gales, ice, fog and, for six months of the year, almost perpetual darkness. The chances of crews of sunken ships surviving were minimal. In summer the perpetual night of winter was succeeded by perpetual day, which, if slightly better in one respect, meant that there could be no respite from enemy attack. The wartime voyage took from ten to fourteen days, during most of which the ships were within easy reach of German air and U-boat bases in North Norway, while land-based air support from Britain or Iceland could only be provided for a short time at the commencement of the voyage when it was least needed. Once the Germans woke up to the fact that a large volume of supplies was regularly being ferried to the Russians by this means and took active steps to prevent it by air and U-boat attack, the convoys were bound to incur very heavy losses. If, in addition, heavy surface ships were to join in, then losses would almost certainly become unacceptable.

Although *Scharnhorst* and *Gneisenau* were no longer available, the Germans still had, in addition to *Tirpitz*, two pocket battleships, *Scheer* and *Lützow*, and two heavy cruisers, *Hipper* and *Prinz Eugen*, and about a dozen large destroyers. They could form a powerful squadron.

The Admiralty and the Commander-in-Chief of the Home Fleet, Admiral Tovey, had several causes for anxiety. They not only had to guard against the threat to the Arctic convoys, but also against the possibility of a break-out by one or more of the German ships into the Atlantic, where the damage they could do to Allied ocean convoys was immeasurable. Moreover, the Home Fleet was constantly being called on to detach ships for special operations in other theatres. *Prince of Wales* and *Repulse* had already been sent to the Far East at the insistence of the Prime Minister, and other valuable ships were required from time to time for operations in the Mediterranean or elsewhere. There was no safe margin of numerical superiority.

To fight a convoy through to North Russia, the Royal Navy was now going to have to provide three separate forces: first a strong close escort of destroyers and small craft to defeat attacks by U-boats and, until the advent of small aircraft carriers later in the war, by aircraft (this close escort would accompany the convoy right through to its destination): secondly, to ward off attacks by the Germans' large destroyers and cruisers, a covering force of from two to four cruisers (initially, these also went right through to Russia, but repair facilities at Murmansk were so primitive, and Russian co-operation so grudging, that it was decided that it was not justifiable to risk these valuable ships, of which there were never sufficient, so far to the east, and the covering force was directed to turn back once the convoy had passed Bear Island): finally, a distant covering force of at least two battleships and a fleet aircraft carrier to meet the threat now posed by *Tirpitz* and the pocket battleships. This distant covering force had somehow to cruise in an area which would enable it to intercept the Germans if they made a sortie, but at the same time avoid approaching too closely to the Norwegian coast and so render itself liable to the full weight of attack of the enemy's land-based aircraft.

Accurate information about the enemy's movements and intentions was obviously essential if all these complicated movements were to be dovetailed into the slow progress of both the outward- and homeward-bound convoys, which usually left their respective ports on the same day and passed each other about halfway through their voyages. Air reconnaissance was extremely difficult due to the distances involved, to the lack at this time of sufficient suitable aircraft and above all to the often appalling weather. The network of Norwegian agents, which was later to prove invaluable, had not, early in 1942, been fully established or trained and equipped. Submarines were stationed off the Norwegian coast, to

report and attack if possible, but theirs was a difficult and dangerous task, especially as the nights grew shorter.

A possible source of information was the link established by the
British Naval Attaché in Stockholm, Captain Henry Denham,
with the Swedish Secret Service, which had given us the first positive clue to the sailing of *Bismarck* in 1941. On that occasion the
information had originated with the sighting of the German
squadron by a Swedish cruiser, but the Swedes had another highly
reliable source of intelligence. At this time, all the German tele-
graph and teleprinter lines to their naval, army and air force commands in Norway passed through Sweden, and the Swedes had
succeeded in tapping them and in breaking a number of the Germans' ciphers. Thanks to the exceptionally friendly relations which
Denham had established with Major Törnberg, he was often provided with the results of the work of the Swedish cryptanalysts. In
order to avoid arousing the suspicions of the Swedish Security
Service, Denham had to meet his contacts in parks and public
places and neither they nor he could commit anything to paper.
All the information passed over had to be memorized until Denham could get back to the Embassy and signal to D.N.I. in London. There was normally a time lag of between twenty-four and
forty-eight hours before his reports were in the hands of O.I.C. It
was, however, an extremely valuable network with intelligence
right from the horse's mouth. Nevertheless, like the other sources
mentioned earlier, it was not something that could be taken for
granted when formulating our plans.

As was the case prior to Jutland, and as with *Bismarck*, precise
and early warning of the enemy's intentions and movements was
a pre-requisite for effective counter-action. Fortunately this was
often forthcoming as a result of our break into cipher Hydra,
which had not been affected by the complications introduced into
the Atlantic U-boat traffic by Triton. Hydra was not only used by
the patrol vessels and minesweepers but also by the U-boats based
in Norway, and by the heavy ships except when on special operations, when cipher Neptun came into force. But this, too, had
now been partially penetrated.

Although B.P. had largely mastered the technique of breaking
the daily changes in the cipher settings, delays of between four
and forty-eight hours did occur. There were major changes every

forty-eight hours and minor ones every twenty-four. It was the major ones that caused the problem and once these were broken the lesser change was usually cracked without delay. There were, therefore, occasions when we were 'blind' for up to twenty-four or more hours, after which we would rapidly catch up again and enjoy perhaps as much as thirty-six hours current reading. It was a matter of luck whether we were 'blind' or 'current' at a critical moment. It must also be remembered that, unless information was forthcoming from Stockholm, we could not learn anything of messages despatched by landline, nor could we become aware by any means at all of instructions given in writing. In short, even our best intelligence sources could not be relied upon to give a complete and continuous picture of what was happening, let alone of what was going to happen, on the other side of the North Sea.

Tirpitz actually sailed from Wilhelmshaven, so avoiding inquis-itive eyes in the Kattegat, on January 12, 1942, and reached Trondheim early on the 15th. Towards the end of February she was joined by *Scheer* and *Prinz Eugen*, although the latter ship was torpedoed and damaged by a British submarine. Admiral Tovey appreciated that an attack on an Arctic convoy in the waters between Jan Mayen and Bear Island was a distinct possibility, and so was not surprised when another submarine, *Seawolf*, reported *Tirpitz*'s departure from Trondheim on March 6, when the out-ward PQ.12 and the homeward QP.8 were already at sea. The Germans, as we knew from their Air Force code, had already lo-cated the outward-bound convoy by one of their long distance Focke-Wulf Kondor aircraft, so that it was a more than reasona-ble deduction that *Tirpitz*'s move presaged an attack on it rather than an attempt to break out into the Atlantic. Tovey therefore sailed the Home Fleet to take up a covering position south-west of Jan Mayen and began searches with aircraft from *Victorious*.

It is unnecessary to attempt to follow the various moves and counter-moves which ensued. Suffice it to say that in the next six days the Germans failed by the narrowest of margins to find PQ.12, while the Home Fleet would not have been in a position to attack *Tirpitz* with aircraft from *Victorious* had not the Ad-miralty intervened, on the basis of Denning's deductions from Special Intelligence, to correct the faulty appreciation of the enemy's whereabouts and intentions on which Admiral Tovey was working. Unfortunately the attack, when launched, failed and *Tirpitz* was able to make good her escape and return unscathed to Trondheim.

Both sides drew serious conclusions from this episode. Admiral Tovey protested strongly about the interference by the Admiralty, but as Captain Roskill has pointed out, 'the intelligence derived by the Admiralty* and sent out to the fleet flagship was, we now know, more accurate than the appreciations made afloat. Neither the signalling of the intelligence nor the issue of orders, when intelligence available in London indicated that assumptions on which our forces' movements had been based were wrong (as happened on the evening of the 8th March), is open to criticism'. The all-but-successful results of the Admiralty's intervention must have had a profound effect on Sir Dudley Pound, whose natural propensity to try to control operations at sea from the Admiralty was already pronounced. He had, on this occasion, been proved right and the man on the spot wrong. He had, however, been well served by O.I.C. and B.P., who fortunately had been able to provide cast-iron information and sound appreciations just when required. No awkward gaps in the flow of Special Intelligence had intervened at a vital time.

The next four convoys in fact sailed without another move by the German heavy ships, but in the course of their voyages two British cruisers were lost, and the First Sea Lord must have been worried at this depletion of his strength of these valuable ships. It was decided that they should not in future accompany the convoys right through to their destinations.

It was certainly now obvious that the movement of the German heavy ships to North Norway was not merely a potential but a very real threat to British convoys and their escorts of destroyers and cruisers. The sailings of the convoys could not be concealed from the Germans for more than a day or two at the most, and it seemed clear to Pound and Tovey that, sooner or later, a major disaster was bound to occur, particularly if the convoys continued to sail throughout the summer months of perpetual daylight. Placing himself in Raeder's position, and not understanding the hand-

* It was, of course, Special Intelligence but Roskill could not refer to this at the time he was writing.

icaps under which his opponent was working vis-à-vis Hitler, Pound felt sure that another sortie by *Tirpitz* was inevitable. He made firm representations to the War Cabinet that the convoys should at least be postponed until next winter, but strong pressure from President Roosevelt on Churchill caused him to be overruled and preparations for PQ.17 had to go ahead. At least Pound received some small bonus from this since the Home Fleet, temporarily depleted by the demands of the Madagascar landings, was reinforced by the U. S. Task Force 99, consisting of the battleship *Washington* and the cruisers *Tuscaloosa* and *Wichita*.

On the German side there had been equal apprehension. It was realized that they had had a very narrow shave during PQ.12 and that *Tirpitz* had been lucky to escape crippling damage from the carrier-borne aircraft. Hitler, above all, was greatly alarmed and issued specific instructions that *Tirpitz* was not again to be risked unless the British aircraft carriers had first been located and attacked, so that they would no longer pose any threat to his prestige-laden battleship. However, although Admiral Tovey suspected that the Germans would be reluctant to run further risks, neither he, nor anyone else on the British side, could be sure of this; it is indeed a fact that Raeder was still anxious to use *Tirpitz* aggressively if he could find a suitable opportunity and if he could persuade Hitler to let him do so. As so often, when the time came O.K.M.'s nerve failed, and the qualifications they added to their instructions to their Fleet Commander would almost certainly have inhibited him, as they did his successors, from taking the bold offensive action that would have come naturally to, and been expected from, any British admiral in similar circumstances. But this was not known to us at the time. From the British point of view the threat remained a very real one, something most definitely to be taken into account.

By the middle of June both sides were making plans in connection with the sailing of the next convoy, the ill-fated PQ.17. On the east side of the North Sea the Germans now had *Tirpitz, Scheer, Lützow* and *Hipper*, with some eleven destroyers and three large torpedo boats in North Norway. Preparations had been completed, as we knew thanks to our Swedish friends and Captain Denham, for Altenfjord, just south of Norway's most northerly point, the North Cape, to be used as an advance base for at least two heavy ships. Hitler, of course, wished to have his cake and eat it. Although his instructions about *Tirpitz* still held good, he had nevertheless perversely indicated to Raeder that a successful attack on the supply route would not be unwelcome. Raeder, who fully appreciated the possibilities and who realized that, at the very least, *Tirpitz* would represent a greater threat if she was showing signs of activity rather than just swinging to a buoy in Trondheim, made plans, with the code name Rösselsprung (Knights Move), which were to be put into force as soon as PQ.17 was located at sea. *Scheer, Lützow,* and six destroyers had moved up to Narvik, conveniently placed for a quick sortie at the right moment, but *Tirpitz* and *Hipper,* with four destroyers, remained for the moment at Trondheim. This would leave them but little time to sail and make contact with the convoy, after the process of locating both it and the British aircraft carriers and also of obtaining the Führer's permission had been completed. Raeder therefore gave instructions that as soon as it had been established that the outward-bound British convoy had passed a certain position, the Narvik squadron was to move still further north to the advanced base at Altenfjord, while *Tirpitz* and *Hipper* were to leave Trondheim and proceed to Westfjord, the entrance to Narvik, thus reducing the distance they would have to steam once Hitler's permission for an attack had been obtained. Nevertheless, despite this bold front, Admiral Schneewind, the fleet commander, was warned, as has already been indicated, to use the utmost caution and to avoid the risk of any reverse.

On June 14, Schneewind issued his plans and four days later all Denham's hard work was repaid when he was able to send the following Most Immediate signal to D.N.I.:

'Plan to attack next convoy.
1. Air reconnaissance to locate eastbound convoy when it reaches Jan Mayen. Bombing attacks will then be made.
2. Pocket battleships and six destroyers will move to Altenfjord and *Tirpitz* and *Hipper* to Narvik area. Both may be expected to operate once convoy has reached 6 degrees east. Simultaneous attack when convoy on meridian of Bear Island by two surface groups supported by U-boats and aircraft. Graded A.3.'

He followed this with another signal giving the dispositions of the German Air Force in North Norway.

This was an accurate summary of the German intentions. Neither Pound nor anyone else on the British side was aware of the restrictions imposed by Hitler, so the signal reinforced all the First Sea Lord's worst fears. About this time he talked by telephone to Tovey in his flagship at Scapa. No record of this conversation was made and so it is not clear how far the discussion centred on this latest and alarming piece of intelligence. Tovey however recalled that, to his dismay, Pound mentioned that in certain circumstances he felt the only course of action open to him might be to order the convoy to scatter, to prevent its annihilation by the powerful German battleship. The effect of an order for a convoy to scatter is for its constituent ships to abandon their close and disciplined formation, and to proceed on separate, predetermined and diverging courses to their individual destinations. It is a recognized tactic for a convoy attacked by a superior surface force on the broad oceans, and had indeed been used successfully in 1940, when convoy HX.84 and *Jervis Bay* had been attacked in the North Atlantic by *Scheer*. But on that occasion neither enemy aircraft nor U-boats had been involved and the merchantmen had a vast area in which to disperse and hide. In the Arctic, as Tovey was well aware, it was certain that both U-boats and aircraft would be engaged, the close escort would be powerless to protect their charges once they had scattered, while the area in which they could do so was much more restricted because of the ice edge and the Norwegian coast than had been the case in the Atlantic. It had repeatedly been proved that even the most weakly escorted convoy stood a better chance if it maintained its cohesion and formation in the face of U-boat and air attack, but this was just what the First Sea Lord seemed to envisage abandoning. Tovey was horrified and described the proposal as 'sheer bloody murder', but his protests do not seem to have made any impression on Pound.

Nevertheless when PQ.17, consisting finally of thirty-four British, American and Russian merchant ships, with three rescue ships, carrying in all 157,000 tons of tanks, aircraft and other war supplies for the Russians, did sail, it had been provided with the strongest protection possible in the circumstances prevailing. The close escort consisted of six destroyers, four corvettes, three minesweepers, four trawlers, two anti-aircraft ships and two submarines all under the command of a most experienced officer, Commander J. E. Broome, R.N. Four cruisers, of which two were the American *Tuscaloosa* and *Wichita*, under Rear-Admiral L. H. K. Hamilton, comprised the close covering force. His instructions were to go as far east as Bear Island, but not any further unless he received fresh instructions. Admiral Tovey, flying his flag in *Duke of York*, with *Washington* and *Victorious*, constituted the distant covering force, which, as before, was not expected to go much further east than Jan Mayen. Eight British, one Free French and four Russian submarines were positioned off the North Cape and special air patrols arranged.

Both PQ.17 and the returning convoy QP.13 sailed on June 27. Their voyages were comparatively uneventful for several days. PQ.17, on which the enemy were concentrating their efforts, was not sighted by the G.A.F. until the afternoon of July 1. By the 2nd, the outward and homeward convoys were passing each other roughly mid-way between Jan Mayen and Bear Island, the former shadowed now by both aircraft and U-boats but not yet attacked by either, although an unsuccessful air attack was shortly to be launched. Admiral Hamilton and his cruisers were in close proximity, although out of sight of the convoy, and the Home Fleet was further south in the vicinity of Jan Mayen.

So far as the Germans were concerned, the convoy having been sighted, *Tirpitz*, *Hipper* and their destroyers were preparing to leave Trondheim, which they did at 8 P.M. on the 2nd, reaching Westfjord at about 2 P.M. the next afternoon, the 3rd. They left there after a few hours and reached Altenfjord at about 10 A.M. on the 4th. In the process three of their four destroyers struck an uncharted rock and took no further part in the operation. *Lützow*, *Scheer*, and their five destroyers did not leave Narvik until around midnight on the 2nd, and reached Altenfjord about 10 A.M. on the 3rd. *Lützow* also ran aground and she too was out of action.

In the meantime, throughout July 3, PQ.17 proceeded successfully on its way. The first air attack was beaten off without loss and the U-boats also achieved nothing. It was not until early on July 4 that the convoy suffered its first casualty, when a single ship was sunk by another air attack. Nothing further developed until eight-thirty that evening when two dozen torpedo aircraft appeared and managed to sink two ships and damage a third. Despite this, the convoy and its escort were in good heart and confident that they could fight their way through to their destination provided their ammunition lasted. Earlier that day the Admiralty had given Hamilton discretion to proceed further east than laid down in his orders if he considered the situation warranted it, but Tovey saw no reason for any departure from the agreed plan and in turn signalled to Hamilton that 'once the convoy is east of 25 degrees East or earlier at your discretion you are to leave the Barents Sea unless assured by the Admiralty that *Tirpitz* cannot be met'. At 6 P.M. Hamilton reported his intention to reverse course at eight o'clock, but at 7:30 P.M. he received a signal, telling him that 'further information may be available shortly. Remain with convoy pending further instructions'. Just over an hour and a half later, Hamilton received a second signal from the Admiralty which read 'Most Immediate. Cruiser force to withdraw to westward at high speed', and some fifteen minutes after this a further signal, 'Immediate. Owing to threat of surface ships convoy is to disperse and to proceed to Russian ports', followed almost at once by a largely technical amendment, which was however prefaced Most Immediate: 'Convoy is to scatter'.

There was only one conclusion to be drawn by the recipients of this succession of signals; the Admiralty's 'further information' must be not only that *Tirpitz* was at sea, but that she would appear over the horizon at any moment. This certainly was the view held by both Hamilton and Broome. The former immediately complied with his instructions and prepared his squadron for an inevitable but highly unequal battle. Commander Broome at first had some difficulty in persuading the Commodore of the convoy that there was not some mistake about the order to scatter, but once this had been put into effect, it seemed to Broome that there was little or nothing his six destroyers could do for the rapidly dispersing merchantmen, and that his best course of action would be to join the cruisers in a death or glory attempt to keep the big German ship away from the convoy. He therefore instructed the smaller vessels and the two submarines of the close escort to continue to Murmansk while he himself took his destroyers back at maximum speed to join Hamilton. In the meantime Admiral Tovey, who was cruising north-west of Bear Island, was unaware that Broome had joined the cruisers, nor had he any information about the whereabouts of the German surface forces. In the event it was not until nearly noon on the following day, the 5th, that Raeder succeeded in getting Hitler's approval for them to sail and it was only at three o'clock that afternoon that *Tirpitz*, *Scheer*, *Hipper*, and nine destroyers reached the open sea. By then the individual ships of the widely scattered convoy were being subjected to merciless attacks by aircraft and U-boats, against which they were virtually defenceless. Twenty-three of them and one of the rescue ships were eventually sunk; only eleven and two rescue ships finally managed to struggle into port. Long before this the Germans had realized that there was nothing for the big ships to do and had ordered them to return to harbour.

We must now return to the Admiralty to try to discover why these disastrous orders were issued. The first thing that must be remembered is that the German signals were being regularly decrypted for periods of forty-eight hours at a time, with gaps between those periods of between four and forty-eight hours. The second point to be borne in mind is that those signals were W/T signals. Instructions to *Tirpitz* as long as she was anchored at Trondheim would not have been sent over the air, but communications between ships anchored in Westfjord and Altenfjord were at this time made by wireless. We knew from previous experience that once the heavy ships put to sea on operations, even if they themselves maintained strict wireless silence, there was a steady stream of instructions and information sent to them from their shore command, just as was the case with the Admiralty and our own forces. The absence of any such flow of signals was a fairly, if not completely, conclusive indication that they were still in port or at anchor in some fjord.

Early on July 3, we began to decrypt the Special Intelligence traffic for the period from noon on the 1st to noon on the 2nd, and this was followed, as usual and without much delay, by the signals for the next twenty-four-hour period. By the afternoon of the 3rd, therefore, we were reasonably well up-to-date as regards information revealed by Special Intelligence. We knew of the Narvik squadron's arrival in Altenfjord that morning, and had also learned of the *Tirpitz*'s departure from Trondheim the previous night, a fact that was also confirmed by one of our P.R.U. aircraft, but the *Tirpitz* group was not actually located by air reconnaissance that day. More worrying still was the fact that B.P. were now faced with the difficult task of breaking in to a new forty-eight-hour period of Special Intelligence and it was never possible to be sure in advance how long this process would take.

The night of the 3rd to 4th was an anxious one for those in the Admiralty, and this anxiety deepened as the forenoon of the 4th came and went without any further news. B.P. although fully aware of all that was at stake, had not so far hit the jackpot, and to add to our difficulties air reconnaissance failed from 11 A.M. to 5 P.M. The convoy, although all had gone surprisingly well with it so far, was now entering on its most critical phase. It was, we knew, being shadowed by both U-boats and aircraft, and was gradually proceeding further away from the distant protection of the Home Fleet. The cruiser force would have to leave it within the next few hours.

There were, however, some slight indications that the Germans might not yet have sailed from Altenfjord. We knew, once more from G.A.F. signals, that the Home Fleet had not been located for the past twenty-four hours. Although we were, of course, unaware of the restrictions imposed by Hitler, it was a reasonable inference that the Germans would not risk their ships without establishing the whereabouts of the Allied battleships and carrier. Secondly, there had been no reports from any of the Allied submarines patrolling off the North Cape of any movement out of Altenfjord towards the convoy. Neither of these two facts was conclusive. There was also one other pointer, no more than a straw in the wind. Although we had not, at this time, succeeded in establishing an agent in Altenfjord itself, we did have a man at its entrance, Porsa, who could observe all comings and goings. Unfortunately he did not report regularly so that the absence of any news from him could not really be taken as evidence that no movement had occurred.

Then, at long last, around 7 P.M., the eagerly awaited news was received in O.I.C. that the break-in had been made and that decrypts for the twenty-four hours which had ended at noon that day could be expected very shortly. This was the basis for the signal to Hamilton at 7:30 P.M. instructing him to remain with the convoy for the time being as fresh information might become available shortly. It is possible that this signal was originated by Captain Eccles, the Director of Operations (Home), who had immediately been given the good news by Denning. He was a frequent visitor to O.I.C. and fully conversant with its methods and the information available to it. It would have been natural for him to keep all options open until the First Sea Lord could be summoned to study the situation in person. By the time Pound arrived in O.I.C., B.P., which in such situations normally concentrated first on decrypting the most recent signals and those which from their outward appearance seemed to be urgent operational ones, had teleprinted some valuable and alarming news. This was that *Tirpitz* and *Hipper* had indeed joined *Scheer* in Altenfjord that morning. They had not therefore proceeded direct from Trondheim towards the convoy. The alarming information was that their accompanying destroyers had been instructed to refuel immediately on arrival. This was, to some extent, to be expected, but it did rather strengthen the view that a move against the convoy in accordance with the original plan was imminent. Exactly how long the refuelling would take could not be known.

Denning was nevertheless quite convinced in his own mind that the German ships had not yet sailed, and in this view he was supported by his chief, Clayton, and by Hinsley in the Naval Section at B.P. His main reason was the entire absence of any signals from Gruppe Nord, the shore command in charge of naval operations in Norway, which always occurred when the big ships were at sea and which had been such a feature of *Tirpitz*'s earlier sortie against PQ.12. In addition there was the lack of any reports from our own submarines† and the other facts already referred to. Unfortunately, the First Sea Lord did not give Denning the opportunity to explain the reasons on which his convictions were based. Instead Pound seems to have confined himself to a few direct questions to which the answers could only be short and factual. Donald McLachlan, who admittedly was not able to refer to Special Intelligence in his book *Room 39*, gives the following account of the scene with the First Sea Lord posing the questions:

† It is of interest to note that when the German squadron did in fact sail on the following afternoon, it was reported by British and Russian submarines and by reconnaissance aircraft.

The dialogue, based on the recollections of two witnesses was of this order:

1 SL: Do you know if *Tirpitz* has put to sea?

Denning: If *Tirpitz* has put to sea you can be sure that we should have known very shortly afterwards, within four to six hours.

1 SL: Can you assure me that *Tirpitz* is still at anchor in Altenfjord?

Denning: No. I shall have firm information only when *Tirpitz* has left.

1 SL: Can you at least tell me whether *Tirpitz* is ready to go to sea?

Denning: I can at least say that she will not leave in the next few hours. If she were on the point of sailing the destroyer escort would have preceded her and made an anti-submarine sweep. They have not been reported by our submarines patrolling off Altenfjord.

Pound has been described by some as an autocrat. He was certainly a very reserved man and never revealed to others his thought-processes. When he had reached a decision and was ready to issue instructions he would speak, but until that moment he was accustomed to keeping his own counsel. This, and the fact that he was an Admiral of the Fleet and the professional head of the Service, made it very difficult, if not downright impossible, for Denning or for that matter Clayton, to force their own views on him when he did not give them an opportunity to express them. Denning regrets bitterly that he did not do so, but looking back it is hard to see how, in the circumstances, he could have done more. When Pound left Denning's room to visit the U-boat Tracking Room, Clayton and Denning were profoundly anxious that a decision which they both considered unnecessary and mistaken was about to be made. The First Sea Lord wanted positive evidence; all they had to offer was negative intelligence.

The Tracking Room plot confirmed what we already knew from open evidence, that U-boats were in contact with the convoy and that they also represented a threat to the cruisers. It did not reveal, because of course no such instructions had been issued, that U-boats should expect their own surface ships in the area. Such a warning would certainly have been issued, had *Tirpitz* then been approaching the convoy. Indeed a little later a decrypt signal was received in O.I.C. informing U-boats that their own surface forces were not at that time in the area, but this was possibly after Pound had left to return to his own office.

At eight o'clock that evening the First Sea Lord called a staff meeting to review the position. Exactly what views were expressed at this meeting cannot now be precisely established, although it appears that most of those present did not favour scattering the convoy at once. The Vice-Chief of Naval Staff, Admiral Moore, however, expressed the view that if the convoy was going to scatter, orders for it to do so must be issued quickly because it was running out of sea room in which to carry out such a manoeuvre. The contrary views put forward do not seem to have influenced Pound, and it is probable that the meeting followed the usual pattern of those over which Pound presided: 'After listening to what people had to say, he would take up the signal pad and draft the action, which he had already decided to take, filling in all details of "addressed to", "repeated to" and so on.'‡ Certainly the meeting was not a long one for the first signal, that ordering the cruisers to withdraw at high speed, went out just after nine o'clock, and that ordering the convoy to scatter some twenty minutes later.

Clayton, who had attended the meeting, returned to O.I.C. greatly depressed. By this time Special Intelligence had been flowing in for more than two hours and now included signals for the current twenty-four hours. The only positive information revealed was the signal to U-boats already referred to, but sufficient time had also now elapsed to substantiate fully Denning's and Hinsley's theory that the big ships could not be at sea because there were no signals addressed to them. Denning discussed the situation again with his chief and persuaded him to return to the First Sea Lord to try to get him to change his mind. It must have required considerable moral courage to do so, but, regrettably, Clayton was unsuccessful. Pound felt that he had already weighed all the evidence presented to him, and he had come to the conclu-

‡ See Godfrey: *Memoirs*. Typescript.

sion that it was insufficient to rule out the possibility that *Tirpitz* was at sea. If she was, and if she had sailed at the first possible moment, she could be in a position to attack the convoy in the early hours of the next morning. He was not prepared to countermand the orders which he had given and which, in all probability, were being executed at that very moment.

This then was the sequence of events which led to the fatal decisions being taken.

With the benefit of hindsight it is very easy to criticize the First Sea Lord. He made it clear at his evening meeting on July 4 that the responsibility for the decision was his and his alone. Events proved that it was a gravely mistaken decision, but at the time, and with the evidence then available to him, could he have acted otherwise?

The movements of the German ships up to the morning of the 4th, revealed to us by Special Intelligence, had conformed so exactly to the plan outlined in Denham's signal that, with no knowledge of Hitler's restricting orders, it apparently seemed certain to Pound that the combined German squadron would sail as soon as the destroyers had refuelled and that it might therefore fall upon the convoy in the early hours of the following morning.

It was certainly right, whatever view one took of this possibility, to withdraw the cruisers immediately. They had already proceeded further eastward than had been originally intended and now their return passage was threatened by U-boats. Better staff work would have made the reasons for the order and the use of high speed clear to Hamilton, but that the instruction was necessary cannot be disputed. But was it essential, in the face of the existing and great threat from U-boats and bombers to order the convoy to scatter without at least allowing a little more time to elapse during which further information, even if it was only negative information, might emerge? Was it necessary to scatter the convoy at all? Its instructions included provision for it to reverse course towards the Home Fleet in the event of danger from the German surface ships. Why was this not adopted?* The attachment of two submarines to the close escort had been specifically intended to provide some defence against heavy ship attack in the absence of the close and distant covering forces. Why was this apparently

---

* Perhaps because of insufficient fuel.

ignored? If cruisers were not expendable, other occasions had demonstrated that destroyers were, and Commander Broome's ships would surely have given a good account of themselves.

One is left with the uncomfortable feeling that the First Sea Lord's mind was made up long before he came down to O.I.C. that evening, perhaps even before the convoy sailed, and that the purpose of his visit was merely to confirm that no positive intelligence had come to hand which would compel him to cancel a course of action upon which he was already resolved.

One must ask whether Clayton and Denning could have done more to press their views on the First Sea Lord. Almost any other senior officer of the Naval Staff would have cross-examined Denning at much greater length, but that was not Pound's way. Nevertheless Denning had stated his views clearly and firmly, and Clayton had returned a second time to reiterate those views to Pound. It is hard to see what more either of them could have done.

Criticism in previous accounts of PQ.17 has been centred on Pound's interference with the men on the spot: Tovey, Hamilton and Broome. But Pound felt that the decision was such a grave one that it was unfair that anyone except he himself should have to accept responsibility for it. Was not his biggest error his failure to accept the advice of his own experts? He was not a frequent visitor to O.I.C. and does not seem to have understood the weaknesses as well as the strengths of Special Intelligence; that it did not always reveal the whole picture of what was happening 'at the other side of the hill'. He did not give due weight to the depth and extent of Denning's background knowledge.

Great man though he was, Pound 'could not delegate or shed the habits of a staff officer'.† To make matters worse he was typical of the Executive officers referred to in Chapter 1, 'incapable of realizing that there was any work which he could not do'. He attempted to act as his own intelligence officer, to evaluate personally and to accept or reject the scraps of information available. But, as was the case with Captain Jackson at the time of Jutland, there was more to it than he supposed. His rejection of O.I.C.'s views led to disaster.

† See Godfrey: *Memoirs*. Typescript.

9

July–December 1942.
The Indian Ocean and Torch

I t is now time to return to the U-boat war. The increased building and training programme was finally beginning to bear fruit. The 140 U-boats operational in July 1942 had increased three months later to 196. Despite diversions to the Mediterranean and the Arctic, Dönitz at last had a really substantial force available for operations in the Atlantic. He was now able, at one and the same time, to concentrate Wolf Packs of up to twenty boats against the North Atlantic and U.K.-West African convoys, to continue the campaigns in the Caribbean, off Freetown and off Brazil and to fulfil his long-deferred wish to attack the focal area off Cape Town.

In the middle of August he sailed four large Type IX C-boats* and a U-tanker from French ports for this purpose. They were followed at intervals by four new and even larger U-cruisers of the Type IX D2 class. They were allowed to attack anything they encountered until they had reached latitude 5 degrees South, but from there on they were to restrict themselves, as the Paukenschlag boats had done before them, to large and valuable targets. It was important that the British should not receive any indication of their ultimate destination. Special Intelligence had given us forewarning of the attack on the United States seaboard, but with

* These were 740 tonners with additional range.

the 'black-out' through which we had been groping since February, it was surely asking too much to expect Winn to produce an equally accurate prediction about Dönitz's latest objective.

It is therefore of interest to note that on August 3, before the first South Atlantic boats sailed, Winn, in considering the disposition of U-boats in the Freetown area and the possibility that some of them might be moved towards Ascension, should have gone on to say 'It is possible that U-boats may proceed even further south. (In December 1941 four U-boats were sent to operate off Cape Town, but had to return at once owing to the sinking of their supply ships.)'† Once again Winn and Dönitz were thinking along the same lines.

The departure of the four boats and the Milch Cow did not, of course, go unnoticed in the Tracking Room. It was a fair deduction that they were destined for operations in distant waters, but was it to be the Caribbean, Brazil, Freetown or the Congo? Brazil was now at war with Germany and there were pickings in plenty to be had off Recife; or would Dönitz be tempted to go for the vital meat trade off the River Plate, despite Argentina's continued neutrality? There were many possibilities to choose from. Winn, however, had a hunch. From the outset he felt that it was the Cape, and so we started to plot the four boats south-west and then south for the South Altantic and South Africa.

The precise route the U-boats would take could only be a matter of conjecture, but almost exactly a month after the boats had sailed we were proved right in our general appreciation, but terribly wrong in our estimate of the enemy's exact positions. On September 12, U.156 torpedoed and sank the liner *Laconia*, just south of the Equator. She was carrying servicemen and women and children, and 1,800 Italian prisoners of war back from the Middle East. There were many survivors, and the U-boat's commanding officer, Kapitän Leutnant Hartenstein, did all that he could for them, taking some on board and helping others to reach the rafts and lifeboats. He immediately broke wireless silence to report to Dönitz and followed this up with messages *en clair* in English on the international wave band. Other U-boats were ordered to the scene, but before the rescue operation could be completed, U.156 was attacked, fortunately unsuccessfully, by American bombers

† See Chapter 6 for sinking of *Atlantis* and *Python*.

from Ascension. Dönitz arranged for Vichy French warships from Dakar to relieve the U-boats of their unwelcome passengers, but then, perhaps not unnaturally, issued a general instruction that such rescue attempts must not be undertaken in the future. For this he was indicted at Nüremberg.

In the meantime the U-boats were again free to continue their interrupted passage, and Winn had to decide whether all this activity should be taken as confirmation of his estimate. The position where *Laconia* had been sunk was not conclusive evidence; it was equally consistent with a movement to the western as to the eastern South Atlantic. Might it not in either case have caused yet another postponement of the venture? On September 21 Winn wrote in his weekly report, 'W/T evidence of half a dozen U-boats 200 miles N.E. of Ascension where the *Laconia* was sunk on the 12th is probably connected with the collection of the surviving passengers and Italian prisoners of war. Most of these have in all probability been picked up by French warships'. This was not very forthcoming, but on the same day he had in fact signalled the Commander-in-Chief South Atlantic that a 'southward movement of U-boats seems imminent', on receipt of which such precautions as were possible were set in train at Cape Town. On September 28 Winn had to report: 'There is still no indication of the whereabouts of the half dozen U-boats which were near Ascension ten days ago, but they may be in the eastern South Atlantic. It is consistent with but not confirmatory of this view that two fishermen reported seeing eight men landing from a U-boat about 200 miles north of Cape Town'.‡ Winn still held to his view that an attack on Cape Town was intended, but the entire absence of any first class evidence to substantiate this was worrying. According to our plot the Germans should have arrived by the end of the month: where were they? At the beginning of October the German propaganda machine seems to have got its wires crossed with U-boat Command, for despite the secrecy with which the operation was supposed to be surrounded and the entire absence of any activity up to this time, it put out a statement about U-boats in Far Eastern waters. On October 5 Winn reported: 'There have been no further reports from the South At-

‡ This report does not seem to have had any truth in it and was typical of many which we received throughout the war.

lantic and no real clue to the whereabouts of the ten U-boats estimated south of the Equator towards the end of September. A German broadcast has mentioned the arrival of U-boats in "Far Eastern waters". There is as yet no evidence to support this statement, but the appearance of up to six German U-boats in the Mozambique Channel by mid-October is theoretically possible'. Confirmation came two days later when the first attack was made off Cape Town. The U-boat concerned was in fact the first of the U-cruisers which had caught up the other boats during the course of the long voyage. She was herself immediately sunk but thereafter our lack of escort vessels enabled the remainder to fulfil all Dönitz's expectations, and it was some months before the situation could be brought under control. Even then German U-boats, relying on U-tankers in the Atlantic and, further east, on supply ships and on the use of Japanese ports, continued to operate in the Indian Ocean with varying success right up to the end of the war. The last two survivors were taken over by the Japanese when Germany collapsed.

This episode has been described in some detail because although a comparatively small number of U-boats was involved and the outcome was not a happy one for us, since far too many valuable ships were lost, it is such a good example of Winn's work at a time when only the minimum of help could be provided by Special Intelligence. It shows the almost uncanny way in which he seemed to read Dönitz's mind, his ability to piece together an accurate picture from fragmentary and nebulous evidence, and perhaps above all his courage in maintaining for nearly two months and in the face of some scepticism a theory for which confirmatory evidence was for so long lacking.

Before returning to the battles on the North Atlantic convoy routes, a number of other developments must be mentioned. Our knowledge of the times of departure of the U-boats from their German, Norwegian and French bases enabled the Tracking Room to make accurate forecasts upon which Coastal Command could carry out offensive patrols, both on the northern exit routes and in the Bay of Biscay. Although none of Coastal Command's aircraft had so far been fitted with 10cm radar, they had been equipped with the Leigh Light, a searchlight devised by Wing Commander Leigh, which in conjunction with their existing radar sets enabled them to surprise and illuminate U-boats on the surface at night. A number of successful attacks were made which considerably disconcerted Dönitz until his U-boats could be equipped with the French Metox radar search receiver to give them adequate warning of an impending attack. The number of interceptions then declined sharply until, when Bomber Command's needs had been met, the new 10cm radar sets were at last supplied to Coastal Command early in 1943. These sets, a variety of which had already been fitted in the surface escorts, completely baffled the Germans for a long time and were probably the most decisive single British development in the U-boat war. For the second half of 1942, however, although the passage of U-boats to and from their bases was seriously incommoded,* it was in no way halted.

By this time Coastal Command were well supplied with medium-range aircraft. Although suitable for the offensive patrols just mentioned, they were of limited value for ocean convoy escort work. Even the longer range Catalinas and Halifaxes could not operate more than four or five hundred miles from their bases, but the very long range Liberator could give cover to convoys for eight hundred miles. In the autumn of 1942 Coastal Command had only one squadron, the famous 120 Squadron—sixteen aircraft of these utterly invaluable American machines. It was quite impossible to give distant cover to all the convoys which were crying out for it. There was still a large gap in the air cover of the Atlantic, stretching from south of Greenland to the Azores. On the Tracking Room plot large red circles extended from Iceland, Northern Ireland, Cornwall, Gibraltar and Newfoundland, showing the limits of air cover that could be provided. Outside these lines was the 'Black Pit', where U-boats could run on the surface in daylight, and refuel from their Milch Cows without fear of surprise from aircraft. Dönitz's strategy was to station a group of U-boats just inside the normal limits of air cover to wait for, say, a westbound convoy. Once sighted it would be pursued by the whole group until it at last gained the protection of aircraft stationed in Newfoundland. The U-boats would then withdraw, replenish with

---

* The Tracking Room estimated that the submerged passage of the Bay of Biscay then ordered would add five days to the length of time previously required.

fuel, torpedoes and supplies from a U-tanker, and then return to lie in wait for the next east-bound convoy.

In the autumn of 1942, the B.Dienst was working with great efficiency and decrypting more and more of the Allied routing instructions. It was ironical that, just as the Germans could not provide their U-boats with comprehensive orders before they sailed, and were compelled to issue frequent fresh instructions once they were at sea, so the Allies played into the hands of the B.Dienst in exactly the same manner. A general route was prepared for each convoy before it sailed but it necessarily had to be issued well in advance, and was almost always modified, once the convoy had got to sea, in the light of the latest situation—which included the state of the escorts, the weather conditions and estimates made by the Tracking Room of the U-boats' positions. These fresh orders had then to be signalled to the Senior Officer of the Escort and the Convoy Commodore. The new route was often given by means of reference points, but unfortunately these could sometimes be unravelled by the Germans, who built up a very good picture of the general routes used and the convoy cycles, as well as often obtaining a precise position through which a particular convoy would pass. Add the fact that Dönitz had sufficient boats to spread them out on three or four separate and extensive reconnaissance lines, and it is surprising that as many convoys got through without being intercepted as was in fact the case, but speed in decrypting was, of course, essential for the Germans— frequently they were too slow.

On October 12, Winn wrote: 'Of the 100 or more German U-boats now at sea in the Atlantic, between one-third and two-thirds are in the North Atlantic between the latitudes of the Azores and Iceland and between 25 degrees and 45 degrees West and it is remarkable that any convoy should pass through this area without being intercepted. The majority are reported but very effective assistance has been rendered with increasing frequency by aircraft from Iceland, and it has repeatedly been demonstrated that timely air cover can effectively break down the shadowing routine and enable convoys to draw clear'.

The Allied routing authorities had a further difficulty. The British were extremely short of reserves of bunker fuel. This was the reason why convoys had to be routed on the most direct Great

Circle routes and large diversions were out of the question, not stubbornness as the Germans supposed, or fear of compromising Special Intelligence as has recently been suggested by a writer† who ignores the fact that Atlantic U-boat Special Intelligence was not at this time available.

For one class of ship, however, diversions were not only possible but essential. These were the 'Monsters', six of the world's largest passenger liners ranging from the two *Queens*, the *Mary* and the *Elizabeth*, of over 81,000 tons, to the *Mauretania* of 35,000 tons, which were now engaged in ferrying large numbers of American troops from New York to the Clyde as an essential preliminary to the opening of the 'Second Front'. The *Queens* carried, in addition to a crew of more than 1,000, over 15,000 troops on each trip. They and the others ran independently, relying on their speed for safety. The sinking of any one of them would have been the equivalent of a major defeat in a land battle. It will be easily understood with what care their routes were planned and with what attention the progress of their six-day voyages was followed both by OP.20 in Washington and O.I.C. in the Admiralty. With their great speed, diversions were not a problem provided the dangers ahead of them could be detected in time. It says something for the accuracy of the plots in the two tracking rooms that although the Monsters crossed and re-crossed the North Atlantic incessantly from the middle of 1942 up to D Day, and indeed thereafter, they were very rarely sighted and not one was lost.

Throughout September and October, attacks on Allied convoys between Britain and America and Britain and West Africa continued. Losses on both sides mounted. Some convoys were steered clear of danger, others had to face mass attacks by up to twenty-five U-boats. In some cases the escorts, particularly if the destroyers were fitted with the latest radar sets and if air cover was available, inflicted unpleasant losses on the U-boats. In other instances the balance was in favour of the Germans. Put at its lowest, the Submarine Tracking Room did succeed in keeping some convoys clear of the Wolf Packs and when it failed to do so, at least the situation was recognized immediately, so that whatever additional support could be organized did reach the scene with the minimum of delay.

† See A. Cave-Brown: *Bodyguard of Lies.*

On November 8, the Allies launched Operation Torch, the invasion of North Africa, at Algiers and Oran in the Mediterranean and at Casablanca and Port Lyautey on the Atlantic coast of Morocco. All the troops, their weapons, supplies of ammunition, petrol and food, were carried in convoys direct from Great Britain and the United States. It required intricate and very careful planning. For example, the six assault convoys for the Mediterranean, consisting in all of 158 merchant ships and 52 escorts, with speeds varying from seven to thirteen knots, sailed from the Clyde between October 22 and November 1. Six slower advance convoys of 84 ships and 40 escorts sailed between October 2 and 30. The routing of this vast armada was planned at the latest possible moment in forty-eight hours of intensive work by Commander R. A. Hall,‡ the head of the Movements Section of Trade Division, in co-operation with Winn.

Towards the end of September Winn produced an estimate of the maximum U-boat threat to Torch. Obviously any considerable and successful attack by U-boats on the assault convoys would gravely prejudice the outcome of the operation. Winn stated that, provided the enemy had no prior knowledge of the invasion, he would be unlikely to have more than two U-boats to the west of Gibraltar, a focal point through which all the British convoys would have to pass, on D Day. By D+2, however, the total could rise to ten and by D+4 to seventeen. If Dönitz took immediate steps to sail boats from Biscay ports, the figure for D+4 could be increased to twenty-four and by D+8 to thirty-two. Furthermore if, at this stage, U-boats outward-bound from Germany and those already operating in mid-North Atlantic were directed to the area, the total could rise to as many as forty-nine by D+11. He added that 'it should be noted that drawing on the last two categories would mean a material but temporary diminution of the U-boat effort against the [trade] convoys, and it is considered that at the end of the first ten days, the enemy would be compelled to take a decision whether or not to reduce further his campaign against trade and supplies in order to add still more to the force in the Gibraltar area, which as mentioned might reasonably amount to 50 U-boats'. It was also appreciated that there might be a maximum of thirty-one Italian, six French and six German U-boats in

‡ See Chapter 10.

the Western Mediterranean. This was an accurate estimate of the possibilities, but of course the precise outcome largely depended on the enemy's reactions and these could not be known in advance. The Naval Staff appear to have taken, perhaps wisely, the most unfavourable view of the possible situation and acted on the assumption that there might well be fifty German U-boats concentrated west of Gibraltar before D Day, presumably on the basis that the Germans must get wind of Allied intentions at least eleven days before the landings. Although they did not do so, Dönitz did in fact have a group of ten U-boats west of Gibraltar towards the end of October, whose presence was suspected by the Tracking Room at the time, but then, by a stroke of great good fortune, he diverted them to the neighbourhood of Madeira to attack a north-bound trade convoy. The Germans remained in blissful ignorance of Torch right up to the moment that the landings started. Their reaction was then much as Winn had predicted, except that some of the boats rushed to the scene were ordered into the Mediterranean and those off Gibraltar and Morocco were so roughly handled by the very strong anti-submarine forces which, as a result of Winn's forecast, had been assembled there, that Dönitz managed to persuade O.K.M. not to compel him to divert all his strength away from the North Atlantic to what he rightly considered a subsidiary theatre. Nevertheless the reduction of the forces available for his main objective, the attack on the trade convoys, was a significant factor in keeping Allied losses of shipping in the North Atlantic down in the next two months.

In fact, the situation was highly favourable to the Germans for a third 'glückliche Zeit'. In order to provide the necessary protection for the British convoys and covering forces of battleships, aircraft carriers and cruisers involved in Torch, the Atlantic convoys had to be largely stripped of their surface escorts, including all the escort carriers which were at last becoming available and which could have closed the Atlantic air gap. The convoy cycles had to be opened out drastically, and shipping from the Cape and West Africa had to be routed independently across to Trinidad to join the American coastal convoy system, which was at long last functioning comprehensively and efficiently, for Halifax. Roskill remarks that this was a 'feat which would have been quite impossible but for the centralised control of shipping exercised by the

Admiralty', and, one might add, the extremely close and effective co-operation now existing between the Tracking Room and Hall's Trade Movement Section.*

If losses in the North Atlantic in November and December were, thanks to the German preoccupation with Torch and Allied counter-measures, kept down to reasonable proportions, the same could not be said for the distant 'soft' spots, and total sinkings of merchant shipping by U-boats in November amounted to 729,000 tons. For the whole of 1942 the losses from all causes reached the staggering total of nearly eight million tons, while by the end of the year and in spite of a better rate of killing in the last six months, the operational U-boat fleet had risen to the frightening figure of 212. Another 181 were engaged on trials and training and over 70 new boats were now being commissioned each quarter.

It was clear that the Battle of the Atlantic would soon reach a climax. The Allies would have to summon up all their reserves of skill and determination, to concentrate all their available ships, escort carriers and aircraft, and to hasten the supply of 10cm radar and new anti-submarine weapons if they were to have any chance of survival. The performance of the Tracking Room, whether good or bad, might well tip the scales one way or the other. The gods must have decided, at this moment, to amuse themselves at the Tracking Room's expense, for on a single day in December they removed with one hand the lynch pin of our organization, and with the other restored to us our most precious source of intelligence.

Mention has already been made of the inadequate staffing of the Tracking Room at the beginning of 1942. During the year the volume of work we were called upon to handle rose by leaps and bounds, but there was no comparable increase in the number of staff to deal with it. By this stage of the war, every trained and able-bodied officer was required for sea duty to man the vastly expanded fleet. The only additional help that could be obtained was by means of the transfer of a R.N.V.R. Sub-Lieutenant from the Mediterranean Section to the Tracking Room. The individual concerned, Eric Fiske, soon proved himself to be an exceptionally able and dedicated member of the team, earning promotion before the end of the war to the acting rank of Lieutenant-Com-

* See Chapter 10.

mander, but one man could not do the work of four, however hard he tried. The flow of talented male civilians had long since dried up, and although some women graduates were now being recruited to try to fill the gap, the idea that they should be given posts of real responsibility was only slowly and reluctantly beginning to gain acceptance. Because the Admiralty, despite its operational role, was a Civil Establishment, the Civil Service Union fought bitterly against the appointment of W.R.N.S. officers or ratings. We did receive some help from the posting of Temporary Assistant Clerical Officers, both male and female, who did invaluable work and enabled us to undertake some research and organize a better and more comprehensive filing and cross reference system, but for far too long the main burden still had to be borne by the four original watchkeepers, Majolier, Finlaison, Whittal and Wilmot-Sitwell (the latter's death during the war was certainly hastened by over-strain), by Fiske, by Winn's deputy—but above all by Winn himself. A renewed attempt to get more staff was made later in the year and this time it was taken right to the top, but even then it was not until November that the arrival of Sub-Lieutenants McMicking, Naylor and Setter, R.N.V.R. at last permitted the formation of two watches. One, consisting of the original and mainly civilian watchkeepers, handled all information about Allied ships and maintained the plot of Allied convoys and independents; the other, the R.N.V.R. watch, handled all enemy intelligence, whether from Special Intelligence or other sources.

It was, however, too late. At the beginning of December Winn collapsed. His doctor advised him that he was suffering from total mental and physical exhaustion, that his blood pressure was dangerously low, that unless he took a complete and prolonged rest he would never again be fit enough to undertake serious work of any sort, and that in no circumstances could a return to the Admiralty be permitted.

The author has vivid recollections of receiving this calamitous news. Late one afternoon, when Winn was taking his weekly 'rest day', he was informed by B.P. that something for which we had all been praying for months past had at last happened: Triton had finally been cracked. Overjoyed, he at once telephoned his chief to explain in suitably guarded terms that the 'Oracle' could once more be consulted, expecting that Winn would say that he would be round at the Admiralty within half an hour, ready to work throughout the night on the tricky and confusing situation that would certainly be revealed once Special Intelligence started to pour in. It was a most unpleasant shock to be told, quite to the contrary, that he would have to do the best he could on his own, but the thought that Winn might not return at all was far worse. The task of handling Special Intelligence was by no means a simple one, despite impressions to the contrary given in some recent books, but it certainly was not beyond the capabilities of ordinary intelligent individuals. What could not be replaced were Winn's own unique gifts: his ability to read Dönitz's mind, his knack of swiftly sorting the wheat from the chaff, and selecting from a mass of evidence that which was of prime and immediate importance and that which was of real significance: his ability to put forward unpopular or at least inconvenient views and above all his forensic skill in persuading the Naval Staff to accept and rely on his judgement, and indeed also on the judgement of his subordinates. He was certainly irreplaceable in the short term, and time was indeed short.

It was an unpleasant prospect, but fortunately, as was always the case in O.I.C., there was no time to sit about worrying. Within an hour the first Triton messages started to come off the teleprinter and they continued to do so in an unending stream until the early hours of the following morning. It was an exciting and an exhausting night.

In the end the gods relented. Winn, being the man he was, defied his doctor and was back on duty in four weeks, but it had been a very close shave.

10

Triton to the Rescue

THE RENEWED penetration of the Atlantic U-boat cipher did
not immediately enable us to establish the true location of every
U-boat at sea. The decrypts were not right up-to-date nor were
they at first complete. Gradually, however, the picture began to
clear and by the end of ten days we were again reasonably sure of
the enemy's general dispositions. In the process we had to make a
large number of changes in the individual positions previously
shown on our plot. U-boats 'X' and 'Y', which we knew had left
St. Nazaire and Lorient in the middle of November were not,
after all, the two boats we thought had reported Convoy 'A' south
of Iceland three weeks later. That was the work of 'U' and 'V',
while 'X' and 'Y' had in fact joined another group three hundred
miles away. U-boat 'L' was not the one off Trinidad but had torpedoed the tanker off Florida. We had to indulge for some time
in a complicated game of General Post. Nevertheless the following table, extracted from the Tracking Room's weekly reports to
the First Sea Lord for the weeks ending December 7, 14 and 21,
1942, shows that Winn's 'Working Fiction' had resulted in a very
accurate assessment of the number of boats at sea, and in the allocation of approximately the right proportion of the total to the
admittedly large areas into which the Atlantic was divided for the
purposes of the report.

The report for the week ending December 7 was arrived at with the benefit only of that Special Intelligence which had been available since February 1, namely arrivals and departures from French and Norwegian ports. By the end of the next week, Special Intelligence concerning boats at sea had given a good deal of information, while by December 21, the estimates, if not completely up-to-date, were solidly grounded on factual information. In studying the tables, allowance must be made for the movements of U-boats taking place during the fortnight, for example from the Canadian coast back into the North-West Atlantic area, for the passage of boats to and from their bases, and finally for two U-boats sunk in the first week and one in the second.

AREA	Dec. 7	Dec. 14	Dec. 21
North East. Iceland–Ireland	3	3	1
North West. Iceland–Newfoundland	12	21	25
South East. Azores–Cape Verdes	6	5	3
South West. Antilles–Bermuda	7	8	3
Canadian Coast	13	5	5
U.S. Coast	1	0	0
Caribbean–Guiana	4	5	7
Biscay–Gibraltar–Azores	36	36	40
Total North Atlantic	82	83	84
Biscay Ports	82	79	78
Total	164	162	162
South Atlantic	11	10	16
Indian Ocean	1	1	0
Grand Total	176	173	178
[U-boats sunk		2	1]

It should of course be remembered that these weekly reports were merely summaries of the previous week's activities, and that the situation was shown in much greater detail on the Tracking Room plot, which was studied daily, sometimes hourly, by all concerned with the control of Allied forces and the routing of shipping. Inevitably many mistakes had been made in estimating the exact positions of the one hundred odd U-boats at sea in the whole of the vast area of the Atlantic during the period when Triton could not be broken. Looking back, however, after thirty-four years (and allowing for the feeling which those whose ships were suddenly torpedoed in areas thought to be free of U-boats must have had that the Admiralty was staffed by ignorant morons), it must surely be agreed that Winn was justified in his attempts to track every individual U-boat that left port and that the faith of the Naval and Coastal Command Staff in his 'Working Fiction' was not misplaced.

Now, however, Special Intelligence about the Atlantic U-boats was once more available. Surely there could be no excuse for any mistakes, no reason why, with the great volume of signals exchanged every day between Dönitz and his U-boat commanders, every single position should not be pinpointed, the enemy's every move discerned and anticipated? Why should not every convoy, every independently routed ship, be guided clear of danger, every U-boat detected and attacked by aircraft or destroyers, before it had time to do us any damage? This is indeed the view advanced in some recent books. Special Intelligence was *the* war winner: it betrayed to us *all* the enemy's secrets. One might even suppose, to read some accounts, that men, ships and aircraft to do the actual fighting were hardly necessary. Special Intelligence alone would provide. Unfortunately it was by no means as simple as this.

It must again be emphasized that the settings for the Enigma M machine changed daily. We have already seen, in connection with PQ.17, the difficulties which could arise if B.P. were unable to crack the new settings swiftly. During the first period of decrypting the Atlantic U-boat traffic, from June 1941 to the end of January 1942, we read currently for the first six weeks or so, as long, that is, as the captured settings remained in force, and we continued to do so on many days until the beginning of November. From then until the Black Out in February 1942, there were more frequent delays of between one and three days, although there were also occasions when current reading was possible. In broad terms a time-lag of twenty-four hours was not disastrous to us, and even a three-day delay might often mean that successful counter-action could still be taken. Anything more than this greatly reduced the operational value of Special Intelligence, although even a week's delay still contributed greatly to our knowledge and was of inestimable value compared with the absence of any Special Intelligence at all. In twenty-four hours a convoy would be unlikely to cover more than 170 to 240 miles. A U-boat, on the other hand, proceeding on the surface, could cover between 320 and 370 miles in the same period, so that given the greatly increased numbers of U-boats by early 1943 and the very accurate information often supplied to Dönitz by the B.Dienst, really up-to-date intelligence about the latest U-boat movements was essential if evasive routing was to be successful. For the first five months of 1943, during which the Battle of the Atlantic rose to a climax, although there were a good number of occasions when we read the Atlantic traffic currently, there were many others when we were three to four days in arrears and at least two occasions when the delays amounted to so much as seven days. The result was that although many convoys were successfully routed clear of danger, many others fell victims to changes in the positions of the U-boat patrol lines ordered by Dönitz at a moment when we were 'blind'.

It may well be asked how, with such failures, Winn and the Tracking Room could retain any credibility with the Naval Staff. The answer lies in the striking difference between O.I.C. and Room 40, a difference for which Denning, Clayton and Godfrey were largely responsible. Whereas Room 40 was, for much of its existence, a cryptanalysis bureau, shrouded in mystery, whose difficulties and limitations, as well as its virtues, were not properly understood by the Naval Staff and the Commander-in-Chief of the Grand Fleet, O.I.C. was accessible, either in person, by scrambler telephone, telex or signal, to all those who had to take operational decisions. They were fully aware of the handicaps which Denning and Winn had to face, they knew precisely when Special Intelligence was available and when it was not, when it was up-to-date and when it was already stale, what was factual and what was intelligent guess-work. They were conscious of the effort which had gone on in the Tracking Room to marry up sighting reports, D/F fixes, attacks on and by U-boats with Special Intelligence, whether current or a week old, and normally they did not attempt to challenge the experts on their own ground.

Such an attempt was made on one occasion by that very great man, Admiral Sir Max Horton, who, at the end of 1942, had relinquished the position of Flag Officer (Submarines) to take over as Commander-in-Chief Western Approaches from Sir Percy Noble, another splendid character. Horton was dissatisfied with appreciations given him by the Tracking Room which had led to an unsuccessful convoy battle, and attacked Winn at one of the fortnightly U-boat Warfare meetings presided over by the Assistant Chief of Staff (U-boats and Trade). Winn accepted the criticism in good part (indeed he had no option), but suggested that if he could be given half an hour, he would lay out all the intelligence available to the Tracking Room at the time the appreciation was made. The Admiral could then examine it himself and decide what different conclusions he would have come to. When Horton arrived in the Tracking Room he was confronted with a mass of Special Intelligence signals, D/F fixes, sighting reports and the last confirmed positions of the U-boats concerned. 'It's all yours, Sir,' said Winn, 'and your Chief of Staff in Liverpool is in a devil of a hurry for the answer.' Horton settled down, but after a period of intense study turned to Winn and in the words of his biographer, Rear-Admiral Chalmers,* 'confessed that most of it was outside his province. With the old familiar smile, which some called "cat-like", and others "benign", he held out his hand and said, "Good-bye, Rodger—I leave it to you." And thereafter he did.'

An excellent example of the frequent difficulties caused by the irregular flow of Special Intelligence occurred almost immediately after the Black Out was lifted. Just before the end of 1942, the Tracking Room had observed the departure from France of a group of six U-boats, the Delphin group. They were ordered to a patrol line defined by disguised reference points, which was thought to lie either west of Madeira, in which case it was designed to intercept the New York-Gibraltar convoys, or, more probably, so it was first thought, south-west of the Cape Verde Islands, in which case the objective must be independently routed shipping. It was soon established that in fact the first alternative was the correct one, and when orders were issued on January 2 to the Delphin boats to proceed westwards from their original line to mid-Atlantic, and then sweep south in company with a U-tanker, the movement was duly plotted on the Tracking Room chart.

* See W. S. Chalmers: *Max Horton and the Western Approaches*. Hodder & Stoughton.

Then one of those unfortunate delays in breaking the daily changes in the cipher settings intervened and we learned no more from Special Intelligence for seven long days.

On the next day, January 3, Convoy TM.1, consisting of nine precious tankers and a small escort, bound from Trinidad to Gibraltar, was fortuitously intercepted by U.514 shortly after it had started its voyage. Another nearby U-boat was ordered to join the attack, but the escort managed to drive them off with the loss of only one tanker and within twenty-four hours the U-boats had lost all contact. It was immediately appreciated in the Tracking Room that U.514's report† might result in a threat to TM.1 from the Delphin group, but the convoy and the U-boats were some 900 miles apart, enemy contact with the convoy had clearly been lost and the exact movements of Delphin could only be a matter of conjecture.

As soon as Dönitz received U.514's report, he cancelled Delphin's previous orders and instructed the group to proceed at high speed towards the distant convoy. Then another chance sighting, this time by a single U-boat outward-bound for the South Atlantic, of a fast Gibraltar-New York convoy (GUF.3) caused Dönitz to change his plans. The Delphin boats were ordered to pursue GUF.3, but after a time, despite the fact that contact with TM.1 had been lost and that the convoy was many hundreds of miles away, Dönitz decided, against the advice of his staff officers, to chance his arm and concentrate on the tankers. He ordered Delphin to turn east of south until they were about 650 miles west by south of the Canaries and about the same distance north-east of the last reported position of the convoy. They were then to spread out on a patrol line 180 miles in length at right angles to the presumed line of its advance, and to steam towards it at nine knots for twelve hours, reversing course for a like period. It was a typical Dönitz reconnaissance patrol.

As Winn subsequently reported, 'the possibility that such a patrol would be established had been appreciated . . . but it was not expected that it would be placed nearly so far ahead [of the convoy] i.e. to the eastward. There had been no evidence of the intermediate attempt to operate against GUF.3 and consequently

† Although not decrypted at this time, the short signal used disclosed that it was a sighting report. The position was obtained by D/F.

no indications of the whereabouts of the Delphin group which, when last heard of in Special Intelligence, had been moving west with orders to turn south when west of 34 degrees West. It had been correctly appreciated that the convoy was free from shadowing after 1600/4'.

Dönitz had played a hunch, against the advice of his own staff. He was proved right because at 3 P.M. on January 8, TM.1 was sighted by the third boat from the northern end of the line. The flow of Special Intelligence was not resumed for thirteen hours after that and even then it was incomplete for some days. Four more U-boats were set on to the unfortunate convoy, and in the end only two of the original nine tankers succeeded in reaching Gibraltar.

Winn had only returned to duty in the concluding phases of the operation, and it is tempting to ask whether, if he had been there from the outset, he would have been able to predict Dönitz's moves with greater accuracy than his deputy. It is hard to believe that with the entire absence of any information about the enemy's intentions or whereabouts he would have been more successful, but Winn did have a quite uncanny flair for this sort of inspired guess-work. TM.1 was but one example of the unending battle of wits between B.d.U. and the Tracking Room. We lost some and we won some. This was one we definitely lost.

One can readily suppose the sort of strain that such episodes imposed on the staff concerned, whether it was Winn himself, his deputy or the night watchkeeper called upon to take decisions in their absence. We were far removed from the sea, but it did not require a great deal of imagination to picture tankers going up in flames, seamen being drowned or maimed, or invaluable cargoes being lost as the result of faulty forecasts made in the comfort and security of the Admiralty. In the case of TM.1 we had a more than usually personal involvement because the Senior Officer of the Escort was a much-liked and respected Commander who had only just completed a spell of duty in the Room as the representative of the Anti-Submarine Warfare Division. However it was just no good allowing one's imagination to run riot. Decisions had to be taken, never lightly, never without due thought, but taken none the less, and one had to accept the consequences. The only possible way to treat the matter was as though it were a game of chess. Ships or U-boats were pawns. When one of them was sunk it was removed from the board. One side or the other had gained a point, but the game was not over and one had to turn immediately to consider the next move, to try to save the remainder of one's pieces and to take out some of one's opponents.

There were other difficulties, besides the delays in decrypting, which handicapped us in our efforts to pinpoint the U-boat patrol lines and guide our shipping around them. By early 1943 the B.Dienst was working at the peak of its efficiency, decrypting an increasing number of our convoy routing signals and now even the daily U-boat Situation Report, which the Tracking Room signalled to all warships at sea and to all commands involved in the Battle of the Atlantic. Although this was carefully worded to avoid any suspicion that it was based on Special Intelligence, it was at this time a fairly faithful representation, albeit in a condensed and less precise form, of the U-boat positions recorded on our plot. It naturally gave Dönitz a clear insight into our thinking and was of great help to him in circumventing the various moves by which we attempted to outwit him. With these two sources of information at his disposal and, in addition, a greatly increased number of U-boats acting as their own reconnaissance force, it was scarcely surprising that Dönitz often managed to detect our evasive diversions and forestall our moves. But the B.Dienst, like B.P. at this period, had its difficulties and was not always able to unbutton our signals quickly enough for Dönitz to make operational use of the results.

The reader may wonder why, if both sides were reading at least some of their opponent's signals, the fact did not quickly become apparent to both of them. So far as the Tracking Room was concerned, the answer can to some extent be attributed to the lack of staff and the pressure of the unceasing war at sea; there was not time for a proper study of the reasons why U-boat patrol lines were suddenly altered, why this convoy or that independent was intercepted. When so much decrypted information came in three or more days old, attention was inevitably concentrated on getting our plot up-to-date with the absolute minimum of delay so that immediate action could be taken. Each minute lost in assessing evidence and taking decisions might well result in disaster. As was the case in Room 40, what was not of immediate operational importance had to be put on one side for later study and usually, before this could be undertaken with the thoroughness and in the detail that were really required, the next crisis was upon us and the study had to be abandoned. New battles had to take precedence over old ones. Nor were such painstaking investigations, calling for the very careful comparison of the timing of the enemy's moves in relation to our own, really a responsibility of O.I.C. It does seem that there was a gap here in the organization of the Intelligence and Signal Divisions and perhaps in that of the Government Code and Cipher School as well. Then again, both sides were careful to phrase their signals to their own forces in such a way as not to reveal the source of the information on which they were based. Where, on the British side, signals referring specifically to decrypts had to be made, they were, as already noted, classified Ultra and made with a one-time pad cipher, which the enemy never cracked. One must also remember that neither side was achieving a constant timely penetration of the other's ciphers, and the very mistakes which this fact caused made it less readily apparent that any decrypting was taking place. Nevertheless within two months of the breaking of Triton, Winn did begin to suspect that all was not well with our security, and gave very strict instructions that the daily U-boat Situation Report signals, which went to all ships and authorities concerned, were to be phrased in much more general and less precise terms except where the position of a U-boat or a group of them could be clearly related to D/F fixes or sightings or attacks, when of course these incidents were specifically mentioned. He also raised the whole matter with D.S.D./N.I.D. 10, the joint section responsible for the security of our codes and ciphers. They seem to have been reluctant at first to accept that Winn's suspicions could be well founded, but they were in the end convinced. It took time to produce fresh ciphers and distribute them to all the ships and authorities concerned all over the world, but this was finally accomplished by the beginning of June 1943, and from then onwards the B.Dienst was unable to supply Dönitz with more than a trickle of information.

The Germans too had their suspicions. How far these were responsible for their use of disguised reference points in their signals, to which reference will be made later, or whether these were a sign of their fear of treachery and agents is not clear. In any event, various investigations were made into the security of their ciphering arrangements. In his *Memoirs* Dönitz writes, 'We found ourselves bound to admit that during January [1943] we had not succeeded in finding with our reconnaissance sweeps the convoys for which we had been searching. As a result of these failures we naturally went once more very closely into the question of what knowledge the enemy could possibly have of our U-boat dispositions. . . . We repeatedly checked our security instructions in order to ensure as far as possible that our intentions were not being betrayed. That a widespread spy network was at work in our bases in occupied France was something we obviously had to assume. An efficient intelligence service must in any case have been able to ascertain the distribution of U-boats among the various bases, the dates of their sailing and return to port, and possibly also the sea areas allotted to boats proceeding on operations. [How wrong he was!] Our ciphers were checked and re-checked, to make sure that they were unbreakable: and on each occasion the head of the Naval Intelligence Service at Naval High Command adhered to his opinion that it would be impossible for the enemy to decipher them. And to this day, as far as I know, we are not certain whether or not the enemy did succeed in breaking our ciphers during the war'.‡ If the British were unduly slow in rec-

‡ In correspondence with the author, Admiral Godt (Dönitz's Chief Operations Officer and his successor as B.d.U.) and Captain Meckel (his Staff Officer for Communications and Electronics), writing on the instructions of the Gross Admiral, made the point that suspicions that the Allies had knowledge of U-boat dispositions and rendezvous were aroused again and again. It was felt that there could be only two possible reasons for this, cryptanalysis or treachery.

The possibility that German signals were being decrypted by the British was referred more than once to the Chef des Marine Nachrichtendienstes (Chief of the Naval Intelligence Service). 'B.d.U. was invariably informed in reply that the ciphers were absolutely secure. Decrypting, if possible at all, could only be achieved with such an expenditure of effort and after so long a period of time that the result would be valueless. The suspicion that the enemy was decrypting our signals nevertheless remained acute among B.d.U.'s staff. However, so long as the Chief of the Naval Intelligence Service would not be persuaded that it was occurring, he would not change the cipher. We, of course, naturally could not prove our point because on each occasion our suspicions were almost always capable of some other explanation. As to treachery—a suspicion equally held for long by the staff—we were able to take action. The number of people with knowledge was greatly curtailed. Finally, apart from

ognizing that some of their ciphers had been penetrated, they did finally accept the fact and introduce the necessary changes. The Germans on the other hand just could not believe that their splendid system was not foolproof.

The use by Dönitz of disguised reference points gave us considerable trouble. The German Navy used a gridded chart, similar in effect to that used on A.A. and R.A.C. road maps. Positions were given by reference to this grid system, not by latitude and longitude. Thus position AB1234 would indicate point, say 55 degrees 30 minutes North, 25 degrees 40 minutes West. This of course presented no problem to us once a portion of a gridded chart had been captured and the whole reconstructed. But in November 1941 the Germans started transposing these letters, square AB becoming, for example, XY while a figure would have to be added to or subtracted from the numerals, so that 1234 would appear in the text of the signal as, say, 2345. These transpositions were changed at regular intervals. Then again dispositions would be ordered by means of a bearing and distance from a reference point, say Point Blue, whose exact position was contained in written orders issued before sailing. It was this type of concealment which had prevented us establishing immediately whether the Delphin's first patrol area was near Madeira or further south near the Cape Verde Islands and such situations occurred frequently. In some cases the key to the new disguise was quickly spotted. A U-boat, which had reported its position using the old reference system just before the change to the new one took place, might come up again and so give the game away. It might be that an accurate D/F fix would be the clue or an order from B.d.U. himself which only allowed one interpretation. But there were many occasions when no such help was immediately forthcoming and two or more solutions were apparently possible. If one chose correctly all well and good, but if one was wrong, then convoys thought to be steering clear of danger could well be heading into it, and diversions might do more harm than good. In most such doubtful cases all the various possibilities were shown on the plot. On one occasion we successfully solved a disguised grid reference and diverted a convoy clear of

B.d.U.'s staff, only the S.K.L. (the Naval Staff in Berlin), and even there only a small circle, had knowledge of U-boat signal traffic. On B.d.U.'s own staff very strict security measures were introduced.'

a waiting patrol line, only to find that the C.O. of one of the U-boats involved had not been as clever as we had and had misinterpreted the disguised grid reference given in his orders and blundered into the convoy in consequence.

Some explanation must now be given of the organization and work of the Movements Section of Trade Division. At the beginning of the war this section was not responsible for routing or diverting merchant shipping. Like the Tracking Room at that time, it merely recorded, it did not influence events. Routes were prepared and issued by another section of Trade Division and diversions from those routes were rarely if ever attempted. The Movements plot was a plot pure and simple, and its staff had no executive authority. Although it was housed in the sub-basement, it was quite separate from the Operations plot and was some distance away from O.I.C. Anyone, therefore, wishing to see a complete picture of the position at sea, had to visit three different plots, Operations for our own warships, Trade for our merchant shipping, and O.I.C. for estimates of the enemy's dispositions.

However by the time the move was made to the Citadel in 1941, the need for a Master plot, at least for all our own vessels, with executive powers and working closely with O.I.C. both for the purposes of evasive routing and for offensive operations, was clearly realized by the Director of Trade Division, Captain Schofield, and the Director of the Operations Division (Home), Captain Eccles. The Operations and Trade plots were amalgamated and were housed in a large room next door to the Tracking Room with direct access to it and separated from Denning's sections only by the width of a corridor. All routes, both for warships and merchantmen, were now prepared by the Main Plot's staff, and all diversions of convoys and independent ships in the Atlantic were initiated by them. They worked, naturally, in close and intimate co-operation with the staff of the C.-in-C. Western Approaches in Derby House at Liverpool, who controlled the escort forces and who issued the routes prepared by Trade Movements. Diversions were always planned and normally signalled by the Admiralty, but always with the agreement of Western Approaches where the latest position concerning the escort's fuel and ammunition and so on was available. At first sight this might seem a rather cumbersome arrangement, with three individual organizations, Trade Movements, O.I.C. and Western Approaches all involved. In fact like many great British compromises it worked extremely well, due mainly to the personalities of the officers concerned.

When the Operations and Trade plots were amalgamated, the man put in charge was Commander R. A. Hall, R.N. Dick Hall was Blinker's son, and it was something of a coincidence that after starting the war as a Naval Control Service Officer first at Rotterdam and then at Sunderland, he should come to the Admiralty, and then, after some eighteen months, find himself responsible for an organization that was to work so closely with his father's old Division that in some respects it might have been part of it. A large and genial man with a face that has been described as 'fresh and plump in which a majestic nose recalls the features of his famous Admiral father', he inspired immediate confidence in all who met him.

Hall, and his two assistants, Lieutenant-Commander Cater, R.N. and Lieutenant-Commander Hewitt, R.N.V.R., had full access to the Tracking Room, and were in and out of it twenty times a day so that they were as familiar with its work as any of Winn's own staff. The working relationship was so close that one never had to waste time with lengthy explanations; a few words sufficed to put Hall in the picture, and off he would hurry back to his own room to confer with Western Approaches or Operations Division about what action was desirable to meet whatever new and unexpected situation had just been revealed in the Tracking Room.

It must sometimes have been very tempting for him to dispute conclusions drawn by Winn or his deputy, often on far from conclusive evidence, but he never did so and was indeed the most loyal supporter of the 'Working Fiction'. When Admiral Edelsten, the Assistant Chief of Staff (U-boats and Trade), gave orders in 1943 that no ships were ever to be routed against the advice of the Tracking Room without his own express permission, he was only setting the official seal of approval on a procedure which Hall and his assistants had long followed. When things went wrong, as inevitably they did from time to time, there was no backbiting, no recriminations, no 'passing the buck'. All Hall's energies would then be concentrated on trying to extricate his precious ships from whatever new danger had just beset them. With two such masterful personalities as Winn and Hall in daily contact with each other, it would not have been surprising if serious clashes had occurred, but although they did not always agree (indeed one A.C.N.S., when turning over to his relief, remarked, 'If ever these two stop bickering, we shall lose the war'), they in fact remained great friends and worked throughout in the closest harmony. Hall's staff, which had originally consisted almost entirely of retired naval officers, eventually built up to a strength of thirty, of whom no fewer than twenty-one were girls, who were responsible for maintaining the plot in three watches of seven. An average of three thousand incoming signals passed through the section daily. Many tributes have been paid to the feats of Winn and the Tracking Room and the contribution they made to the successful outcome of the Battle of the Atlantic. Practically nothing has been said about Hall and his team, but without their unremitting and devoted labours the best of intelligence would have had little practical value.

By the beginning of 1943 the Tracking Room staff totalled eleven men and three women. There were six R.N.V.R. officers: Winn, his deputy and the four watchkeepers responsible for enemy intelligence; three civilian watchkeepers maintaining the plot of our own vessels; two further civilians engaged on research and records, and three girls dealing with typing and filing. In addition, although not directly responsible to Winn, there were six D/F plotters, in three watches of two, and an observer from the Anti-Submarine Warfare Division, who was normally an active service R.N. Commander. During the day, therefore, there would be eight to eleven people in the Room (depending on who was having a rest day), and at night-time two Tracking Room and two D/F watchkeepers. It still could not be said that the section was over-staffed.

A typical day would start between seven-thirty and seven forty-five, with the arrival of Winn and his deputy (unless some crisis had kept one or other of them in the Admiralty all night). Their first task would be to study the information, from all sources, which had come in during the night, and then to plot the U-boats on to their estimated positions at noon that day. Depending on the complexity of the situation, this would take from half an hour to an hour. No sooner had this been completed than it was time for the first conference of the day, a three-way hook-up on the scrambler telephone with Western Approaches and Coastal Command. The former were usually represented by the Chief of Staff and the Staff Officer (Convoys), Derek Crosse (late of the Tracking Room), and the latter by the Naval Liaison Officer, Captain Peyton-Ward, R.N., and the Senior Air Staff Officer. Sometimes the two Commanders-in-Chief would also join in. In 1944, when the pattern of the U-boat war had altered, the hook-up became five-way with the addition of Combined Headquarters at Plymouth and Rosyth. Winn would give the latest plotted position of the U-boats, and discussions would then follow about convoy routes and diversions, the movements of support groups* and plans for air escorts and offensive patrols. This usually took twenty to thirty minutes, and was followed quickly by the appearance in the Tracking Room of the Assistant Chief of Staff (U-boats and Trade), accompanied by the Directors of the Trade, Operations and Anti-Submarine Warfare Divisions and sometimes by the A.C.N.S. (Home) or (Foreign). Most of these senior officers slept in the Admiralty at night and formed the habit of dropping in to the Tracking Room just before they turned in, for a chat with the night watch and a last look at the situation. They were therefore well-informed of the current situation, but always anxious to hear Winn's views and ideas as to how things might be expected to develop in the next forty-eight hours and, if any major change in the situation seemed likely, in the rather longer term. Because all those concerned made such frequent visits to the Room during the course of each twenty-four hours, this conference also did not often last more than thirty minutes. It was in fact a briefing session before the main ten o'clock meeting of the Naval Staff which was presided over by the Vice-Chief of Naval Staff.

The first two hours of the day, even during the comparatively quieter phases (and there were precious few of them in the first five months of 1943), was a period of intensive and high-pressure work, demanding great concentration, speedy thinking, and quick

---

* Support Groups of from six to eight ships were formed as additional anti-submarine vessels became available. They did not form the original escort of convoys, but, as the name implies, were directed to the support of any convoy seen to be in danger.

and precise answers to the many questions raised by the skilled and well-informed audience. However, once they were over, Winn was generally able to relax a little and settle down to a more detailed study of the night's reports, to discussions with Hall about the routing of future convoys or with his own staff about specific questions which they had been investigating. It was inevitable, both because of Winn's temperament and his training at the Bar, that delegation did not come easily to him. Nor did the nature of the job readily lend itself to this. The man in charge had to see and consider every scrap of information himself; he could not rely on ready-made solutions to individual parts of the jigsaw presented to him by his staff. In the process we all developed an uncanny short-term memory. For two or three months it was not difficult to recall, without reference to the files, such details as the date a particular U-boat left port, the time, day and position of the sinking of another, the characteristics of this commanding officer or the precise wording of a general order issued weeks before by Dönitz. Then, as one's mind was called upon to deal with fresh facts, and the old ones lost their significance, they would subconsciously be transferred to the 'memory bank' to be brought out again only when something else pressed the right 'key'.

By noon the daily U-boat Situation Report signal had to be drafted and despatched, and Special Intelligence exchanged with Knowles in Washington and his opposite number in Ottawa, Lieutenant-Commander McDiarmid, R.C.N.V.R. Co-operation with both organizations was now extremely close, and both the American and Canadian officers had paid visits to O.I.C. So far as Ottawa was concerned, we supplied the Canadian Tracking Room with all the Special Intelligence they required in the same way as we did British naval commands at home and overseas, that is to say digested and processed, not raw. The system worked well and we never received any complaints that they were insufficiently informed. The Americans, on the other hand, had their own cryptanalysis service working closely with B.P., and Knowles received Special Intelligence in the same form and as quickly as did the British Tracking Room. A unique feature of the co-operation with the Americans was the establishment, with the full approval of the 'High-Ups' on both sides, of a direct signal link between the two Tracking Rooms on the understanding, scrupulously observed, that the messages exchanged were seen by no one other than Winn, Knowles and their two deputies. These messages ensured a completely free and unfettered exchange of ideas and information between the two organizations in which, if necessary, disagreement could be frankly expressed without offence being taken. This might not have been the case had the signals appeared, for example, on the desk of the irascible Admiral King or our own Andrew Cunningham. An example that comes to mind was Winn's signal to Knowles at a time when we had begun to suspect that the Germans were reading our Daily Situation reports, and when the American version seemed to us to be too detailed and accurate, 'Your 1157/9, too true to be good'.

Knowles was, of course, responsible for promulgating information to ships and commands in the American zone of control,† while we and the Canadians did the same in our zones. It was most unusual for there to be any significant difference between the plot in OP 20 and that in O.I.C., and if there was, it was soon resolved by friendly discussion. There were doubtless many examples of close Anglo-American co-operation and indeed of the actual integration of British and American staffs during the war, but none can have been closer or more successful than that between the two Tracking Rooms. Integration was simply never necessary: both organizations worked as one.

Reverting to the normal day (if ever there was such a thing) in the Tracking Room, the afternoon might well be spent in preparing the Weekly Report on U-boat Activities for the First Sea Lord or appreciations for the Joint Intelligence Committee, in studying the latest accounts of the interrogation of prisoners of war or in dealing with the many visitors requiring information, such as the editor of the Weekly Intelligence Report, the Staff Officer (Intelligence) to Flag Officer (Submarines) or Captain Peyton-Ward from Coastal Command. Occasionally there would be a visit from a V.I.P. such as General Smuts, or once from Sir Stafford Cripps, when he was charged by the Prime Minister with an investigation into the conduct of the Battle of the Atlantic. He appeared to be

† The Atlantic was divided into various zones in which the British, Canadian and U.S. authorities exercised control over all naval and merchant ships. These zones varied at different times. See Roskill's *War at Sea* for more detailed explanations.

satisfied with his cross-examination of his fellow lawyer, Rodger Winn, much, one suspects, to the relief of the senior members of the Naval Staff, who retired discreetly to the background. Once a fortnight, Winn, or in his rare absences his deputy, had to attend the fortnightly meeting of the Anti-U-boat Warfare Committee, which was presided over by the Assistant Chief of Staff (U-boats and Trade), and comprised the Commander-in-Chief Western Approaches and his Chief of Staff, the Air Officer Commanding-in-Chief Coastal Command and his Senior Air Staff Officer, the A.O.C.s of 15, 18 and 19 Groups, and the Directors of the Operations, Trade and Anti-Submarine Warfare Divisions of the Naval Staff. It was a formidable array of high-ranking regular officers for mere R.N.V.R.s, who had to open with a résumé of the past fortnight's events and a forecast of the likely developments during the next two weeks. Once again an accurate memory and the ability to state one's case clearly and firmly were essential, but these were qualities in which Winn excelled and if his views were sometimes challenged or the conduct of his section occasionally criticized, it was done fairly and with courtesy.

All the time, of course, the Room's primary functions had to be performed, because the Battle of the Atlantic did not cease for a single moment, day or night, throughout nearly six years of war. A fresh rush of Special Intelligence might start to pour off the teleprinters, requiring immediate attention. The first decrypt to arrive was often not very informative. It might well be four or five days old and already completely overtaken by events. It might on its own be meaningless. 'Group Ritter is to advance its patrol line one hundred and fifty miles on a line of bearing of 85 degrees.' Not knowing which U-boats formed 'Group Ritter' or where their original patrol had been, one was not much the wiser. Signals might only be weather or fuel reports from a single boat on passage and hundreds of miles away from any potential victim or attacker, although in this case one had at least the first piece of the jigsaw, even if it was an unimportant one. Gradually, however, the pace would quicken and the trickle of decrypts would become a torrent. Each one would have to be quickly scrutinized to decide whether it was sufficiently up-to-date and informative to justify an alteration in our plot, and if it did, whether it was necessary to call in Hall from next door to discuss a diversion. Perhaps it would be necessary to speak to Western Approaches, or the Home Fleet, or Coastal Command on the scrambler to enable them to plan escort reinforcements or alter the patrols planned for the next day or night. All the time Winn, his deputy or the duty watchkeeper had to decide whether the information was sufficiently firm and up-to-date to justify action, or whether it would be better to wait a little longer until the picture became clearer and mere theories had crystallized into facts. All this was against the background of hundreds of ships at sea relying on our efforts to steer them clear of danger areas, and with the knowledge that every minute might well make the difference between success and failure.

On most days Winn would leave the Room around 8 P.M., after a twelve-hour working day, but naturally if a crisis had blown up in the late afternoon, it would be much later than this. After his illness, D.N.I. had secured for him the use of an Admiralty car to bring him to work at 7:30 A.M. and to take him home again at whatever hour he could force himself to hand over to his night watchkeeper. Even so it was a rather more gruelling regime than is normally associated with Whitehall Warriors, and one which, when coupled with his physical disabilities, called for iron determination and dedication. He had them in full measure.

Winn, it is perhaps not surprising, was not always an easy man to work for. He drove his staff hard and could be biting if our performance and judgement fell short of his own very high standards. Nevertheless what was said on such occasions was said privately. In public he gave all of us his wholehearted backing and insisted that the Tracking Room spoke with a single voice. The result was that, from the Vice-Chief of Naval Staff downwards, senior officers came to place as much, or very nearly as much, faith in the advice of the junior R.N.V.R. Sub on night watch as they did on Winn's own prognostications during the day. He was not only popular with his staff but deeply respected by them, and every man and woman in the Room was concerned to save him strain and to do their best to maintain our reputation and his. There was, of course, some friction from time to time. The pressures were very great and it would have been surprising if, in the circumstances, with a dozen or so men and women thrown together, more or less by chance, with different backgrounds, ambitions and temperaments, everything had always been sweet harmony. What is remarkable is how seldom this did occur and how unimportant it was. People work best under pressure and every single member of the Section gave of his or her best, a best that was in fact much more than could reasonably have been expected of them.

11

January–May 1943.
Climax of the Battle
of the Atlantic

THE FIRST five months of 1943 saw the climax of the Battle of the Atlantic. The struggle swayed to and fro, the advantage lying first with one side and then with the other. In January, thanks partly to exceptionally severe weather but also to increasingly successful evasive routing, shipping losses caused by U-boats were only just over 200,000 tons; in February they rose to 360,000 and in March they soared to 627,000 tons; in April they dropped back to 328,000 and in May fell still further to 264,000. The U-boats, however, were having to pay a heavier price for their successes. Six boats were sunk in January, nineteen in February, fifteen in March and again in April, and no fewer than forty-one in May. This was a total of ninety-six boats, and although during the period the total U-boat fleet actually increased from just under to just over four hundred boats, it was a rate of loss which no service in the world could sustain. Towards the end of May, Dönitz threw in the sponge and withdrew from the North Atlantic convoy routes. It is true that he attempted a come-back in the autumn and that even after this he never, right up to the very last day of the war, abandoned the struggle in one form or another, but the two sides were never again so equally matched nor the battle so ferocious as in those five months, and above all in March. In that month ninety-five ships were sunk by U-boats, seventy-two of them in convoy, and only six U-boats paid the penalty at the hands of the convoys' sea and air escorts. It appears that the British Naval Staff were almost in despair. It seemed that our one 'sure shield', the convoy system, was failing, and in a much-quoted sentence the Admiralty subsequently expressed the opinion that 'the Germans never came so near to disrupting communications between the New World and the Old as in the first twenty days of March 1943'. As Captain Roskill has written,* 'They must have felt, though none admitted it, that defeat then stared them in the face.'

This, curiously enough, was never a view held even privately by the Tracking Room. Curiously, because on the walls of the Room graphs and statistics showed all the relevant information: Allied shipping losses and replacements, ships sunk in convoy and those sunk sailing independently, U-boat kills and the ever faster flow of new boats from the Baltic, the tonnage of supplies imported into Britain, troops transported from America, air and surface forces available for offensive and defensive patrols, the numbers of Very Long Range aircraft and of Escort Carriers, which were slowly but surely closing the Atlantic air gap, all the data by which the success or failure of the battle could be judged. Less curiously, perhaps, because Winn and his staff had by now the real feel of the struggle and could sense the desperate efforts, the gambler's last throw, which the enemy was making to achieve his purpose. Not only were we aware of the increase in the numbers of Allied forces and the greatly improved weapons, and above all the 10cm radar, with which they were now being supplied, but we were alive to every sign, the slightest nuance, not only of the faltering morale which began to manifest itself among the growing proportion of U-boat C.O.s and crews thrown straight into the heat of the conflict on their first war cruise, but also of the anxiety and lack of confidence displayed by Dönitz himself in his exhortations and admonitions to his U-boats at sea.

As early as February 8, Winn remarked in connection with the return of an outward-bound U-tanker, due to defects, that 'an increase has been noticeable of late in the incidence of incapacitating

* *War at Sea.*

defects developing during outward passage of the Bay of Biscay'.†
Not that the threat from the U-boats was under-estimated. On
February 2 Winn had produced a paper headed 'Admiral Commanding U-boats' future strategy. An appreciation for the period
May to August 1943'. After referring to Dönitz's recent appointment, in succession to Admiral Raeder, as Commander-in-Chief
of the German Navy, and after pointing out that he now had
nearly two hundred boats operating from Atlantic bases, Winn
asked how Dönitz would apportion their efforts during the coming summer. His conclusions were as follows:

'1. That for the next four months the U-boat effort will be increasingly concentrated in the area between Newfoundland and
Iceland.

'2. That until losses exceed 15% and also the number of ships
sunk average for four months on end less than half a ship per
U-boat cruise, there will be no big change in policy. In the North
Atlantic in December and even more obviously in January, the
latter condition has been satisfied but on the other hand no
U-boats have been sunk [in that area].

'3. That if the switch comes it will be sudden and practically
complete as was the case when the U.S.A. entered the war and the
whole effort was shifted to the American seaboard, the change
taking effect within six weeks of the new situation arising.

'4. That in such case the new focal area would be:
      (a) Curaçao
      (b) Trinidad
      (c) The Caribbean passages
      (d) Natal
and in particular the area between the Azores, Madeira and the
Canaries and the open sea routes between the Caribbean, Bermuda and the Azores.

'Diversionary activities off Cape Town, Freetown, Libreville and
the Plate and in the North-Western Approaches would be necessary to obviate a countervailing concentration of escorts in the
new areas of attack.

† A few weeks later a special report was prepared detailing these abortive
sailings.

'Extreme mobility of anti-submarine aircraft and surface ships is an essential condition of preparedness for the coming phase.'

This was a truly remarkable forecast, showing not only an understanding of how Dönitz was thinking at that very moment, but how he would react when the adverse conditions, which Winn clearly anticipated, actually arose. It fell short of complete accuracy only in under-estimating the speed with which the Allied victory in the North Atlantic would be achieved.

In February, in a report on an unsuccessful attack on a convoy (HX.175), Winn drew attention to the following points:

'(a) Failure on the part of three U-boats, all new, to make a successful attack on a convoy of twenty-three ships and five escorts.

'(b) The large number of torpedoes fired without success. (Schroeter's [a U-boat Commander] claim is untrue if our interpretation of the grid is correct).

'(c) Failure of our escorts, two American destroyers and three corvettes, to detect a number of attacks on the convoy before they took place.

'(d) Fear of air attack, both by U-boats and B.d.U. The attack mentioned by Zimmerman [another U-boat C.O.] was purely imaginary. There were Hudson aircraft carrying out a sweep in the vicinity, but no attack was made.

'(e) The value of aircraft in making a U-boat dive with the result that on re-surfacing the U-boat might be twenty miles astern of the convoy. Even if they do not sight a U-boat, aircraft near a convoy are a great deterrent.'

On February 22, Winn reported that 'up to noon on February 20 when ON.166 was first reported the week had been most successful as only one convoy, ON.165, had been intercepted and the resultant operation had resulted in the loss of only three ships and the almost certain destruction of two U-boats. . . . Since the beginning of the month a total of nine U-boats has been destroyed plus one highly probable: this rate of killing is well above the average and highly satisfactory, although it must be borne in mind that during the same period twenty new U-boats started their first operational cruise'. A week later the Tracking Room report stated: 'In respect of the number of German U-boats sunk the month of February has achieved a record, for it is clear from Special Intelligence that seventeen have disappeared.'‡

In March an event took place which, but for really brilliant work on the part of B.P., could have had the most serious consequences. For some time past we had been aware that the Atlantic U-boats were being supplied with a later and improved version of the Enigma M machine fitted with four instead of only three rotors. It had taken time to equip all boats with the new machine and until the process was completed the three-rotor system remained in force. We anticipated that the introduction of the fourth rotor would present our cryptanalysts with a stupendous problem and when, on March 8, Dönitz instructed the boats at sea to start using the fourth rotor at midnight that night, it seemed that the worst had happened. On the 9th, Admiral Edelsten, Assistant Chief of Staff (U-boat and Trade), reported to the First Sea Lord that what had so long been feared had now occurred and that the Tracking Room was likely to be 'blind' for a considerable period, perhaps for months.

It could not have happened at a worse moment. Despite the better rate of killing, U-boats were now pouring out from the Baltic training grounds in a flood, and Dönitz had over a hundred at sea in the Atlantic of which the Tracking Room estimated on March 15, that 'the record number of sixty-six is in the North Atlantic north of 50 degrees North mostly between 20 degrees and 35 degrees West', i.e. south-west of Iceland and east of Newfoundland. This was an accurate estimate as no fewer than three groups, Raubgraf of nine, Stürmer of eighteen and Dränger of eleven boats, were spread on extensive patrol lines waiting for the next east-bound convoys from New York. Others were on passage or otherwise available to reinforce these thirty-eight boats if the opportunity should present itself. To divert both east-bound and west-bound convoys clear of such concentrations was well nigh impossible without absolutely precise and continuous knowledge of their dispositions. Admiral Edelsten's alarm was fully justified.

However, in the event, by a tremendous feat of cryptanalysis,

‡ In fact, the total eventually proved to be nineteen.

B.P. succeeded in solving the new problem which confronted them in a matter of days and the flow of Special Intelligence continued with no greater interruptions than those to which it had been subjected since December. Nevertheless these interruptions were themselves serious. The delays in cracking the daily changes in the settings varied at this particular time from three to seven days. That might not have been so serious but for the superb efficiency of the B.Dienst, who frequently, although not invariably,* were able to supply Dönitz with decrypts of our signals diverting convoys in time for him to move the U-boats across the new track of the convoy concerned.

Such indeed was the case with convoys SC.122 and HX.229, which were intercepted by the Stürmer group on March 16, and pursued eastwards across the Atlantic for four days. The HX. or faster convoy overtook SC.122 and the two convoys coalesced into a great mass of nearly one hundred ships. The Raubgraf and Dränger groups joined in the attack, and while the two convoys were in the mid-Atlantic air gap, the forty U-boats concentrated against them were able to achieve the biggest single success ever recorded in the Atlantic. Twenty-one ships were sunk for the loss of a single U-boat.

The Tracking Room had appreciated the possible danger to SC.122. On March 15, its report had stated that 'no Special Intelligence has been received since the 11th March and therefore it is not known with certainty how the U-boats are now disposed. A supply U-boat in 49 degrees North, 31 degrees West has already refuelled half a dozen of the boats which operated against HX.228 and several others are making towards it and are unfortunately likely to encounter SC.122'. Luck on this occasion was with the Germans. SC.122 evaded the first U-boat patrol but, thanks partly to the B.Dienst, the HX. convoy was less fortunate and with the large area covered by the two more easterly Wolf Packs it would then have been difficult, even with more up-to-date information, to have diverted either convoy clear of danger. The Germans did not in fact appreciate for some time that two convoys were in-

* In twenty days in March 1943, one hundred and seventy-five Allied signals to convoys in the North Atlantic were decrypted by the B.Dienst, but only ten of them in time for Dönitz to make operational use of them. See J. Rohwer: *Marine-Rundschau*, June 1976.

volved, which is a good example of how, even with the best service from cryptanalysis, the fog of war could still cloud the issue and leave much to chance. The result was also affected by the fact that some of the ships of the Allied escort groups were unaccustomed to working together and that no air cover could be provided, on the vital days, either by V.L.R. aircraft or by escort carriers. In his report on March 22 Winn wrote, 'Special Intelligence has been received for the period noon 15th to noon 19th but does not give a clear picture of the operations. Convoys SC.122 and HX.229 were heavily attacked between longitude 35 degrees West and 25 degrees West by the largest pack of U-boats which has ever been collected into one area for the same operation. In total forty U-boats were directly or indirectly operating against these convoys, which until a late stage the enemy supposed to be portions of the same convoy'. Although recognizing that we had suffered a severe defeat, Winn certainly did not regard the outcome as the end of the road. The enemy had been singularly well placed and luck had obviously been with him. The next time, and there had been many occasions even in the last two months to justify this view, luck would be on our side. The gaps in Special Intelligence would not always occur at such decisive moments, our guesses might be better, the patrol lines of U-boats would not be so ideally disposed as to prevent attempts at diversions. It was certainly a battle lost but there would be more, and we should win them.

Indeed Winn's next report on March 29, was based on Special Intelligence that was completely up-to-date and he was able to write that 'three convoys in the area south-east of Greenland have been sighted. Neither against SC.123 nor against ON.174 were U-boats able to develop any attack but since PM 27th, HX.230 has been shadowed and a total of eleven U-boats has been identified in contact or in the vicinity. So far as present knowledge indicates, the operation of bringing through these convoys with well-timed assistance from a Support Group has been most successful'. The escort of SC.123 had included, for the first time since 1942, an escort carrier, the U.S.S. *Bogue*, a ship soon to make her mark against the U-boats, and it had also been possible, thanks to more than usually precise knowledge of the enemy dispositions, to switch the support group from one convoy to the next and 'punch a hole through the U-boat patrol line'.

But delays in decrypting and the difficulties in solving the disguised grid references used by U-boat Command were not the only obstacles in the way of diverting convoys clear of danger. It was not always possible to be certain of their exact positions, since the convoys and their escorts naturally maintained wireless silence unless U-boats or enemy aircraft were already in contact. For example, early in April, HX.232 was seen to be heading straight for the middle of a line of ten U-boats: 'When knowledge of this patrol was received the convoy was estimated to be within 60 miles of it, but as events showed was actually 25 miles ahead of the plot and a drastic alteration away failed to keep them clear'.

The battles continued to rage furiously and early in April Winn produced a forecast of the likely strength of the operational U-boat fleet (at that moment 254), for the next six months. Average U-boat sinkings for February and March were put at sixteen, which was 'appreciably above the earlier average', but reinforcements, too, were on the increase. After making a rather conservative allowance for seventy-five further kills up to the end of September, Winn estimated that the total number of operational boats might by then have increased by fifty-one to three hundred and five. In view of the alleged despondency of the Naval Staff at this time, it is interesting to note that Admiral Edelsten (The Assistant Chief of Staff, U-boats and Trade) returned the appreciation to Winn with the following pencilled comment on it: 'Cdr. Winn. I shall be most disappointed if this figure is correct and am prepared to proffer a small wager that the figure will be under 300. Obviously I must have odds offered!'

Edelsten's optimism was justified and there was soon more evidence in German W/T traffic that the strain was at last beginning to tell. On April 19 Winn commented, '. . . such manifestations of concern for the vulnerability of U-boats to air attack are suggestive of an incipient decline in morale amongst at any rate some U-boat crews, and a remarkable signal has been received in which U-boat Command attempted to reassure C.O.s in another respect. It appears that a rumour has spread to the effect that our escorts sometimes leave depth charges suspended from buoys with a time release causing them to explode after the escorts have moved away. This device, it was said, was "pure bluff, and it should be realized that bangs do not mean danger. The man who allows his healthy warrior and fighting instincts to be humbugged ceases to have any powers of resistance to present day enemy defences".'

From now on, the Tracking Room's reports gave more and more examples of the growing anxiety and loss of confidence felt by Dönitz and his men. After a 'remarkably feeble operation' from April 21 to 24, against HX.234, it was noted that 'the U-boats engaged have made repeated and bitter complaints about the ubiquity and efficiency of the aircraft which were constantly with the convoy on April 24. There was no attempt to fight back at these aircraft such as has been evident on two of three occasions recently, particularly in the Bay of Biscay. To stay up and fire at attacking aircraft is a method of avoiding attack enjoined by the U-boat Command with increasing emphasis of late, but congenial only to the bolder type of C.O. whose absence from the HX.234 engagement was conspicuous. The outstanding impression felt on reading recent U-boat traffic is that the spirit of the crews which are at present out on operations in the North Atlantic is low and general morale is shaky. There is little doubt that B.d.U. shares this impression for he has been comparatively restrained in expressing his none the less evident disappointment, and was very quick to snatch the excuse for an encouraging broadcast supported by von Bülow's† claim to have sunk an auxiliary aircraft carrier.' In fact Bülow had failed to hit the carrier, H.M.S. *Biter*.

At the end of April a convoy battle took place which, although by no means the last in the long struggle, was probably the most decisive fought and which deserves to be remembered long after the ill-fated PQ.17 is forgotten. The west-bound ONS.5 was attacked by two packs of U-boats with a combined strength of forty-one boats. The convoy was delayed by a tremendous gale and the escort depleted by shortage of fuel but two Support Groups were despatched to give assistance, and strong air patrols organized. Twelve merchant ships were lost but seven U-boats were sunk, five of them by the surface escorts. Winn recognized the significance of the victory which the sea and air escorts had won in this 'last

† A U-boat Commander.

Extracts from weekly B. Dienst reports during April and May 1943 to B.d.U.
and others stressing Allied H/F D/F activity. The last example shown is a decrypt
of the U-boat Situation Reports which were signalled daily to all allied ships and
authorities concerned with the Battle of the Atlantic. By permission of *Motorbuch Verlag, Stuttgart*

Rodger Winn. A charact[...]
picture, although taken in[...]
Godfrey Argent

Captain Kenneth A. Knowles, in
1945, when he was head of the
American Tracking Room.
Private Collection

The M-4 (naval) Enigma machine with four rotors, put into service on 1st March 1943. *Bibliothek für Zeitgeschichte, Stuttgart, West Germany*

The telex message from N.S. (Naval Section) B.P. to I.D.8.G. (Denning's section of O.I.C.) of the decrypt of the German order to *Scharnhorst* to sail and attack JW .55B. The pencilled word Ultra shows that O.I.C. had signalled this information to C.-in-C. Home Fleet. Note the German time of origin. *Public Records Office, London*

U

Battle Group

/DH (2)
TO: I D 8 G   Z IP/ZTPG/194876
FROM: N S

5205 KC/S   T 00   1527   T O I 1500/25/12/43

FROM: ADMIRAL NORTHERN WATERS

TO: BATTLE GROUP

         ADMIRAL POLAR COAST.

MOST IMMEDIATE

'OSTFRONT' 1700/25/12.

———— will be referred to in English
as "EPILEPSY."

0025/26/12/43+++EE/FA

Ultra.

ERATIONAL INTELLIGENCE CENTRE SPECIAL INTELLIGENCE SUMMARY

U/BOAT SITUATION

Week ending 24.5.43   O.I.C./S.I.600

NORTH NORWAY (Based on Z information up to 24.5.43)		17.5.43	24.5.43	Increase or Decrease
Hammerfest		2	3	+1
Narvik		1	2	+1
Bergen		7	5	-2
Trondheim		4	2	-2
Bear Island area	Total	5	4	-1
		19	16	-3

NORTH ATLANTIC (Based on Z information up to 24.5.43)				
On passage N'about		3	3	-
N.E.area (E. of 30 W)		4	6	+2
N.W.area (W. of 30 W)		52	32	-20
SE area (Azores - Cape Verdes -Freetown)		1	6	+5
SW area (Azores - Antilles - Bermuda)		-	2	+2
Canadian and U.S.Coast and on passage.		2	6	+4
Caribbean - G. of Mexico - Guiana		1	1	-
Biscay - Azores - Madeira - Gibraltar		42	32	-10
Biscay ports	Total	87	99	+12
		192	187	-5

SOUTH ATLANTIC (Based on Z information up to 24.5.43)				
Brazil - Freetown		7	2	-5
S.Atlantic on passage		2	2	-
Capetown area	Total	2	1	-1
		11	5	-6

INDIAN OCEAN (Based on Z information up to 24.5.43)	4	5	+1

BLACK SEA (Based on Z information up to 24.5.43)	6	6	-

MEDITERRANEAN (Based on Z Information up to 24.5.43)				
In port		16	14	-2
At sea	Total	8	8	-
		24	22	-2

L.28146/79619 10M 11/42 S.E.R. Ltd. Gp. 671.

The first page of the Submarine Tracking Room's report to the First Sea Lord for the week ending May 24, 1943. Although the sub-headings show that the decrypting was completely up-to-date for all areas, the withdrawal of the U-boats from the North Atlantic convoy routes was not yet apparent. There were no plus signs on the O.I.C. typewriter and the typist's ink strokes have not come through clearly in the photograph. *Public Records Office, London* large-scale engagement'. It was, he reported, 'a critical incident in the North Atlantic campaign: the heavy punishment inflicted for results which in the circumstances must have seemed meagre to B.d.U. may well have contributed to the recent drop in U-boat morale . . . Over forty separate attacks appear to have been made by the U-boats whilst the escort forces carried out approximately the same number of counter-attacks on U-boats. In addition to the U-boats sunk, five U-boats reported severe damage, twelve U-boats reported varying degrees of lesser damage, and on twenty separate occasions U-boats reported being driven off or forced to dive. This was possibly the most decisive of all convoy engagements and the enemy no doubt referred to it in a subsequent general message in the following passage: "Our heavy U-boat losses in the past month are attributable primarily to the present superiority of the enemy's location devices and the surprise from air which these have made possible. More than half our total losses have arisen as a result of this surprise . . . losses in actual combat with convoys have been small, except in one case where particularly unfavourable conditions prevailed, and even of these losses some were caused by air." '

Dönitz was down but he was not yet out. On May 10 the Tracking Room estimated that there were 126 U-boats at sea in the North Atlantic, sixty per cent of the strength available, the highest number ever known. Three U-tankers were supporting them and thirty of the boats which had operated against ONS.5 were refuelling and repairing damage in the western North Atlantic after their pursuit of that convoy. It was noted that 'the apparent gap through which SC.130 [the next east-bound convoy] has been routed is rapidly closing: it will be touch and go whether this convoy scrapes through'. The Senior Officer of the escort, (Commander P. W. Gretton R.N.), was one of our most successful Escort Commanders, and had just been involved in the ONS.5 operation. He was about to get married and pass the word to the Commodore of the convoy that 'it was most important that, throughout the long eastward journey the convoy should maintain, or if possible improve on, its rated speed. The Commodore promised his full co-operation, and it is pleasant to record that, although four groups of U-boats were concentrated to attack the convoy between the 15th and 20th, and the air and surface escorts were heavily engaged with them, no ships were lost. The convoy made excellent progress, and the Escort Commander steamed into Londonderry in ample time to keep his appointment.'‡ Five U-boats were sunk in the course of the operation. This time a note of real desperation had been apparent in Dönitz's signals to his U-boats. 'The convoy absolutely must be found again. Do your best. Success must come tonight'. Later two of the most senior and experienced commanders engaged were ordered to report exactly what had occurred since, said Dönitz, 'we can see no explanation for the failure'. To Winn this was 'further evidence that U-boat morale and efficiency are declining'.

On May 24, Dönitz at last recognized that the battle on the convoy routes must be abandoned, at least until new weapons and better defences against our radar had been found, and he withdrew his forces to what he hoped would be less dangerous areas west of the Azores. On the same day, and before this move became known to us, Winn wrote: 'During this month 26 German U-boats have been sunk. The April total is now assessed at 15 and the total since January 1st is 80. In the last three months 51 U-boats have started their first war cruise while fifty-six have been sunk, resulting for the first time in any three month period in a net decrease in operational numbers. Morale and efficiency are flagging and growing apprehension is clearly felt of air attack. Both V.L.R. aircraft and carrier-borne aircraft have contributed immensely to the safety of convoys in recent weeks. Temporarily the balance has been tipped in favour of the defenders in the Battle of the Atlantic, using as they have been enabled to do offensive methods and weapons in their defence of convoys.'

It seemed, after so many months of bitter struggles, too much to hope that the enemy had given up the fight, even for a time, and when, after a delay of seven days, Special Intelligence disclosed Dönitz's withdrawal signal, its true significance was obscured for a few more days due to difficulties in solving the disguised grid reference by which it was ordered. 'The major problem in estimating the present U-boat dispositions is the uncertainty as to the locality of an area to which on May 24 a group of fifteen U-boats was ordered to transfer. These U-boats were to arrive during the afternoon of the 31st at a position which is variously and incon-

‡ See Roskill: *War at Sea.*

clusively interpreted as either south of Sable Island [some 200 miles east of Nova Scotia] or about 600 miles south-west of the Azores. It is by no means clear that either of these positions was intended but they appear the most probable of many possibilities. In the absence of any subsequent Special Intelligence or any other relevant evidence the matter remains an open speculation.'

Within a few more days, however, it was clear that the Azores position was the correct one and that the northern North Atlantic was almost clear. 'As a result of this movement to the south-west the number of U-boats north of 50 degrees North has fallen to under ten, and three of them have been ordered to carry out a W/T ruse so as to give the impression that the convoys in this area are still liable to heavy attack.' The change had taken place even more suddenly and completely than Winn had predicted. Winn also noted the frantic efforts being made to replace the loss of experienced officers. 'A recent "Most Secret" message from the Naval Personnel Department of the Supreme Command of the Navy has demanded the names of anyone from other arms who could be released to train as U-boat commanding officers.' The battle was over and the enemy was licking his wounds. Dönitz told his men that the withdrawal was only temporary, 'and that the battle in the North Atlantic—the decisive area—will be resumed' but, in Captain Roskill's words 'the victory here recounted marked one of the decisive stages of the war; for the enemy then made his greatest effort against our Atlantic lifeline—and he failed. After forty-five months of unceasing battle of a more exacting and arduous nature than posterity may easily realise, our convoy escorts and aircraft had won the triumph they so richly merited'.

It is right to emphasize that the victory was won at sea by the men of the Royal and Allied Navies and Merchant Marine, and by the aircrews of Coastal Command, the Fleet Air Arm and the U. S. Navy. Scientists, engineers, shipbuilders, weapon designers, operational research specialists, cryptanalysts and intelligence officers all played their part, but it was the fighting men and Merchant Navy crews who bore the brunt of the battle and who deserved most of the credit for its outcome.

What contribution did the Tracking Room make to a campaign that was at least as vital to the Allied cause as the Battle of

Britain? We certainly did not succeed in routing all convoys clear of danger, or in anticipating all the enemy's moves. Many mistakes were made and grievous losses were suffered as a result. But if the outcome of the struggle did hang on a knife-edge, if the Germans did in fact fail only by the narrowest margin to sever our communications with the New World, without which the country would have starved and the invasion of Europe have been inconceivable, then perhaps the many prescient forecasts made by Winn, from the attack on the American seaboard in January 1942 to his appreciations in February 1943, did, in his words, help 'to tilt the balance' in our favour. Emphasis has been laid on a number of convoy operations when we were, for one reason or another, unable to make successful diversions, but, to coin a phrase, 'happy is the convoy with no history'. There were many such. The well-known German historian, Professor Jürgen Rohwer, who 'probably knows more about the Battle of the Atlantic than anyone else alive',* wrote in his book, *The Critical Convoy Battles of 1943*: 'Nevertheless Commanders Winn and Hall and their American opposite number Captain Knowles did succeed in routeing 105, or about 60 per cent, out of the total number of 174 scheduled North Atlantic convoys running between the middle of May 1942 and the end of May 1943 clear of German U-boat patrols so that they were not intercepted. Of the 69, or about 40 per cent, which were intercepted either by design or by chance sighting, 23 escaped without loss. 40 suffered comparatively minor losses, mostly stragglers. Only 16 convoys lost more than four ships from the actual convoy formation.' This is surely a tribute of which the staffs of the British, American and Canadian Tracking Rooms and their respective Trade Routing Departments can feel proud.

* Vice-Admiral Schofield in a letter to the author.

12

June–December 1943.
Dönitz Tries Again

THE WITHDRAWAL from the northern Atlantic convoy routes in May did not, of course, mean an end to the U-boat war. Quite the contrary. Dönitz still had over four hundred U-boats, of which half were operational. Nor was he as yet completely convinced that pack attacks on convoys were impossible. His move of fifteen of the survivors of the May battles to the area west of the Azores was an attempt to catch the New York-Gibraltar traffic off guard, and he had some grounds for supposing that the soft spots off Freetown and Brazil and in the Indian Ocean could still be made to pay good dividends. Winn's warning in February that the utmost mobility of Allied anti-submarine forces would be necessary in the event of a sudden change in the enemy's strategy was more than usually perspicacious.

It was, therefore, most fortunate that at this precise moment the Americans carried out a far-reaching and extremely effective re-organization of their anti-U-boat effort. By mutual agreement the British and Canadians assumed complete responsibility for the New York-Halifax-U.K. routes, while the Americans concentrated on the New York-Gibraltar convoys, the Trinidad-U.K. oil convoys and the whole of the western South Atlantic. They also made an internal change which was of at least equal importance when they created the Tenth Fleet. This was not a fleet in the normal sense of the word: it possessed no ships and only limited personnel. It was an administrative move which gave effect, in a typically U.S.N. way, to the need to centralize and co-ordinate the various organizations concerned with the anti-U-boat war. It gave to the Tenth Fleet, in more precise and legal terms, the powers which in practice were wielded in the British Admiralty by the Assistant Chief of Naval Staff (U-boats and Trade): the Tenth Fleet's relationship with the Commander-in-Chief Atlantic Fleet, who continued to exercise control over the escort forces, both sea and air, was analogous to that of the Admiralty with the Commander-in-Chief Western Approaches and with the Air Officer Commanding-in-Chief, Coastal Command. Orders were very rarely issued, but requests or suggestions were equally rarely ignored. The creator and Commander-in-Chief of the Tenth Fleet was Admiral 'Ernie' King, who thus lent to it his own prestige and authority in the same way that those of the Admiralty were behind the A.C.N.S. (U.T.). Tenth Fleet did not, on the whole, consist of new departments: it took over old ones, among them Admiral Metcalf's Convoy and Routing Division, A.S.W.O.R.G., the American equivalent of the British Anti-Submarine Warfare Division, and, of great interest to O.I.C., Kenneth Knowles' OP 20 Atlantic Operational Intelligence Section. Knowles now wore two hats: he remained part of the Cominch organization, but, as part of the Tenth Fleet, was also head of one and the same section under the designation F.21.

The increase in authority and stature which this gave to Knowles and his men was of great importance, and put him firmly on a par with his opposite number Rodger Winn, just at a time when the combination of Special Intelligence and the new German dispositions would offer him full scope for his great talents as an intelligence officer. He was fortunate, too, that the effective head of the Tenth Fleet, placed there as Chief of Staff by Admiral King, was Rear-Admiral Francis S. Low, an extremely able and dynamic officer under whom Knowles had served on the China Station and for whom he had a great respect and admiration, feelings which were reciprocated by Low. Low was no anglophobe and relations with the Royal Navy took a distinct turn for the better.

The first evidence of the Tenth Fleet's efficiency was not slow in emerging. The escort carrier *Bogue*, which a few weeks before had been protecting the SC. and HX. convoys, was now shifted to the New York-Gibraltar ones. Not only were these successfully routed clear of the waiting U-boat patrols but two U-boats were promptly sunk, one of them a minelayer acting as a U-tanker. In July a concerted effort was made against these Azores U-boats by two more American 'hunter-killer' groups, centred round the escort carriers *Santee* and *Core*. In that month and in August the three carriers and their accompanying destroyers sank thirteen more U-boats. The victims included three minelayer-tankers and one U-tanker proper, a very serious blow to the German supply organization to which we will return later. The July sinkings, seven between the 13th and the 30th, were remarkable, amongst other things, for the fact that they were achieved despite the entire absence during the first three weeks of the month of any Special Intelligence, the longest single delay in breaking new settings, except for the 1942 'Black Out', ever experienced. It is true Special Intelligence had already revealed the general area of the patrols and in some cases given a good idea of refuelling rendezvous, but past freedom from interference from the air had bred over-confidence in the Germans and their W/T discipline was at first lax. It was a triumph for Knowles and for his D/F team, for the mobility of the hunting groups and the vastly increased area of search which their carrier-borne aircraft enabled them to cover; a striking contrast to the dismal situation in which the American defences had found themselves only twelve months earlier.

Nor was it only around the Azores that the Americans struck at the U-boats. In the same three months they sank seven U-boats off Brazil and five off their own coast, in the Caribbean and off Trinidad, while other kills were also achieved by American aircraft loaned to the British off Iceland, in the Bay of Biscay and to the west of Portugal. It was a splendid achievement and complete justification for King's creation of the Tenth Fleet.

It was not until the last week in August that the full effects of the American onslaught became apparent. The Tracking Room was then able to report that 'the loss of the supply U-boat west of the Azores on the 8th August is now confirmed. As a result two outward-bound U-boats were ordered to take over the refuelling of a dozen U-boats homeward-bound from the Caribbean and Freetown areas. One of these 740-tonners was itself sunk, possibly by aircraft from *Card* on the 11th August. Owing to the ever stricter enforcement of W/T silence, the Germans did not become aware of these losses for some time, and they were eventually compelled to detail a new U-Kreuzer outward-bound from Germany to the South Atlantic-Indian Ocean to refuel seven or eight U-boats eight hundred miles south-west of the Azores on 23rd August. This U-Kreuzer has a fuel capacity of about 500 tons but will probably have to hand over 150 to 200 tons in the course of this operation. As a result of these difficulties U-boats have had to leave patrol so as to reach base without refuelling. No U-boats remain in the Caribbean or off Brazil and not more than three in the West African area.'

Despite the greater number of U-cruisers and 740-tonners with good endurance which the Germans now possessed, their far-distant operations were largely dependent, as we have just seen, on their ability to refuel their boats at sea. In the Indian Ocean it was still possible to use surface tankers, but in the Atlantic only U-tankers could operate with any hope of safety. Ten of these Type XIV boats had been built and up to the end of May only one of them had been sunk. In addition there were eight mine-layers of the XB Type, which could also be used as supply boats if the need arose, making a total of seventeen. It may seem strange that greater efforts had not previously been made to eliminate these invaluable aids to long-distance U-boat warfare. Back in December 1942, in the first week of the resumed flow of Atlantic U-boat traffic, the Tracking Room had remarked that 'three supply U-boats are known to be at sea, two of them returning empty. The supply U-boats are worked as hard as our own tankers and the enemy appears to have over-estimated his powers of supplying operational boats, several of which have been in great difficulties owing to shortage of fuel. U-boats returning from distant waters have been ordered to exercise the utmost economy in fuel'.

There were, however, insuperable difficulties both in pinpointing the refuelling rendezvous and in providing forces capable of proceeding swiftly to these remote areas and finding the U-boats when they got there. It was not until three things had occurred— the shift of the centre of operations to the area west of the Azores with the relaxation of all pressure in the north, the advent of escort carriers, and the renewed flow of Special Intelligence—that this could even be attempted. There was also a grave risk that we should compromise Special Intelligence by too obvious and concentrated efforts, and O.I.C. did indeed voice concern about this to F.21 when the *Bogue-Core-Santee* operations were in full swing. Our concern was not unreasonable: we had, after all, a good deal more experience in handling Special Intelligence than our opposite numbers in Washington, but in the end, thanks to German over-confidence in the perfection of their ciphering arrangements and their under-estimation of the efficiency of the Allied D/F organization, Knowles was proved right and no harm, except to the unfortunate U-boats, resulted. As a matter of fact, although the Americans accounted for five Milch Cows and reserve tankers in more or less deliberate hunts between June and August, an equal number were sunk, fortuitously one might say, while on passage in the Bay of Biscay, and three more on the northern exit routes during the major offensive waged by Coastal Command on passage boats at this time. By October Dönitz was left with but two U-tankers and three reserve minelayers. It was as devastating a blow as that which Raeder had suffered when the surface supply ships were mopped up in June 1941, and as on the earlier occasion, 'intelligence' had played a notable part in it.

Mention was made in an earlier chapter of Coastal Command's efforts to attack U-boats outward- or homeward-bound in the Bay of Biscay during the summer of 1942 and how, after some initial successes, the Germans overcame the problem by means of an efficient radar search receiver. By early 1943 most of Coastal Command's anti-submarine aircraft had at last been fitted with the new 10cm radar, against which the U-boats' search receivers were ineffective, and in June the A.O.C.-in-C., Air Vice-Marshal Sir John Slessor, took the opportunity given by the withdrawal of the U-boats from operations against the northern convoys, to concentrate his aircraft on the northern and southern exit routes in an all-out campaign which has come to be called the Bay Offensive. Once again this was planned on the basis of the Tracking Room's estimates of the positions of the outward- and homeward-bound boats, and patrols were shifted day by day and night by night to follow the U-boats' progress and to take advantage of the latest tactics ordered by B.d.U. We were greatly aided by the Germans' failure to recognize the true cause of our aircraft's ability to locate them and by the various mistaken methods with which they sought to fight back. In particular Dönitz's orders to his boats to stay on the surface and fight it out with their new and more powerful anti-aircraft armament, and his attempts to sail boats in groups, provided the airmen with a wealth of targets, dangerous ones though they were.

In the middle of June, for example, the Tracking Room was able to inform Coastal Command that 'U-boats on passage to and from the Bay of Biscay are now proceeding in groups of up to six when east of 18 degrees West. Their orders are to remain on the surface during the day relying on their combined H/A fire to drive off aircraft'. Thus, each time that Dönitz ordered new tactics in an effort to give his U-boats some chance of survival, the necessity of informing those boats already at sea betrayed his intentions to us in sufficient time for counter-measures to be devised and put into effect. After a somewhat slow start the battle rose to a pitch of fury, the British throwing in Support Groups and cruisers, the Germans fighters and bombers fitted with their new glider bombs, until once again Dönitz had to admit defeat and cancel for the time being all outward-bound sailings. At the same time homeward-bound boats were instructed to creep submerged along the Spanish coast, inside territorial waters. In June, July and August, twenty-five U-boats were sunk in the Bay Offensive and four more on the northern transit routes. Another forty-five were sunk in other areas to bring the total losses to seventy-four for a loss to the Allies of only fifty-eight merchant ships. It was, for Dönitz, just as disastrous a period as the previous three months had proved to be.

In considering, during May, areas to which he might transfer operations after abandoning the northern Atlantic, Dönitz had not of course forgotten the Indian Ocean. He already had seven U-cruisers there, one of which, as we knew, had brought out the Indian nationalist leader Subhas Chandra Bhose and transferred him to a Japanese U-boat, a mission with which we were unfortunately unable to interfere. By June one U-boat had to start its return voyage due to engine defects, and one had gone to Penang, where the Japanese had set up a base for the Germans. One had been sunk and we learned from Special Intelligence that the remainder were beginning to run short of food. The Germans, however, had two tankers, *Charlotte Schliemann* and *Brake*, available

for use as supply ships, and with the facilities existing at Penang
and Singapore, and preparations now being made for another base
at Soerabaya in the Dutch East Indies, Dönitz felt confident of
being able to maintain, and indeed reinforce, his campaign in a
vast ocean where, due to the demands of other areas, British resources both of sea and air escorts had to be spread woefully
thinly. (No fewer than forty-eight ships had to be transferred
from the Eastern to the Mediterranean Fleet for the invasion of
Sicily.) Allied merchant ship traffic was heavy and the port facilities in East Africa, the Red Sea and India very inadequate, so that
to avoid congestion, large numbers of ships had to be sailed independently.

Towards the end of June ten specially modified 740-ton
U-boats, the Monsun group, left Biscay ports bound for the Cape
and the Indian Ocean. Had all ten arrived in their operational
areas the results could have been very serious, but three of them
were sunk early on and two more, due to the loss of the Milch
Cow destined to supply the group, had to hand over fuel to the
remaining five. Thus only half the original number managed to
reach the Indian Ocean. On their way south they had been spread
out on a wide front and had, we were interested to learn, made
use of kites to raise a look-out three hundred feet in the air and
give a range of vision of twenty miles. These kites were given the
code-name of Bachstelze or Water Wagtail (the Germans were
never very original in their use of code names). For most of this
time Special Intelligence was, as already noted, 'very fragmentary
. . . and in many instances belatedly received'. Nevertheless warnings were sent to the Commanders-in-Chief South Atlantic and
East Indies and as much shipping as possible gathered into convoy or diverted. The delays in receiving Special Intelligence frus-
trated any attempt to prevent *Charlotte Schliemann* refuelling the
U-cruisers already in the Indian Ocean or *Brake* the five new-
comers when they arrived. In the latter instance the Tracking
Room had the melancholy satisfaction of proving the C.-in-C.
East Indies wrong when he held, contrary to our advice, that the
U-boats would operate for several weeks before refuelling, but the
argument was largely academic as it would have needed much
more timely and precise information and an escort carrier to re-

peat the successes of the Americans in the Azores area, and neither was available.

Once the Monsun boats had filled their tanks they separated to widely dispersed areas, and although some of these did become known to us, it was a most difficult task to hunt down individual boats, which, contrary to Atlantic practice, were given wide discretion by B.d.U. and rarely used their own wireless. Indeed the Tracking Room could do little from such a great distance beyond signalling such information as Special Intelligence did reveal, to help the C.-in-C., who in any case had his own Intelligence Centre at Colombo. Although merchant shipping losses were never really serious they were a constant worry and continued to impose a great strain on our forces until these could be augmented at the beginning of 1944. By that time Triton was being decrypted with far fewer and much shorter delays, with the result that *Charlotte Schliemann* was caught and sunk at the end of February and *Brake* just over a week later. Thereafter the activities of the surviving U-boats were considerably restricted, while the loss of U-tankers and further successes by American hunter-killer groups in the Atlantic restricted and then finally prevented reinforcements reaching them. Nevertheless the campaign was continued until 1945, when some boats were ordered back to Germany and the last two were handed over to the Japanese when the final collapse came. The operations in the Indian Ocean were a good example of the difficulties, even when Special Intelligence was available, of finding and killing U-boats which were working individually and on their own initiative without indulging in a large volume of wireless chatter.

All this, however, anticipates events. Irritating though these far-distant campaigns were, the centre of attention remained in the North Atlantic. At the end of July Winn produced a paper giving his ideas about the options open to Dönitz. He began by pointing out that, although the enemy had been driven from the convoy routes by an unacceptable rate of loss, he must be well aware that Allied ability to survive and to mount a military offensive was completely dependent on bringing to Britain a continuous supply of food, men and munitions from the western hemisphere. Dönitz must therefore have withdrawn only with the hope of living to fight another day. Since then, however, he had suffered nothing but further disasters. Referring to the Bay Offensive, Winn wrote, 'day by day, group by group, one after another, U-boats, Commanding Officers and crews have been subjected to the experience of being hunted, pounced upon and driven to an extent and with a continuity which human flesh and blood inspired by no national victories cannot possibly be expected to endure.' Dönitz would surely only throw his forces back into the struggle in the North Atlantic if he assessed the chances of successful resistance by the German Army and Air Force to an invasion of France as being minimal. 'It would be the last dying struggle of the caged tiger for the enemy to send back in September and October into the North-Western Approaches, his main U-boat forces, unless in the meantime, he acquires by sheer good luck, or the brilliance of some unknown inventor, the antidote and the panacea to all those well-proven weapons which he now knows, or must suspect, that our armoury contains. If, and only if, by the equinox all hope is lost, there will be a sudden, drastic, and for him, fatal contest staged in the North Atlantic.' In such circumstances, Winn estimated that Dönitz might commit so many as 150 U-boats, but he felt that the 'contest would be quickly decided'.

Winn concluded by calling for offensive measures to keep the enemy off balance. 'The time is ripe for confident, optimistic and bold enterprise, even if heavy losses on the North Atlantic convoy routes were to be suffered. The morale of the Merchant Navy is now so high, and the force of escort vessels available now so considerable, that for a limited time heavy losses could be accepted, and no fear need be felt as to the ultimate outcome.'

He must have had some qualms about the propriety of a mere intelligence officer encroaching on the field of future strategy for, rather unusually, before sending his appreciation to Admiral Edelsten, for whom it was destined, he submitted it for comment to Denning and Clayton. They both considered that he had overstepped the limits of his responsibilities and that the turn of phrase employed, while perhaps acceptable from the Prime Minister, would be found less felicitous when coming from an officer in charge of one section of the O.I.C. Winn agreed with them and filed the paper with a pencilled note: 'A purely personal view'.

Nevertheless he did discuss his ideas verbally with Edelsten, who in fact incorporated many of them in an appreciation, which he wrote and circulated to the Naval Staff in August, which forecast a renewal of the convoy battles. Nor were Winn's views so very wide of the mark. Dönitz was indeed counting on new weapons, both offensive and defensive, to enable him to renew the battle. A new radar search receiver had been produced and great store was set by an acoustic torpedo, the Zaunkönig (or the Wren) to riposte against the escort vessels. There were also new and better types of U-boats being planned, although none was yet in commission. Dönitz did not, however, under-estimate the sacrifices which he would demand from his men. 'I finally came to the bitter conclusion that we had no option but to fight on. The U-boat arm could not alone stand aside and watch the onslaught, of which it had hitherto borne the brunt, now fall in all its fury as an additional burden on the other fighting services and the civilian population. . . . The question was—would the U-boat arm itself appreciate the bitter necessity of continuing a campaign in which there was no longer any chance of major success, and would it be prepared to do so in a spirit of selfless devotion to duty?'

These remarks, taken from Dönitz's *Memoirs*, in fact refer to the month of June before the U-boats had been subjected to the full blast of Coastal Command's Bay Offensive and the American onslaught west of the Azores. How much more anxiously must he have repeated the same questions to himself at the end of August! Dönitz need not have worried about the reactions of his commanding officers and crews. They were the pick of the German Navy and there was probably no more dedicated and highly motivated body of men in the Armed Forces of the Third Reich than the U-boat crews. Although we in the Tracking Room could observe signs from time to time that confidence in their weapons was faltering, and that some of the U-boat commanders on their first war cruise were perhaps less ready than their comrades had been in the past to press home attacks, the U-boat men never gave up the fight right up to the last day of the war. They were always ready to believe Dönitz's promise that, if only they would hold on, new weapons and new U-boats would turn the tide; they never ceased to make the sacrifices which he called for, and this despite the fact that, out of 39,000 members of the U-boat Arm engaged on operations throughout the war, fatal casualties reached the dreadful total of 28,000.

By the end of August Dönitz was ready to resume the battle. Accepting the long delay imposed by submerged passage of the Bay of Biscay by the southern route along the Spanish coast, he sailed a group of nine U-boats and a U-tanker from France, followed in early September by another thirteen and six from the North Sea. Once again the Germans were counting heavily on surprise, and all boats were enjoined to exercise the utmost caution until they had reached their patrol line. They were all equipped with the new search receiver, with increased anti-aircraft armaments and with a number of the new acoustic torpedoes. It was to be a sudden and surprise attack, and the primary target was to be the escort vessels not the merchant ships.

It seems amazing now that the Leuthen boats (for this was the code name for the group) should not have been issued with precise orders before sailing. After all, this was not a matter of regrouping U-boats already at sea, but was an operation with boats fresh out of port, carefully thought out and long-prepared. Despite renewed doubts about the security of their cipher, the U-boat Command had again come to the conclusion that it was inviolate and that our ability, which they had by now observed, to locate whole patrol lines, was due to some miraculous airborne location device of whose precise nature they were unaware. It was a fatal misapprehension.

On September 13, the Tracking Room reported that 'Special Intelligence is available for five of the first nine days of September. The greatest problem is the whereabouts of some twenty U-boats which have recently left Biscay ports . . . very strict W/T silence has been ordered and U-boats were informed on 6th September that "during the present waiting period" the main object was to avoid being observed. Without further information it is impossible to be sure of the ultimate aim of the operation but if the waiting area is north of the Azores it might be a resumption of attacks on convoys, while if close to the Islands it may be designed to prevent any move against them by the Allies'. (Negotiations with the Portuguese had just been concluded and the Azores were in fact successfully occupied on October 8.)

Two days after this report was written, Dönitz issued orders to the Zaunkönig group to take up a patrol line by the evening of the 20th. The line was some 350 miles in length with its northern end about the same distance south-west of Iceland. This order was not decrypted until the 18th but this would not have mattered much had not Dönitz used 'a new type of grid reference employing fixed points defined in the sailing orders of the U-boats'. Unfortunately the Tracking Room estimated the position to fall about a hundred miles south of the actual line taken up by the Zaunkönig group, and although convoy ONS.18 was diverted it was not sufficient to keep it clear, nor was the faster ON.202, which was following behind and overtaking ONS.18, routed far enough north. Despite this error, we were well aware of the nature of the new attack which the enemy was planning. Dönitz had once again been unable to resist the temptation to issue an eve of battle exhortation. In this he referred to the new weapons and radar defences with which the U-boats had been provided and urged them to remain undetected until the last moment, but then to 'decimate' the escorts. In consequence the convoys, which had already been provided with strong escorts, were given additional air cover, and a Support Group, originally intended for operations in the Bay of Biscay, was rapidly diverted to the area. The descent of fog at a critical moment was a lucky bonus for the British.

Although the Allies had also developed an aerial acoustic torpedo, indeed one of the U-boats engaged in this operation was sunk by one, they did not have precise advance warning of the German Zaunkönig. Interrogation of prisoners of war in August had revealed that the Germans were also experimenting with some such weapon, and an antidote had been prepared and was subsequently rapidly issued to the Allied escort forces. It is, however, only fair to record that initially the Germans did achieve the surprise they were seeking with this weapon. On September 20, when the battle was just starting, Winn reported that 'the major development evidenced this week has been the resumption of U-boat operations against convoys. It is evident that the enemy fully appreciates that it is only in the North Atlantic convoy lanes that the U-boats can vitally affect the outcome of the war. He has sent them back with exhortations to valour and possibly with new equipment. It remains to be seen whether the talk of a new weapon means anything. If the U-boat which torpedoed H.M.S.

Lagan early today was the one she was closing, the nature of her damage may indicate the use of some type of acoustic torpedo but there has been no indication in Special Intelligence that such a device has been perfected'.

The operation was by no means the unqualified success for which Dönitz had been hoping. Although six merchant ships and three escorts were sunk and one escort damaged, three U-boats were sunk and six more damaged. In a long analysis of the operation, issued on September 27, Winn remarked: 'Thus 45% of the U-boat force was incapacitated permanently or for a substantial period. . . . It is considered; (a) that the enemy command had extremely high hopes of achieving an outstanding triumph by a surprise renewal of attacks and by their use of their new torpedo; (b) that in the early stages both the command and the individual U-boat commanders were elated and pleased with the results; (c) that as it was fully appreciated that the convoy had a very strong escort despite the presumed absence of knowledge that any encounter was probable, and as casualties became known this elation faded and the laudatory summary which was addressed to the survivors was probably rather designed to stiffen their valour than inspired by belief in or gratitude for their alleged achievements.' Winn, rightly or wrongly, was always inclined to ascribe the worst motives to Dönitz.

U-boat Command was naturally anxious to receive detailed reports concerning the performance of the new 'wonder weapon'; they could not know that the Tracking Room, using the data supplied in the reports which they demanded from the U-boats, was producing an even better analysis, better because we could discount the wildly if understandably exaggerated German claims of the effectiveness of Zaunkönig. Four days after the U-boats had been called off, an analysis giving the following details of all acoustic torpedo attacks on the two convoys was in the hands of the Director of the Anti-Submarine Warfare Division: Time of attack, Position, U-boat, Tube, Real Inclination, Running Time, Remarks (Target, Range, etc.), Claim (Explanation: Possible target). Such a report, which could only have been compiled on the basis of Special Intelligence, was, of course, of enormous value in perfecting the 'Foxer', the device towed astern of the escort vessels which attracted the acoustic torpedo and caused it to explode harmlessly.

The Germans were now in a much less favourable position than they had been at the beginning of the year. There were far more surface escorts available for every convoy, the groups were accustomed to working together, their tactics had been developed and refined, and new weapons like the Hedgehog,* and above all the 10cm radar had nullified all the U-boats' old advantages when operating on the surface at night or in poor visibility. Support Groups could now reinforce any convoy threatened and could stay behind and hunt, for up to eight hours if needed, any U-boat which had been compelled to dive. Above all, the advent of the escort carrier and the long-awaited supply of additional V.L.R. aircraft, coupled with the occupation in October of the Azores, meant that the Atlantic Air Gap had been closed, so that continuous air cover could be given throughout its voyage to any convoy in the whole of the North Atlantic. On the Intelligence side also, the balance had swung decisively in our favour. The change in our ciphers introduced in June had taken away Dönitz's best, indeed almost his only, source of information, just at a time when B.P. had so perfected their techniques that delays in breaking new cipher settings became ever shorter. From the beginning of October onwards, more and more traffic was decrypted currently and by December current reading became almost continuous, with such delays as did occur limited to twenty-four or at the most forty-eight hours. Gone were the days when evasive routing was restricted by the limits of the escorts' fuel or the absence of air cover. No longer could the B.Dienst enable Dönitz to frustrate any diversions we did make by timely switches of his patrol lines. It was he who was now groping in the dark while our picture became so clear that convoys could be diverted, Support Groups transferred, air cover increased or reduced in accordance with the daily or even hourly demands of a situation in which, as Dönitz said, we could see his cards without his being able to get so much as a glimpse at ours.

He did not, of course, admit defeat quickly. With the number

* A form of mortar for throwing a salvo of mortar type A/S bombs ahead of the ship instead of dropping them over the stern. The Hedgehog was replaced by the Squid, an even more formidable ahead-throwing depth charge mortar.

of U-boats still at sea, interception, sometimes as a result of accurate anticipation, sometimes because of a fortuitous encounter by a U-boat on passage, continued. But our confidence in the ability of the sea and air escorts to drive off attacks was now so great that in some cases risks were deliberately accepted. At the beginning of October, 'the engagement of SC.143 with a known group of U-boats was deliberately accepted in order to ensure a safe passage for HX.259, a larger and more weakly escorted convoy, and the result achieved in bringing through the two convoys for the loss of one merchant ship and one escort and in sinking three U-boats may justly be considered highly satisfactory'. Two weeks later 'Convoy ON.206 was fortuitously intercepted on the afternoon of 15th by a U-boat on passage from Norway and contact was maintained until late on the 16th, by which time several reports had been made of the other convoy ONS.20. The convoys were so placed when intercepted that it was impossible to evade the advance of the main pack of U-boats which had been formed near 30 degrees West. Therefore they were so handled that the enemy would be likely to split his force between them. In actual fact though both were simultaneously being shadowed the enemy made the appreciation that there was only one convoy, ONS.20, and that the other body was a decoy group. In consequence, when this fact became known in the Admiralty on the morning of the 17th, the Support Group with ON.206 was sent back to ONS.20 and arrived before dark on the 17th in time to catch and severely damage a U-boat lying in wait ahead of the convoy. So far as can be judged at present we have lost one merchant ship and two Liberator aircraft and four U-boats have been sunk, three by aircraft and one by H.M.S. *Byard*.'

Dönitz's renewed attacks on convoys were not confined solely to the U.K./U.S.A. route. With the failure of the B.Dienst, the U.K.-Gibraltar traffic offered him a better chance of successful interception, particularly as he was able once again to obtain a modicum of co-operation from the G.A.F. It was less easy for us to 'make use of evasive routing for the convoys', wrote Winn in connection with convoys SL.139 and MKS.30, 'and they actually followed a route quite favourable to the U-boats'. There were some hard battles, but the truth of the matter was that Allied air and sea defences were now so strong that the Germans had an almost impossible task. Our ability, thanks to up-to-date Special Intelligence, to detect any threats in good time and so ensure the maximum support for any convoy in danger undoubtedly helped enormously, but as on the more northerly routes, it is likely that victory would have been achieved, albeit at greater cost in ships and lives and less swiftly, even if no Special Intelligence had been available at all.

In October, Knowles, in F.21, again saw an opportunity to strike at U-boats on passage or refuelling west and south-west of the Azores, and this was something that did owe a great debt to Special Intelligence. Despite his losses in this area in July and August, Dönitz had no option but to try to refuel his U-boats bound to or from distant waters, and he therefore sent out one of his last three U-tankers at the beginning of October. Back came the U.S. escort carrier *Card* and promptly sank first the U-boat requiring fuel and then the Milch Cow. Moving north-west and joined by *Core* and *Block Island*, the U.S. hunter-killer groups then sank two more U-boats and a reserve minelayer tanker. It was only with the greatest difficulty that the remaining U-boats managed to return home. The fleet of U-tankers and minelayers, which only five months before had consisted of seventeen boats, was now reduced to five, of which only two minelayers were to survive the war.

The Germans again became really alarmed at the rapidity with which we seemed to be able to detect their refuelling rendezvous, as can be seen from the following extract from the Tracking Room's report for the week ending the 18th October: 'The activities of U.S.S. *Card* in the area near 48 degrees North 29 degrees West have been very unsettling for the enemy who has been so impressed by the insecurity of existence of supply U-boats nowadays that he has provided two special "Flak"† U-boats for the protection of the tanker boat and is investigating the possibility of using only dark hours for effecting transfers of supplies. Apart from the fact that a supply U-boat was attacked unsuccessfully during the night of 12th/13th and was again attacked and claimed by *Card* as probably sunk about 0930/13th and that *Card* claims, in all, three certain kills and three probables, nothing is known of events in the refuelling area despite the fact that Special Intelligence is entirely up-to-date. As there is a complete ban on

† Anti-aircraft.

W/T within 250 miles of the fuelling point no boat has spoken, which in itself implies that no boat was fuelled early enough to be now so far as two hundred miles from the fueller. Since the fuelling should have begun on the 12th it is obvious that the operation has been gravely hindered if not prevented. There is a relief supply boat of the minelayer type in the neighbourhood and recourse may ultimately be had to him'. This was a good example of one of the occasions, which were to become more and more frequent, when we knew as much if not more of the actual U-boat situation than Dönitz did.

By November the Germans were finding it increasingly difficult to locate convoys, and when located to keep contact with them. Attempts were made to concentrate attacks on the first night so as to take advantage of surprise before reinforcements could reach the scene. These tactics brought little success and a plan was then adopted of scattering U-boats like a chequer board across a wide area of the Atlantic. 'This policy of dispersion,' wrote Winn on November 15, 'must have been dictated by despair of finding convoys which had consistently eluded the concentrations throughout the fortnight, but it was explained to the U-boats as an expedient to obviate the tendency of large patrols to premature detection by enemy radar. A novel note of quasi apology and simulated frankness thus appeared. . . .'

In the Tracking Room another R.N.V.R. watchkeeper, the New Zealander, Sub-Lieutenant McKay, had now been obtained, thus releasing Eric Fiske to reinforce Winn and his deputy during the day and to carry out special investigations of one sort or another into the mass of Special Intelligence that was being received. Our civilian researcher, Dr. Wood, specialized on the Baltic traffic, and weekly statements of the whole U-boat fleet were being issued, divided into three classes: (1) non-operational, i.e. under construction, school boats, probably withdrawn from service, and freight carriers; (2) pre-operational in the Baltic by classes and types; and (3) operational by classes and types. Against each category the increase or decrease for the week was noted. In addition full reports on every major convoy operation were prepared as soon as the complete Special Intelligence became available, and as long as there were major operations on which to report. These special reports were drawn up entirely from the German point of view and the narrative included all the relevant signals made to and from U-boats, with appendices listing all U-boats which had been in contact with the convoy in each day and night period of the battle, and a list of all damage suffered. They were designed for the benefit of the Anti-Submarine Warfare Division and were to be compared with the reports received from Allied forces, in order that an assessment could be made of the relative success of the various tactics and weapons used by the sea and air escorts. The reports rarely included much information about Allied counter-measures, but are probably now one of the most detailed and comprehensive records of the German side of convoy battles in existence.

At the beginning of December, the first of a series of tables showing the months of experience in operational command of all U-boat commanders was issued. It read as follows:

Length of time in months	Number of C.O.s	Percentage
Under 3 months	50	30%
4– 6	27	16%
7– 9	30	18%
10–12	21	13%
13–15	24	15%
16–18	7	3%
19–21	4	2%
22–24	4	2%
25–27	1	1%
	168	

Average number of months in operational command: 8.1 months.

It was yet another example of the completeness of our knowledge of the U-boat Arm, but also showed the frighteningly short span of active life that could be expected by the average German submariner by this time in the war.

Perhaps it would be fair to close this chapter with one last quotation as typical of the situation in the North Atlantic at the end of 1943. On December 27, the Tracking Room report contained the following remarks: 'These patrols have been subjected to minor modifications which have made evasive routing of shipping difficult, but the only interception achieved by the enemy was the result of the failure of one U-boat to understand the disguised reference point for his patrol line. In consequence he was patrolling two hundred miles further west than either the Germans or ourselves anticipated'. We had come a long way since the unfortunate onslaught on convoy TM.1 in the first days of January.

13

The End of
Scharnhorst and *Tirpitz*

AFTER THE disaster of PQ.17 there had been something of a lull in the Arctic, but in August 1942, when some destroyers were returning from a mission to Murmansk, Denning became aware from decrypts that the German minelayer *Ulm*, on the way to an operation off Spitzbergen, was in the neighbourhood of Bear Island. There was absolutely no other evidence to disclose her whereabouts and Ultra signals could not, of course, be sent to private ships. Nevertheless the chance to get a little of our own back was too good to be missed, and so the destroyers were ordered by the Admiralty to alter course to 225 degrees and sweep through a given area in line abreast ten miles apart. No explanation was given for these instructions. The destroyers were however informed that no British or Allied vessel was in the area. Years afterwards one of the officers concerned told Denning that he was completely mystified when, a few hours after receipt of the Admiralty's signal, they suddenly sighted *Ulm*, alone in the Arctic wastes, and sank her.

At the beginning of September 1942 one last PQ. convoy was run. It was given a large 'fighting' escort of fleet destroyers and, for the first time, an escort carrier. The Germans made no move with their heavy ships and, despite furious attacks by bombers and U-boats, PQ.18 battled its way through. Fifteen of its ships were sunk but at the cost to the Germans of forty aircraft and three U-boats. The demands of Operation Torch then necessitated the postponement of any further convoys until the end of the year, by which time the German Air Force had been compelled to transfer most of its Norwegian-based striking force to the Mediterranean.

In a contribution to a Joint Intelligence Committee appreciation in September, Denning had written in connection with the German surface ships that 'the discipline and morale of officers and men continues to be exceptionally high, but on proceeding to sea is tempered by the fact that they believe their chances of operating successfully against the British naval forces are slight, and they are mainly imbued with a spirit of determination to fight and die in accordance with the highest traditions of the German Navy'.

We were, by now, becoming aware of restrictions imposed on the movements of the German heavy ships by the growing shortage of fuel oil, but we were still not fully conscious of the inhibiting effects of Hitler's refusal to allow reasonable risks to be taken. His continued insistence on the avoidance of damage in engagements, even with inferior forces, ironically led to the resignation of Raeder and his replacement as Commander-in-Chief of the Navy by Dönitz.

When the Arctic convoys were resumed at the end of 1942 under the new designation JW., outward, RA., homeward, Raeder determined on another sortie by surface ships. *Tirpitz* was refitting at Trondheim and *Scharnhorst* had not yet completed repairing the mine damage suffered during the Channel Dash, but the pocket battleship *Lützow* and the heavy cruiser *Hipper* were available, and were sent out under Admiral Kummetz to attack JW.51B on New Year's Eve 1942. The British covering force under Admiral Burnett consisted of two 6-inch gun cruisers, a very much weaker squadron than the German one, and to make matters worse the convoy, which was maintaining strict wireless silence, had been delayed by a gale and was 150 miles astern of its plotted position. Kummetz very nearly achieved a spectacular success. He intercepted the convoy and for several hours was held off only by the bold and brilliant tactics of the destroyers of the escort under Captain Sherbrooke. When Burnett and his cruisers finally reached the scene, the need to avoid damage seemed paramount to Kummetz and he hauled off after his flagship had been hit and retired quickly to Altenfjord. Hitler had been led to expect a glorious victory (a U-boat had signalled 'I see nothing but red', which caused some hilarity in the Submarine Tracking Room). A breakdown in communications left him without any more news long after the British communiqué had justifiably claimed a considerable success for the weaker British force. Hitler was so enraged that he insisted all Raeder's heavy ships were useless and must be scrapped, their guns used for coast defences and their crews drafted to other and more aggressive arms of the Service. Considering that it was Hitler's own instructions which had led Kummetz to display such caution, one's sympathies must lie with Raeder. Despite Hitler's pleas he insisted on resigning.

It might have been supposed that Dönitz, who had for years been demanding that greater priority should be given to his U-boats, would be delighted to carry out Hitler's orders. In fact, when he came to assess the situation, he was compelled to agree that Raeder's views had much to commend them. At the very least, the mere existence of the German heavy ships tied down quite disproportionate British forces urgently required in the Mediterranean and the Far East. Dönitz finally persuaded an aggrieved and reluctant Hitler to permit him to retain the most effective of the big ships in commission.

Early in 1943 *Scharnhorst* completed her repairs and made two attempts to reach Norway. On each occasion her intentions were revealed by Special Intelligence and she was quickly located by the R.A.F. Twice she decided that discretion was the better part of valour and turned back to Germany before an attack could be launched against her, but on a third attempt bad weather came to her assistance and she managed to join *Tirpitz* and *Lützow* in Altenfjord.

The danger presented by this powerful force at a time when the British Home Fleet was depleted by the demands of the Mediterranean and of the Battle of the Atlantic, caused a temporary cancellation of further convoys. It was obvious to the British that quite exceptional measures would have to be taken to sink or damage the two big German ships before Arctic convoys could be resumed. The first attempt to achieve this was Operation Source, the celebrated attack by 'X-craft', midget submarines, on September 22, 1943. *Scharnhorst* had just moved her berth and escaped, but at 8:31 A.M. the Battlegroup (i.e. *Tirpitz*) signalled that a midget submarine had been destroyed inside the net barrage and that four prisoners had been taken. At 9:12 A.M. the destroyer *Erich Steinbrinck* reported a heavy explosion sixty metres to the port of *Tirpitz* and this was followed immediately by a second explosion causing the intake of a considerable quantity of water. At 10:48 A.M. *Tirpitz* requested the provision of a ship capable of carrying out electric welding. Photographic reconnaissance later showed that although *Scharnhorst* and *Lützow* had both shifted their berths, *Tirpitz* had not followed suit and that she was surrounded by oil. It was clear that serious damage had been done and this was confirmed when we learned from Special Intelligence that the troop transport *Monte Rosa* was bringing workmen to carry out repairs on the spot, which suggested that the battleship was incapable of moving south to Trondheim or Germany. Repairs in fact took six months. Not long after this *Lützow* required a refit and, despite accurate knowledge from Special Intelligence of her intentions, managed to get back to Germany successfully. The result, however, was that the once formidable Battlegroup had been reduced to a single effective ship, *Scharnhorst*.

We now come to an operation which was as traumatic for the Germans as PQ.17 had been for the British. Although it has been suggested* that the supplies of tanks and aircraft ferried to Murmansk at such cost in lives and ships to the British (and to the Germans) were in fact of little value to the Soviets, Hitler and his High Command regarded the interruption of the convoys as a matter of great importance. By the autumn of 1943 the German Army in Russia was facing disaster. The greatest tank battle of the war, Kursk, had been fought and lost and the prospects of holding back the Russians seemed increasingly remote each week. Dönitz was desperately anxious that the Navy should do anything within its power to help the hard-pressed soldiers. He had, earlier in the year, issued the following directive regarding the use of surface forces against the convoys to Russia: 'The conditions required for successful operations by surface ships against traffic in the Arctic will occur very seldom, since the enemy, to judge from past experience, will deploy for the protection—immediate and indirect—of

* See Alan Clark: *Barbarossa*. Hutchinson.

his convoys, forces of such strength as will undoubtedly be superior to that of our own forces. Nevertheless there may occur opportunities for attacking unescorted ships sailing independently.
Whenever such an opportunity occurs it must be seized with determination, but with due observance of tactical principles. It may
also sometimes be necessary to attack heavily escorted convoys
with all available forces; orders to deliver such an attack will be
given if the convoy in question is deemed to be of such value that
its destruction is of primary importance to the situation as a
whole'.†

The conditions and tactics for an attack by surface forces had
been the subject of some debate among the various authorities involved. The command structure was complicated. In supreme
command was Hitler himself in his remote headquarters at Ras-
tenburg. Although he interfered much less with the Navy than he
did with the Army, the restrictions he imposed on the use of the
big ships had their effect at all levels, and often caused German
Admirals to act with a caution, not to say timidity, which would
certainly have earned their British opposite numbers severe criticism. Dönitz, the Commander-in-Chief of the Navy, and the
Seekriegsleitung, or Naval Staff, were in Berlin, although Dönitz
sometimes visited Gruppe West in Paris or his old U-boat headquarters in Lorient. At Kiel was Gruppe Nord-Flotte, Admiral
Schneewind, the shore-based Commander-in-Chief of the Fleet
and the controlling authority for all operations in Norway. Under
Gruppe Nord came Admiral Northern Waters at Narvik, and
under him for some purposes but not all, was the man who would
actually have to carry out an attack, Admiral Kummetz, the Flag
Officer Battlegroup. In addition there was the Admiral Polar
Coast at Tromso.

Communications were not good. A message from the Battlegroup at sea to Admiral Northern Waters took, on average, one
hour to reach its destination: to Gruppe Nord-Flotte two hours
and to S.K.L. in Berlin three or even four hours. When, as was
often the case, the final decision lay with Dönitz, by the time all
the authorities had been consulted or had made their views
known, the situation might have altered completely. *Tirpitz*, still
undergoing repairs, was lying in a branch of Altenfjord, Kaafjord.

† See Dönitz: *Memoirs*. Weidenfeld & Nicolson.

She was connected to the land telex and telephone systems. *Scharnhorst*, on the other hand, was lying in another branch of Altenfjord, Langfjord, and communication with her could only be effected by boat or by W/T. This fact was to prove of great importance.

In November, Kummetz went on sick leave and his place was temporarily taken by the Rear-Admiral Destroyers, Admiral Bey. Both Bey and Schneewind seem to have been doubtful whether, during the dark days and almost perpetual gales of winter, favourable conditions for an operation by *Scharnhorst* were likely to arise. These conditions included far-reaching aerial reconnaissance to locate a convoy in good time and to establish with certainty that the Home Fleet would not be in a position to interfere either during or after the onslaught on the convoy, favourable weather which would permit the German destroyers, which although larger than their British counterparts were worse seaboats, to operate, and sufficient visibility to enable *Scharnhorst*, whose radar was inferior to that of her opponents, to make the best use of her superior armament. The G.A.F. were not enthusiastic. Their big Blohm and Voss flying boats were both vulnerable and valuable and their radar sets susceptible to icing; no guarantee of really effective reconnaissance could be given. Nevertheless none of those concerned ruled out the possibility of a sortie.

There were four alternatives. The destroyers could be sent out on their own; *Scharnhorst* could accompany them but only to provide distant cover against British cruisers; *Scharnhorst* and the destroyers could operate together; *Scharnhorst* could operate on her own. In every case tactical surprise and precise knowledge of the British dispositions were essential.

On December 19 and 20, Dönitz visited Hitler and secured his agreement to an operation against the next convoy that could be located, provided the chances of success seemed reasonable. *Scharnhorst* had been brought to six hours notice and Schneewind had issued operational orders under the code name Ostfront. The G.A.F. were asked to carry out intensive reconnaissance. The British convoys were now being sailed in two sections in order to reduce their size, and JW.55A was in fact at sea as these preliminary moves were being made. Under the cover of Force 1, consisting of the 8-inch cruiser *Norfolk* and the 6-inch cruisers *Belfast*, wearing the flag of Admiral Burnett, and *Sheffield*, it reached Murmansk on December 20. The Germans learned of its passage too late to organize any aggressive action. The Commander-in-Chief Home Fleet, now Admiral Sir Bruce Fraser, in the battleship *Duke of York* accompanied by the cruiser *Jamaica*, forming Force 2, had also gone right through to Murmansk to confer with the Russians. He quickly returned to Iceland to refuel in time for the second east-bound section JW.55B, which had, left Loch Ewe on the 20th. Burnett remained to provide cover for the west-bound RA.55A which was due to sail from Murmansk on December 23. When it met the east-bound convoy he would take over the latter's protection.

The Germans appear to have felt that, because of the lack of any activity against the first portion of the convoy, the British would be lulled into a false sense of security and would not anticipate an attack on JW.55B. Of course the mere presence of the German battlecruiser in Altenfjord meant that any convoy was liable to be attacked, but the need for Admiral Northern Waters to relay all instructions to *Scharnhorst* by W/T meant that we had more than just suspicions to go on. We were well aware from Special Intelligence that the U-boats and the G.A.F. were making strenuous efforts to locate the convoy and that *Scharnhorst* was at six hours' notice. Although none of the German signals affecting *Scharnhorst*'s last operation were decrypted completely currently, and many of them were not decrypted at all, B.P. managed to unbutton a sufficient number quickly enough for Denning in O.I.C. to keep Fraser and Burnett clearly informed of their opponent's intentions and moves.

Just after midnight on December 19/20, Denning was awakened in the Admiralty and shown four decrypts whose contents he immediately signalled to Fraser and Burnett. The first was from Admiral Northern Waters to *Scharnhorst*, originated at 6:23 P.M. on the 18th, bringing her from six to three hours' notice. The second, also made by Admiral Northern Waters at almost the same time, was to Air Officer Lofotens and read as follows: 'Urgently request air reconnaissance against convoy which is certainly to be assumed and against heavy group which is probably at sea. Battlegroup is at three hours' notice'. The third signal had also been originated on the evening of the 18th and was addressed to the Battlegroup, but its 151 groups were in Offizier (officer only) cipher and were not decrypted. The last intercept received in O.I.C. that night had been originated sixteen hours later than the other three. It was from Air Officer Lofotens reporting that reconnaissance on the 19th, 'had been cancelled owing to weather at operational aerodrome. One hour's notice ordered for one radar-fitted aircraft'.

These four signals clearly showed the Germans' interest in the convoy and the probability that an operation by *Scharnhorst* was being considered. During the course of the 20th we learned that reconnaissance for that day had also been cancelled, but an earlier signal of the 18th from Admiral Northern Waters in Offizier cipher, which on this occasion was decrypted, instructed the Battlegroup to take 'preparatory measures so that departure would be possible at any time'.

Nothing more was received from B.P. until 11 P.M. on the 21st when we learned that at four o'clock that afternoon Admiral Northern Waters had instructed *Scharnhorst* to revert to six hours' notice, presumably because of the failure of the U-boats and the G.A.F. to locate the convoy. This fact was signalled to Fraser and Burnett. For the next forty-eight hours no further decrypts were obtained, but between seven and ten o'clock on the evening of the 23rd, we learned that *Scharnhorst* had again been brought back to three hours' notice on the afternoon of the 22nd, and that on the 23rd she had once more been instructed to make preliminary preparations for departure.

Further decrypts were received later that night. They showed that the convoy had been sighted on the 22nd and had initially been reported as consisting of troop transports, but this mistake had been corrected after a couple of hours. Another interesting message was from Captain U-boats Norway to boats at sea, passing on a G.A.F. sighting of the convoy on the 23rd and adding that 'it is possible that there is a strong battlegroup at sea'. Admiral Northern Waters informed *Scharnhorst* that the U-boats were not in contact with the convoy. The sighting reports of course explained why *Scharnhorst* had been brought back to three hours' notice and confirmed Denning's suspicions that a sortie was imminent.

The position during the forenoon of the 24th was roughly as

follows. The east-bound JW.55B was south-west of Bear Island and only some 400 miles from Altenfjord. It was being shadowed by aircraft. The west-bound RA.55A was also approaching, but was considerably further north and had not been detected at all by the enemy. Burnett's Force 1, returning from Murmansk, was some distance away to the eastward, while Fraser's Force 2, coming up from Iceland, was an even greater distance away to the south-west. Fraser feared that if *Scharnhorst* were to sail at this moment she might reach JW.55B before either Force 1 or Force 2 could intervene. He therefore took the unusual, but, as it proved, very sensible step of breaking wireless silence to instruct the convoy to reverse course for three hours to narrow the gap between him and it.

His signal was nevertheless accurately D/F'd by three German stations in the Bight and by one at Kirkenes. For some reason (was it wishful thinking?) the German Naval Staff elected to treat the fix as unreliable and, although conceding that it might have been originated by a heavy British covering force giving distant cover in the normal manner, preferred to believe that it was from a position much farther north, possibly from a straggler from the convoy. Captain U-boats, who was temporarily doubling as Admiral Northern Waters, seems to have been less complacent. On the previous day he had warned his U-boats that 'It is possible there is a strong battlegroup at a distance from this convoy', and just before midnight on the 24th Air Officer Lofotens signalled his intentions for reconnaissance on Christmas Day. They included the despatch of two large BV 138 flying boats on 'probing reconnaissance against what is thought to be a battlegroup approaching from the south-west which has been D/F'd'. Subsequently this reconnaissance was increased to three flying boats, one of which was fitted with radar, a considerable effort which would not have been employed unless the threat from the Home Fleet was being taken rather more seriously in the North than it was in Kiel and Berlin. These signals reached O.I.C. within three hours of their transmission and were promptly passed on to Fraser and Burnett, who may well have received them as soon as the Naval Staff in Berlin.

By Christmas Day the German attitude seems to have been confused. Bey and Admiral Northern Waters considered that none of the conditions for a satisfactory sortie prevailed, and that the most that could be undertaken would be an operation by the destroyers on their own. Schneewind and Gruppe Nord-Flotte on the other hand felt that if the Air Force had not established the presence of a heavy covering force at sea during the course of the day, *Scharnhorst* and the destroyers should sail that evening so as to fall upon the convoy at the first glimmer of daylight next morning. It is curious that whereas, during PQ.17, Sir Dudley Pound would not accept Denning's negative evidence that *Tirpitz* was not at sea, Schneewind chose to interpret the much weaker, but equally negative evidence of the absence of any sighting as proof that the Home Fleet was not in a position to intervene.

On the morning of Christmas Day, JW.55B crossed the patrol line of the Eisenbart group of U-boats south-west of Bear Island. One boat managed to get off a report and to maintain contact for a few hours. As a result the rest of the group were ordered to operate against the convoy and *Scharnhorst* was brought to one hour's notice. This signal was not decrypted until the following day, by which time it had been overtaken by events.

So far as the Germans were concerned, everything was now ready and all that was required was final approval from Dönitz. The Gross Admiral had been visiting Gruppe West and was now on his way back to Berlin. The Naval Staff felt that the situation was developing favourably, and although a final decision was left till Dönitz should arrive, the executive order 'Ostfront 5 P.M.' was issued. This went out from Gruppe Nord-Flotte at 2:33 P.M. and was passed on to *Scharnhorst* by Admiral Northern Waters at 3:27 P.M. On his arrival in Berlin Dönitz recounts that he judged the situation as follows:

'A convoy, carrying war material to Russia and protected by a cruiser escort which was no match for our battleship, was sailing through an area within easy reach of our Battlegroup. Its position, course and speed were known. Because of ice in the vicinity of Bear Island which prevented evasive action and the superior speed of the German ships, it could not hope to avoid our attack.

'Our reconnaissance had not discovered the presence of any heavy enemy formation, though that, of course, did not mean that no such force was at sea. But if it were it must have been a long way from the convoy, and the *Scharnhorst* seemed to have every chance of delivering a rapid and successful attack.

'The very considerable amount of war material that a convoy of some twenty ships could carry would add materially to Russia's offensive strength, and that was a thing which our Battlegroup had to prevent whenever a reasonable opportunity occurred to do so. In my opinion, as in that of the Admiral Commanding the Fleet, here was a splendid chance for *Scharnhorst.*'‡

At 7:25 P.M., Dönitz sent the following signal to Bey, who was now proceeding out of Altenfjord in execution of the Ostfront order:

1. Enemy attempting to frustrate the heroic struggle of our Eastern Armies by sending valuable convoy of supplies and arms to the Russians.

2. *Scharnhorst* and destroyers will attack convoy.

3. Tactical situation must be used skilfully and boldly. Engagement not to be broken off with only partial success achieved. Every advantage must be exploited. Best chance lies in *Scharnhorst*'s superior fire power. Therefore endeavour to deploy her. Destroyers to operate as seems suitable.

4. Disengage at your discretion but without question if heavy forces encountered.

5. Inform crew accordingly. I rely on your offensive spirit!'*

In the meantime the weather in North Norway had been deteriorating and the G.A.F. feared that reconnaissance would not be possible on the following day. Admiral Northern Waters felt that in these circumstances and with no information of the whereabouts of the Home Fleet, the operation should be abandoned and telephoned Schneewind to say so. Schneewind eventually spoke to Dönitz but the latter considered that the decision whether or in what manner to operate should be left to the Flag Officer Battlegroup, whom, he felt, had been given wide discretion. He does not seem to have realized the effect that his signal of 7:25 P.M. must have had on Bey. The tragedy was that Bey's departure had been delayed by the necessity of transferring from *Tirpitz*, where he had remained until the last minute so as to be in the closest possible touch by landline with his shore command, to *Scharnhorst*. The trip from Kaafjord to Langfjord in the motor minesweeper

‡ See Dönitz: *Memoirs*. Weidenfeld & Nicolson.
* This signal was not decrypted by B.P.

R.121 took a good two hours. There would have been plenty of time to call the whole thing off.

At 9:16 P.M. when he was in the outer fjords and beginning to feel the full effects of the weather, Bey signalled to Schneewind, 'Reference your suggestion Para 6c. In the operational area probably south-west force 6 to 8. Offensive action by destroyers greatly impaired. Speed Restriction'. The reference was to the paragraph in his operational orders covering the use of the destroyers on their own, and it seems likely that Bey was giving a broad hint that in his opinion the sortie should be cancelled. His signal took a long time to reach Gruppe Nord-Flotte and even longer S.K.L. in Berlin. Both authorities again seem to have felt that previous signals and instructions left Bey with full discretion to act as he saw fit and made no reply. Bey cannot have taken the same view, for he held on North to intercept the convoy. Early next morning he detached his destroyers to search for it. They lost touch with him and took no effective part in the subsequent action. *Scharnhorst* was on her own.

Had the British been as unaware of *Scharnhorst*'s movements as the Germans supposed, things might have turned out differently, although whether Bey could have successfully attacked the convoy with its strong close escort of destroyers and regained the safety of the Norwegian coast without being intercepted by either of the British covering forces is open to doubt. In the event there was no question of surprise.

Just before 9 P.M. on Christmas Day, O.I.C. received an intercept, timed at eleven fifty-eight that morning. It read as follows: 'From Battlegroup to R.121. Emergency. Proceed to *Scharnhorst* in Langfjord. Further orders there'. The exact purport of the message was not clear, but it suggested that something was underway that might well be connected with the battlecruiser's imminent departure, and Fraser and Burnett were promptly alerted. Just after midnight two more decrypts were received which turned this suspicion into a certainty. The first was from Air Officer Lofotens, timed 4:21 P.M. on the 25th, reporting that the convoy had again been sighted at 2:13 P.M. The second, timed 3:27 P.M. on the 25th, was the Most Immediate signal from Admiral Northern Waters to Battlegroup. It read 'Ostfront 5 P.M.' This could only be the executive order to sail in accordance with previous instructions. Hinsley at B.P. must have felt that the operation was doomed, because he telephoned an addition to the telex to Denning, 'This will in future be referred to as Epilepsy'. Once more an Ultra signal was made to the two British admirals, but when, just over an hour later, O.I.C. received *Scharnhorst*'s signal, timed 5:15 P.M. on the 25th, informing the patrol boat V.5903 that she would 'pass outward-bound as from 6 P.M.', it was not felt that it would add anything to the information already in their possession. Denning did subsequently make a mental calculation as to when the British and German forces would have contact with each other, and was rather disappointed when he proved to be twenty minutes out in his reckoning. At 3:19 A.M. on the 26th, one last signal was made by the Admiralty. It was addressed to all authorities concerned including those such as the Senior Officer of JW.55B's escort to whom, for security reasons, the previous Ultra signals could not be sent. It stated baldly that the Admiralty appreciated that *Scharnhorst* was at sea. During the course of Boxing Day another dozen German signals were decrypted, but fascinating though some of them were, none was received in time to be of operational value. O.I.C. had already played its part. It was now up to those at sea.

Admiral Fraser was anxious to be as certain about the position of his own forces as he was about that of the enemy. He again broke silence to order Burnett and the convoy to report their positions. When they had done so he instructed Burnett to close the convoy and the latter to alter to a more northerly course away from the approaching Germans. These signals were also D/F'd by the Germans and should, at the eleventh hour, have alerted them to the danger into which *Scharnhorst* was heading.

Just before 9 A.M. on Boxing Day, Burnett's flagship picked up the German battlecruiser on her radar and twenty-five minutes later he opened fire. *Scharnhorst* was taken completely by surprise, hit and turned away. Burnett, anticipating that Bey would circle round to attack the convoy from a different direction, did not follow. Soon after noon he was proved right and a second brief engagement took place. This time *Norfolk* was hit, but Bey again turned away to the south for the safety of the Norwegian coast. His course actually took him nearer to Fraser, who was being kept fully informed by Burnett, now shadowing the German battlecruiser. At 4:17 P.M., *Duke of York* gained radar contact with the enemy and at 4:50 opened fire. Once again *Scharnhorst* was taken by surprise. At 4:56 she signalled to Gruppe Nord-Flotte: 'Most Immediate. 72 degrees 39 North, 26 degrees 10 East. Heavy battleship. Am in action'. Bey evidently mistook some of Burnett's cruisers for battleships because at 5:22 he signalled that he was 'surrounded by heavy units'. The situation soon became hopeless. At 6:02 a signal went off to 'Admiral of the Fleet and Commander-in-Chief. *Scharnhorst* will ever reign supreme', and this was followed at 6:25 by one to Hitler, 'We shall fight to the last shell'. *Scharnhorst*'s last signal was made at 7:25, stating that she was steering for Tanafjord at 20 knots. It seems unlikely that she was still capable of this speed because, shortly before she had reported it as only 15 knots, and within another twenty minutes, after repeated hits from *Duke of York*'s 14-inch guns, from the lesser armament of the cruisers and from eleven of the many torpedoes fired at her by the British destroyers, she sank. Despite every effort only thirty-six survivors could be rescued.

The loss of *Scharnhorst* continues to exercise the attention of German historians to this day. Admiral Bey and all his officers went down with their ship so that one side of the story is lacking. Bey's tactical handling of the situation has been much criticized but a cardinal error attributed to him was the despatch of the signal about the destroyers just as he was leaving the fjords. It has hitherto been supposed on the German side that this signal was accurately D/F'd by the British and betrayed the fact *Scharnhorst* was at sea. This is not so. W/T reception was often very unreliable from North Norway and it was too much to expect that a sufficiently accurate fix could be obtained to show that *Scharnhorst* had moved fifteen or so miles from her berth towards the open sea. Bey's signal was indeed intercepted but it was not decrypted until nine o'clock the next morning. By that time we had of course learned exactly what was happening from Admiral Northern Waters' Ostfront signal.

The question which ought to be asked is why Bey was sent to sea at all or why he was not recalled. Both he and Admiral Northern Waters considered that the requirements for a successful operation had not been met, in particular because of the failure to locate the Home Fleet, whose presence at sea, and in an area po-

tentially dangerous, they strongly suspected. Why was more attention not paid to the accurate D/F fix of Fraser's signal on the
24th? Why, despite the fact that weather conditions had prevented the extensive reconnaissance called for and that as late as
the 25th the Air Officer Lofotens was still searching for 'the battlegroup thought to be approaching from the south-west', was his
lack of success ignored? It was not until just after midnight of the
25th/26th that the G.A.F. reported, 'within radius of 80 kms no
remote group located', and this was not a large area. This does not
now seem to justify the statement that if a heavy group was at sea,
it must have been a considerable distance from the convoy. On
December 26, the B.Dienst was monitoring traffic between Burnett and Fraser and it appears that Force 2 was actually sighted
that morning, but the fact that the group of ships was seen to
contain one large vessel was not believed and was suppressed.

Of course the Germans could not be expected to realise that
their signals were being decrypted, but the almost casual disregard
of the negative fact that the G.A.F. reconnaissance was far from
comprehensive, and of the positive intelligence provided by their
D/F and Y stations is remarkable.

A complicated chain of command, operational instructions
which seem to have been capable of more than one interpretation,
and delays in communications all led to German mistakes, but
one cannot help having the feeling that Dönitz's burning desire to
relieve the pressure on the German Army in Russia blinded him
to the true facts of the situation, and prevented him from drawing
the right conclusions from the intelligence actually available to
him, in just the same way that Pound's preconceived ideas during
the PQ.17 operation made him deaf to Denning's arguments.

The loss of *Scharnhorst* transformed the strategic situation, and
with hindsight everything that subsequently occurred in North
Norway seems something of an anti-climax. This was not the impression that those concerned on the British side had at the time.
Tirpitz was being repaired in Altenfjord. Should she again become
operational, her destruction would certainly not be accomplished
by one British battleship and a few cruisers and destroyers. In
March 1944 we learned from Special Intelligence that the battleship had carried out trials on March 15 and 16, and four days later
Denning warned the Naval Staff that '*Tirpitz* is unlikely to pro-

ceed to sea for operations against a well-escorted convoy but might do so if she was sure that she had no heavy ships or aircraft carriers to contend with. It is known that the enemy attach great importance to intercepting supplies to Russia and this may influence them to take more than normal risks with *Tirpitz* in her present condition. It should therefore be assumed that *Tirpitz* may be operationally effective and battleship cover for JW.58 should be given'.

It is open to doubt now whether Dönitz, after the fiasco with *Scharnhorst,* would have risked Germany's last battleship in this way, or whether Hitler would have permitted him to do so if it had come to the crunch, but as long as *Tirpitz* was afloat and capable of steaming the possibility could not be ignored.

When JW.58 sailed on March 27, it had been decided that as soon as the convoy was out of danger from surface attack, a strong attack should be launched by the Fleet Air Arm on *Tirpitz* from *Victorious, Furious* and no fewer than four escort carriers. Air reconnaissance by a special R.A.F. unit sent to Russia for the purpose had been arranged, and photographs were flown to England by a Catalina.

We had learned from decrypts that *Tirpitz* was due to carry out full-speed trials on April 1, but shortly before noon on that day further intercepts disclosed that this had been postponed for forty-eight hours. Sir Bruce Fraser and his second-in-command, Admiral Sir Henry Moore, who was to be in charge of the air strike, were immediately informed by Ultra signal. It was obvious that not only was there no danger of surface attack on the convoy but that the battleship's trials might present a good opportunity for the airmen, since when at anchor *Tirpitz* was well protected by torpedo nets and smoke screens. Sir Bruce Fraser therefore decided to advance the date of the planned attack by twenty-four hours to the 3rd. Just before the first wave of aircraft took off from the carriers, Denning was able to send Moore another Ultra informing him that *Tirpitz* would leave her anchorage at five-thirty that morning. She was caught just as the torpedo nets were being opened and the battleship was weighing anchor when all the enemy's attention was concentrated on these operations. The first wave of aircraft were on her before the smoke screen could become effective and in two attacks at least fourteen hits were secured. Unfortunately the heaviest bombs which the carrier-borne aircraft could take seem to have been discharged from too low a height, and therefore did not do as much damage as had been hoped. O.I.C. thought *Tirpitz* would be out of action for six months, but in fact the Germans were able to restore her to a partial degree of operational effectiveness in half that time.

Various other attempts were made by the Fleet Air Arm to dispose of *Tirpitz* during the next four months, but it finally became apparent that their largest bombs were not heavy enough and that only the 12,000-pound blockbusters of the R.A.F.'s Lancasters could be expected to sink her. A force of Lancasters was therefore flown to Russia in September and on the return trip on the 15th, despite fighter defences and a smoke screen, secured one hit and two near misses. We had confirmation of this four days later in a message to all German military attachés, and this time repairs could not be carried out on the spot and *Tirpitz* had to be moved south to Tromsoe. She was consequently within range of operations from this country and on November 12, thirty-eight Lancasters caught her before the smoke screen was functioning properly and when, for some reason, she was without fighter protection. Three hits and two near misses with the giant bombs caused the battleship to turn turtle so that her superstructure rested on the bottom. One thousand of her crew were lost.

O.I.C. had not been able to contribute very much to the R.A.F.'s triumph, but as soon as Denning learned of the success of the attack from the report in flight of a special reconnaissance aircraft, he asked Hinsley at B.P. to look for an emergency German message at the appropriate time. Sure enough he found one timed 9:46 A.M. Accurately guessing the contents, it did not take the cryptanalysts long to find the cipher settings for the day. The signal was from Naval Communications Officer Tromsoe reporting that *Tirpitz* had blown up and capsized. The threat from the last of the big German ships had been finally removed.

14

Denning's Damned Black Magic

ALTHOUGH, AFTER the sinking of *Bismarck* and the escape of the battlecruisers up Channel, the Germans had virtually abandoned attempts to use their regular warships for the guerre de course, they continued for some time to send out disguised merchant raiders. These ships pursued the same tactics as before and remained extremely elusive. We never succeeded in breaking Special Cipher 100 or Tibet, the ciphers used by the raiders, their supply ships and the blockade-runners, while the 'Black Out' in Triton throughout most of 1942 prevented us from gaining the knowledge of the whereabouts of raiders through signals to U-boats which had led to the sinking of *Atlantis* and *Python* in 1941.* The entry of the United States and Brazil into the war did begin to make the South Atlantic a more dangerous area for enemy surface ships, but the Allies still lacked sufficiently precise information about their movements to achieve more than chance interceptions by the limited number of ships and aircraft then available.

At the end of 1941, Raider E, *Thor*, which had been refitting and exercising in the Baltic since her very successful first cruise, sailed for a second operation. She was followed in 1942 by two new raiders, H, *Michel*, in March, and J, *Stier*, in May. All three

* See Chapter 6.

ships broke out down Channel, making short passages from port to port at night and under heavy escort. Their movements did not go unnoticed and all were attacked but unfortunately without success. After brief stops in southern Biscay ports they managed to gain the Atlantic, where they were able to find victims among the independently routed merchant ships. *Stier,* however, both literally and figuratively caught a Yankee† when she encountered the Liberty ship *Stephen Hopkins* in the South Atlantic on September 24, 1942. The American ship opened fire at once with her single 4-inch gun and so damaged the raider that she sank. Unfortunately, *Stephen Hopkins* also sank and only fifteen of her crew survived. *Michel* and *Thor* achieved a certain amount of success during the year, but in November *Thor* was destroyed in Yokohama harbour when the supply ship *Uckermarck,* alongside which she was lying, blew up while her fuel tanks were being cleaned. *Michel* survived for another eleven months, but she too met her end near Yokohama when she was torpedoed by the U.S. submarine *Tarpon* on October 17, 1943. We quickly learned of the identity of *Tarpon*'s victim because we were now decrypting cipher Bertok, that used between the Naval Attaché in Tokyo and O.K.M.

Denning's raider expert, Lieutenant Hutchinson, R.N.V.R., could do little more than his predecessor to forecast the movements of the enemy ships once they were at sea, although he was able to accumulate even more detailed information about their characteristics and tactics, and to issue from time to time further Raider Supplements to the Weekly Intelligence Report. The best opportunity for locating and attacking the raiders and blockade-runners occurred, of course, while they were outward- or homeward-bound in the Bay of Biscay or English Channel, and after earlier failures the British scored a success here in October 1942. The records of this operation are of interest in the way they reveal the interaction of various sources of intelligence: no single source gave, on its own, a complete picture, but in combination and with intelligent deductions by officers with deep background experience of German procedures, they revealed the enemy's plans clearly enough.

† 'The equivalent of "to catch a Tartar" before Yankee lost its derogatory implication.' Brewer's Dictionary of Phrases and Fable.

Raider B, *Komet*, which with Soviet help had reached the Pacific via the north of Russia in 1940, had returned to Germany in November 1941. She then carried out an extensive refit, but in June and July 1942, Denning's Baltic expert, Clements, noticed from Special Intelligence that she was working up in the Baltic. During this period she was, of course, using cipher Hydra, the Home Waters cipher, not Cipher 100 which would only come into force once she had started her cruise in the Atlantic. When she returned to Kiel we identified her by photographic reconnaissance and were able to reconstruct her appearance accurately. This was, however, the only photograph of her to be secured, and despite all Hutchinson's and Clements' care, she might well have appeared unexpectedly in the Channel had it not been for Special Intelligence. As it was, we were able to follow her move from Kiel to Swinemunde in the second half of September, and to detect the obvious signs that she was again about to sail on a war cruise. On September 29, Hutchinson notified all home and overseas commands by Ultra signals of her impending departure. From previous experience he anticipated that she would be given strong escort in the Channel and plans were made for her interception by M.T.B.s and destroyers from Portsmouth and Plymouth. On October 2 Fenley, the expert on the Bight and the Channel, learned that *Komet* was due at Bremen on the 4th, and then on the 7th that patrol vessels would be stationed off Flushing that night to assist the navigation of an unnamed vessel, a procedure often used when important ships were moving in these difficult waters at night. It was assumed that this must be *Komet* and the authorities concerned were immediately warned that she was making for Flushing. Fog and delays in decrypting then intervened and the raider managed to reach first Dunkirk and then, early on the 13th, Le Havre. We had previously noted, both from photographic reconnaissance and Special Intelligence, the transfer of three small destroyers from Brest to Cherbourg and from that port to Le Havre. *Komet*'s next move round Cape Barfleur to Cherbourg was almost certainly planned for the night of the thirteenth, so that afternoon the Commander-in-Chief Portsmouth gave orders for Operation Bowery, involving nine destroyers and twelve M.T.B.s, to be put into effect. Coastal Command flew special patrols and just before 10 P.M. one of them reported the raider in Seine Bay on a course of 270 degrees. The destroyers and M.T.B.s caught her off Cap de la Hague just after midnight, sinking her and damaging all her escorts. The British forces suffered only two minor casualties. It had been an extremely successful operation made possible by accurate intelligence and sound appreciations based on thorough knowledge of German procedures.

The Germans made one last effort to send out another raider. The intelligence pattern was much the same. Hutchinson and Clements had been following a new raider, K, *Togo*, in the Baltic, and on January 23, 1943, Hutchinson issued a warning that this ship would soon attempt a break-out. Four days later we observed that special preparations were being organized to sweep an important unit through our recently laid minefields off Brest, but it was not until the first week in February that Special Intelligence revealed that *Togo* was approaching Ostend and then that she had run aground off Dunkirk. She got off but was bombed and damaged by R.A.F. Whirlwinds off Boulogne. The damage was sufficient to necessitate her return to Germany. Unfortunately further attacks on her were beaten off, but, although it was a disappointment that she was not sunk, at least she was prevented from gaining the Atlantic. It was a significant change from 1940 and 1941 when warships and raiders had reached the sealanes without being detected at all, or even from the beginning of 1942 when *Thor*, *Michel* and *Stier* had forced their way down Channel despite British efforts to stop them. Now only *Michel* was left at sea to operate in the Pacific for a few more months. The raider war was practically over.

Raiders were not of course the only German surface ships at large. Considerable efforts were made to break the blockade and run valuable cargoes between France and the Far East. This occurred in three phases: from April 1941 to May 1942; from August 1942 to April 1943; and from November 1943 to January 1944. In the first period sixteen ships sailed from the Far East, of which twelve arrived in Europe while all six which left Europe managed to reach their destinations. Neither O.I.C. nor the British air and sea patrols had much success. We did from time to time get warning of departures, but the information was often too late to permit effective counter-action to be taken and in general, even when timely intelligence was available, there were no ships or aircraft available to act upon it. In the second phase, however, results were considerably better. Fifteen ships attempted to sail from the Far East but seven were sunk, four turned back and only four reached Europe. In the reverse direction seventeen ships sailed, three turned back, four were sunk and ten arrived safely. As was the case with the raiders, the best opportunities occurred when the blockade-runners were leaving or approaching Biscay ports. There was no information from signals to or from the blockade-runners themselves, but instructions to patrol craft, destroyers and, after December 1942, to U-boats employed as escorts, often gave us a clue to an imminent arrival or departure.‡ One blockade-runner, *Regensburg*, was intercepted on March 30, 1943, in the Denmark Strait because U-boats on passage in the area had been warned of her approach. It was ironical that the very efforts which the Germans made to give their ships protection during the most dangerous parts of their voyages caused their destruction.

By September 1943 the enemy was ready to renew his attempts to beat the blockade, and seven ships were known to be waiting in Biscay ports while five were available in the Far East. One outward-bound ship was bombed and sunk off Lorient in December, but an inward-bound one managed to reach France despite air attacks on her. We were however made aware by Special Intelligence that the Germans were sending out a particularly strong escort of destroyers to meet a second ship, *Alsterufer*. She was attacked and set on fire by a Coastal Command aircraft, while the Commander-in-Chief Portsmouth sailed two cruisers, *Glasgow* and the Canadian-manned *Enterprise* to deal with the ten German destroyers which had put to sea to bring the blockade-runner in. In a running fight three of the enemy warships were sunk, but the remainder managed to escape. The cruisers at first thought they had inflicted greater casualties than was in fact the case, and when Denning reported to the First Sea Lord, by now Sir Andrew Cunningham, that Special Intelligence had disclosed that seven had survived, he retorted fiercely that he preferred the reports of his captains to Denning's 'damned black magic'. He had however

‡ Much information, although not always of a very precise nature, was gleaned from signals to U-boats opening or closing various large areas in the North and South Atlantic to unrestricted attack on independent ships, and also from general information contained in Japanese diplomatic wireless traffic between Berlin and Tokyo.

to accept the evidence supplied next day by photographic recon-naissance.

Early in 1944 three more homeward-bound ships were inter-cepted in the South Atlantic by American warships, and Dönitz decided to abandon any further attempts at blockade-running with surface ships. The British control over the Bay of Biscay and the American watch over the South Atlantic were now too strong, but it is doubtful if the results would have been quite so disas-trous for the Germans had it not been for Special Intelligence. U-boats, some of them specially modified, had to be detailed to take over blockade breaking.

The Germans were not the only would-be blockade-runners. In January 1941 five Norwegian merchantmen had managed to break out of Gothenberg in Sweden and reach Britain. However, when ten more ships tried to repeat the exploit in April 1942, the Ger-mans were more alert, and despite our much greater knowledge of the dispositions of their sea and air patrols, only two merchant-men got through. No further attempts were made for over a year, but by the autumn of 1943 the Swedes were taking a much more benevolent line towards the Allies and the organizer of the earlier operations, Commander Sir George Binney, R.N.V.R., decided that regular runs between Hull and Gothenberg could be undertaken by fast small craft. Five motor gunboats were dis-armed and converted into miniature merchantmen. Flying the Red Ensign they brought back 348 tons of ball bearings and other valuable Swedish products in nine round trips for the loss of only one of their number.

These operations, which were given the code name Moonshine, had a distinct touch of James Bond about them. It was not en-tirely surprising since the first plans were discussed by Binney with Ian Fleming and Denning over dinner in Binney's London flat. Success depended greatly on the supply of accurate meteorological forecasts and of absolutely up-to-date intelligence about the dispo-sitions of the German sea patrols and convoys in the Skagerrak. Thanks to Hydra, Denning was usually able to provide the latter, and several operations were cancelled at the last moment or even after the boats had already sailed because of O.I.C.'s warnings about enemy movements. The occasional appearance of a bottle of Swedish Schnapps in O.I.C. testified to the gratitude of the masters of the blockade-runners for a trip successfully completed.

In the same way the landing of agents by sea in Norway and in France, and indeed all the operations of Allied fast coastal forces, depended greatly on the information supplied by Denning and his experts. Accurate information about the movements of enemy patrol craft and convoys and the swept channels which they used, was not gleaned solely from Special Intelligence. Denning's appreciations were based on the continuous and patient evaluation of dozens of different scraps of information which trickled into O.I.C. over the weeks and months. Photographic reconnaissance, visual reports from Bomber and Coastal Command pilots, signals from M.T.B.s and destroyers, the occasional clue from an agent, a captured chart or the interrogation of a prisoner of war, all these were the pieces from which a mosaic was built up. It stretched from the North Cape down through the Norwegian Leads to the Skagerrak and through the Belts into the Baltic; along the coast of the Low Countries and through the English Channel to Ushant and from there to the Franco-Spanish frontier. Patterns of behaviour were gradually established so that the movements of a German destroyer, the passage of a convoy here or of patrol craft there, minesweeping at this point or air activity at that, would cause alarm bells to ring in the minds of Denning's experts, to be followed by swift action at Bomber, Fighter or Coastal Commands or at Rosyth, the Nore, Dover or Portsmouth.

Few records of this side of O.I.C.'s work have survived. A great deal of the information was passed on the green scrambler telephone or by teleprinter to the Chiefs of Staff or S.O.(I.)s at the naval commands from Scapa down to Plymouth or to the Naval Liaison officers at Bomber and Coastal Commands. As our resources increased, attacks on the enemy's coastal shipping could be laid on at short notice, or for that matter cancelled if weather conditions became unsuitable or the German plans were suddenly changed. For the raid on St. Nazaire, however, as with all other operations requiring advance planning, intelligence had to be supplied at an earlier stage. It consisted of an accurate assessment of the German naval forces likely to be encountered, detailed information about the swept channels and minefields and, at the last minute, the correct recognition signals for the day for a German patrol vessel. By great good fortune this ship was at sea on the night of the raid and Commander Ryder's use of her reply to the challenge that was flashed at him from the shore gained a few precious extra minutes during the dangerous approach through the estuary.

O.I.C. was less successful at the time of the Dieppe operation, when an encounter with an unexpected convoy alerted the German defenders before H hour. Nor could good intelligence guarantee success. At the end of October 1943, for example, O.I.C. warned the Commander-in-Chief Plymouth that a blockade-runner, *Münsterland*, was moving from the Bay of Biscay up Channel. During her passage from Brest to Cherbourg she was due to be escorted by five German destroyers, and the Commander-in-Chief sailed the light cruiser *Charybdis* with two fleet and six Hunt class destroyers to intercept her. On this occasion the victory went to the enemy. *Charybdis* was sunk.

Despite these occasional reverses the balance had now swung definitely in favour of the British, and German movements in the Bay of Biscay and the Channel were increasingly restricted although they were never halted. British successes were due quite as much to the growth in offensive power, both sea and air, as to good intelligence. Nevertheless the fact that reliable information could be supplied undoubtedly influenced the authorities to provide the necessary forces, and each time that O.I.C.'s tips were proved accurate confidence in and the demand for them increased.

One might have thought that this would have been a poor time to change the bowling, but the idea that any regular naval officer might actually be serving his country to better effect in the Intelligence Division rather than at sea had still not gained acceptance in certain quarters. Godfrey had been a believer in the suitability of Paymasters for intelligence duties and had been largely responsible for securing the appointment of Clements, Fenley and Harrison.* What he does not seem to have foreseen was that the Paymaster Director General would continue to regard service in N.I.D. as a handicap rather than a qualification for advancement in the Paymaster branch, and that any individual who did not re-

* Godfrey may have had to appeal to the V.C.N.S., Sir Tom Phillips. Phillips personally instructed a most reluctant Paymaster Director-General to supply three suitable officers.

turn to the fold after a maximum of two years would be regarded as beyond redemption. Denning had in fact served out his allotted span by the time war was declared, and by the end of 1942 the P.D.G. was, to put it mildly, becoming extremely restless. He demanded that Denning must either apply for a normal Paymaster's posting or face the consequences so far as his career was concerned. In a private note to Clayton in June 1943, Denning wrote that he did not 'feel that it is altogether fair that I should be called upon to either:

(1) Apply for a fresh appointment and so abandon a very specialised job in the Operational Intelligence Centre

or

(2) Apply to remain in my present appointment, and so abandon all prospects for further employment.

I am, and always have been entirely ready to serve as and where required: and continue to contemplate service in the Royal Navy as my future career.

'If, therefore, it is decided that it is in the best interests of the Service that I should continue in my present appointment, I submit that this be placed on record together with the above indication, that such continuation is accepted willingly for the good of the Service and not as an escape from sea service.

'Should the importance of my present employment not be considered to justify its further extension, personal consideration of future prospects and promotion would naturally assume greater importance.'†

Clayton was quite clear that Denning's greatest contribution to the war effort would be made in O.I.C. and took the matter up with the D.N.I., Commodore Rushbrooke, who fully shared this view and finally got the question referred to the First Sea Lord himself. A minute came back in Pound's own handwriting in his distinctive green ink: 'This officer is to remain in his present appointment until the conclusion of hostilities in Europe.' Despite his inability to accept Denning's appreciation at the time of PQ.17, Pound recognized the enormous value of his work, but the

† Denning Papers.

decision none the less gave no guarantee that it would not count against Denning in his future career.‡

Clements, Fenley and Harrison, on the other hand, were more junior officers and, invaluable as their work had been, their retention in O.I.C. could not be said to be as vital as was the case with Denning: if Paymasters were not to be allowed to specialize in intelligence, their own interests obviously required to an even greater extent that they should return to the normal duties of their branch. They were all posted to sea in the last quarter of 1943. These episodes do, nevertheless, highlight the weaknesses of a system which demanded the removal of such highly experienced and able officers at a time when the Allies were going over to the offensive and when the invasion of Normandy was less than nine months ahead.

Fortunately replacements were available. Lieutenant Bisset, R.N.V.R., one of Denning's watchkeepers, took over Harrison's work on Norwegian waters and a young archaeology graduate, Margaret Stewart, relieved Fenley while another girl, Ena Shiers, took over Baltic Intelligence. Although a good number of girls, both permanent and temporary members of the Civil Service, had been doing essential jobs in O.I.C. from the outset, they were mostly engaged on conventional women's duties, as secretaries, teleprinter operators, confidential filing clerks, 'secret ladies' scrutinizing and distributing Special Intelligence messages and so on. Margaret Stewart and Ena Shiers were the first to take over duties in O.I.C. from a naval officer and perform what had hitherto been regarded as a man's job. They did not have time for a lengthy apprenticeship. They had to learn 'on the job', and with no naval training, they at first found it all very confusing. Of course they soon picked up the tricks of the trade, but Margaret Stewart always felt that she was up against a certain amount of male prejudice. It might have been easier for her if she had been a W.R.N.S. officer, but owing to the opposition of the Civil Service Union, W.R.N.S. were for a long time not permitted to serve in

‡ To be fair, it does not seem to have done so. Denning subsequently became Director of Naval Intelligence and was appointed, on the formation of the Ministry of Defence, the first Deputy Chief of the Defence Staff (I.) in the rank of Vice-Admiral. It will, however, be seen from Lord Mountbatten's Foreword that he was personally responsible for Denning's appointments to these important posts.

the Admiralty, which despite its operational role was a 'Civil' not a 'Naval' establishment. At any rate the S.O.(I.) Portsmouth was considerably astonished to find himself being briefed over the telephone by a girl, and a civilian at that. He very soon saw that the service which he was getting was in no way inferior to that which he had been accustomed to receive from Fenley.

By May 1944, the surface ships of the German Navy were incapable of interfering to any significant extent with the Allied invasion of Europe. *Scharnhorst* had been sunk, *Tirpitz* was out of action in Altenfjord, *Gneisenau* had been so damaged by the R.A.F. that she and the heavy cruiser *Hipper* had been paid off. *Prinz Eugen*, and the two pocket battleships, *Scheer* and *Lützow*, were either still refitting or engaged in supporting the German Army in the eastern Baltic. Only five large and one small destroyer remained in Biscay ports, while in the Channel there were but five small destroyers and thirty-four E-boats. The effectiveness of the latter was now much reduced by the growth of our own Coastal Forces and by our dominance of the air. Apart from his U-boats,* Dönitz's contribution to the defence of the Atlantic Wall had to be confined to the provision of coastal artillery and the laying and maintenance of large minefields.

It was not therefore possible for O.I.C. to make the same sort of spectacular contribution to the success of D Day which it had been able to do to the various surface ship actions of the preceding three years. Nevertheless, if less obvious, O.I.C.'s work was every bit as valuable.

O.I.C. was involved throughout all the stages of the preliminary planning, and the approach routes to the beaches were chosen on the basis of information it supplied about the German-swept channels and minefields. The approach routes were changed more than once in the light of the latest intelligence available, and a few days before D Day a combined surface and air operation was organized and carried out in Seine Bay to confirm that O.I.C.'s conclusions were completely up-to-date and accurate.

In the initial assault stage of Operation Neptune, 1,213 warships from battleships down to midget submarines, and 4,126 landing-ships and small craft, sailing from ports as far west as Plymouth and as far east as Newhaven, had to follow the British-

* See Chapter 15.

swept channels to a point eight miles south of the Isle of Wight and then steam down the so-called Spout, across the enemy's minefields to Seine Bay and the assault area. The fact that only one Allied destroyer out of the whole of the assault force was lost by mining was a tribute not only to the superb efficiency of the minesweepers, but also to the patient and laborious efforts of Denning's staff in piecing together the many scraps of information which provided such a complete and detailed picture of these German defences.

The German Navy was no more successful than the Army or the Air Force in anticipating the exact time and place of the invasion, but its reactions to it in the early hours of June 6 seem to have been rather swifter and more percipient than those of the other two Services. Because of the destruction by Allied bombing and by the French resistance forces of much of the German land communication system, the Naval W/T network, although also disorganized, was in considerable demand. Thanks to B.P., Denning was able to keep Admiral Ramsay, Allied Naval Commander-in-Chief Expeditionary Force (A.N.C.X.F.), fully informed about the enemy's moves and projected counter-measures. Ramsay made a point of telephoning the Director of Naval Intelligence to express his thanks for the contribution made by O.I.C. to the success of the assault.

The British had recently developed a new type of mine, actuated by the pressure of the displacement of water when a vessel passed over it. There seemed to be no method of sweeping these 'oyster' mines, and the British were reluctant to use them for fear that one would fall into German hands and that its secrets would then be passed to the Japanese. The effects on the American landing operations in the Pacific might, it was thought, be serious. If, on the other hand, the Germans had also developed a similar type of mine, there was obviously no reason why the British should not use their oyster mines as soon as required. Captain Cowie, Director of the Admiralty's Torpedo and Mining Division, and his deputy, Captain Maitland Dougall, were therefore delighted when, shortly after D Day, Denning drew their attention to an obscure reference in a routine German signal to the transport to the French coast of a hitherto unknown type of mine, given the prefix

'D'. 'Eureka,' cried Maitland Dougall, 'D for Druck—pressure mines! The Germans have them and are going to use them. We can do the same and warn our people what to expect.' It was a small example of the dividends to be won from the careful study of routine administrative messages, and a vindication of Denning's theory that valuable intelligence could only be obtained by first establishing a 'norm' and then looking for any deviation from it. It was also one more contrast with the situation prevailing in Room 40 where for so long messages of no immediate and obvious operational importance had, of necessity, been consigned to the wastepaper basket.

A small pre-D Day incident demonstrated the soundness of Denning's insistence that O.I.C. must be the filter through which all maritime operational intelligence should pass. Captain Roskill has pointed out that Admiral Ramsay was more fortunate than some of his predecessors, because he could count on almost any request for men, ships or services being met if this was humanly possible. Some weeks before D Day, Ramsay's Intelligence staff thought, like Sir Max Horton,† that their information should reach them raw and not digested and processed by O.I.C. They formally requested Clayton to see that decrypts were sent direct to them from B.P. Clayton was as reluctant as Denning to agree to this departure from our well-tried practice, but did not feel that it would be right to give an outright refusal. It was therefore arranged that this request should be met for a trial period. Within ten days it was clear that the new system was unworkable. A.N.C.X.F.'s staff had neither the knowledge nor the training to handle the information which poured into their office and the experiment was quickly abandoned.

After the invasion of France, the strength of the German Navy in surface ships with any real offensive capability was so reduced that they had to fall back on belatedly-designed explosive motor boats, human torpedoes and one- and two-man submarines. The endurance of these 'small battle units' was not great and their success meagre. Intelligence about them was handled by Denning's sections rather than by the Submarine Tracking Room, since they were operating in coastal waters far more familiar to Denning's

† See Chapter 10.

men than to Winn's. Warnings of their intended sorties were often revealed by Special Intelligence in time for O.I.C. to alert Coastal and Fighter Commands and the appropriate naval authorities.

However, much of Denning's attention was now concentrated on supporting the intensified efforts of the Navy and R.A.F. to destroy the enemy's convoys creeping along the coasts of the Low Countries, Germany and Norway. These convoys had always been of very great importance to the Germans, and had been constantly attacked by the Royal Navy and the R.A.F. since 1940. However, with the growing breakdown of the German road and rail system under the weight of the Allied air offensive and with the withdrawal of Swedish shipping, which had for so long aided the Axis war effort, the coastal convoy system in the North Sea and Baltic became absolutely vital. Knowledge of the routes used, the timing of the convoys and the scale of protection provided (which remained formidable), was therefore of enormous importance to the cruisers of the Home Fleet, the Norwegian and British M.T.B.s and to the strike aircraft of Coastal and Fighter Commands. Equally Bomber Command's long-standing minelaying campaign had compelled the Germans to devote a great effort to keeping their swept channels clear and, until the last three months of the war, they somehow managed to keep losses down to reasonable proportions. Then the sheer volume of the task became too big, and even in the Baltic the toll of ships sunk began to mount. U-boat training was disrupted, the withdrawal of troops and civilians from the eastern provinces endangered and the complete control of the Baltic, which the Germans had enjoyed for so long, ceased. The information supplied by O.I.C. to those organizing these operations was accurate, up-to-date and complete. It made a significant contribution to the final collapse of the enemy's sea transport system.

An interesting sidelight arising from this constant watch on German traffic by sea, and from the establishment of norms against which any deviations could be judged, was the fact that we detected, before the Ardennes offensive at the end of 1944, a very considerable southward movement of troops from Norway. On October 30, Denning wrote in a report for the First Sea Lord, a copy of which went to Admiral Ramsay: 'The gross tonnage of shipping which has made the passage from Oslofjord to Denmark from the middle of October amounts to 95,000 GRT. It is estimated that this is sufficient to have lifted at least one division from Norway. Elements of the 269th Division previously stationed in the Bergen area have been identified on the Western Front during the last few days and have evidently been transferred from Norway to Denmark since mid-October.' The movements continued throughout November and the first half of December. Precise details of them were reported by O.I.C. each week. On December 16, the day on which the German offensive in the Ardennes actually opened, Denning remarked, 'The Germans are able to move one division and its equipment per week but in view of the quick turn round [of the ships involved] it is unlikely that much heavy equipment is being moved.' Judging by the surprise and initial success of Von Rundstedt's offensive, Eisenhower's intelligence staff cannot have drawn the right conclusions from these reports.

Great efforts had been made by Bomber Command, alerted by Denning, to interfere with this traffic by even more intensive mining of the Skagerrak and the Belts, and many ships were sunk. Partly because of this and partly because the surviving ships were now needed in the Baltic, where large-scale evacuation of German troops and civilians from Lithuania, Latvia, Estonia and Poland was beginning, the traffic then declined.

The last stages of the war produced few surprises. O.I.C. was able to follow the events in the Baltic and the all-out effort of the remnants of the German Navy's surface forces to support the collapsing Eastern Front. Messages from the beleaguered French Atlantic ports, from the Channel Isles and Holland, and from the 'Small Battle Units', which maintained the fight to the last, continued to come in and the increasingly rapid disintegration of the enemy's maritime effort was clearly apparent. Nevertheless there was no repetition of the mutinies of 1918 and discipline and morale in the German surface ships was maintained, as it was in the U-boat Arm, to the very end. The remaining major surface ships, which had been the centre of Denning's attention for five and a half gruelling years, mostly fell victims to the R.A.F. *Hipper* was bombed in dock at Kiel on April 3, and *Scheer* suffered a similar fate a week later. *Lützow* was caught off Swinemunde on April 16, and had to be scuttled. Only *Prinz Eugen,* one light cruiser and a handful of destroyers survived to be handed over to the victorious Allies.‡

‡ See Chapter 15 for the fate of the U-boats.

15

U-boat Warfare.
D Day to VE Day

IN JANUARY 1944, Winn was promoted to the acting rank of temporary Captain R.N.V.R. The proposal to do so originated with Admiral Edelsten, who had been Assistant Chief of Staff (U-boats and Trade) since December 1942. He had almost come to regard the Tracking Room as forming part of his own 'empire' rather than that of the D.N.I. In October 1943 in a minute to the D.N.I., Rushbrooke, and to his two fellow Assistant Chiefs of Staff, Brind (Home) and Servaes (Foreign), he wrote of Winn: 'His experience, wisdom and sound appreciation of the U-boat War have saved this country a vast amount of shipping tonnage and enabled a heavy toll to be taken of U-boats on many occasions. It is not an exaggeration to state that his work is of national importance and very ably shouldered. In my opinion such brilliant service to the country requires further recognition than the O.B.E. awarded to Commander Winn in January 1943, and I should like to see this officer promoted to Captain in the New Year Promotions. I fully realize that the promotion of a temporary R.N.V.R. officer to this rank would be exceptional but the position held by this officer and his responsibilities rank, at least, with those of a Director of a Division.'

His remarks were enthusiastically endorsed by Brind, Servaes and Rushbrooke. Admiral Commanding Reserves concurred and, for once, there was no opposition from the Treasury to the upgrading of the post. It was a great honour for Winn and indeed, as he made clear to his staff, for the whole Tracking Room. It was also in striking contrast to the attitude of Regular Naval officers to the Reserves and to civilians which had prevailed in Room 40's day.

At sea the U-boat war was far from over. Although the number of operational boats had declined in the last six months by forty to 168, new boats were now being commissioned at the highest rate ever achieved, so that the total strength of the U-boat fleet had actually risen by thirty-one to 436. Nor was it only in numbers that there had been an improvement on the German side. In his first report for 1944 Winn remarked, 'It is probable that U-boat morale is for the moment rather higher than of late for three reasons. First the number sunk in December was much lower; only six for certain, of which one was scuttled owing to severe weather damage, plus four possibles.* Second the Gnat [the rather contemptuous British code name for the Zaunkönig acoustic torpedo] habitually explodes at the end of its run or on encountering an adverse set such as a wake and such explosions have been repeatedly and apparently sincerely reported with embroidery of 'sinking noises' as successful attacks on destroyers and other vessels: as a result U-boat Control either credulously or artfully has assessed this weapon as producing sixty per cent hits and has reckoned nearly 50 escorts as sunk or damaged since September. In the third place some actual successes have been achieved'.

The German press had been making very extravagant claims about their new weapon and the number of Allied destroyers sunk, and the section of N.I.D. responsible for propaganda suggested that we should publish the truth to deflate these boasts. The matter was referred to the Deputy Director Intelligence Centre who firmly opposed the idea. 'The failure of this weapon,' wrote Clayton, 'on which such high hopes are based is evidently unknown to the enemy and I suggest it would be most unwise to enlighten them further by denying claims in which they believe.' There can be little doubt that Clayton was right: that the enemy should continue to employ and rely on a weapon that was far from an unqualified success was of much greater benefit to the British than the very problematical effects which might have been

---

* The actual total eventually proved to be eight.

achieved by their 'white', 'grey' or 'black' propaganda organizations.

Within a few weeks of Clayton's minute, we intercepted emergency signals from two U-boats† reporting that they had been torpedoed and were sinking. It was obvious that they had been hit by Gnats fired from other U-boats and Dönitz was compelled to warn his commanding officers to be very careful when firing acoustic torpedoes in bad visibility. Winn commented: 'The Gnat torpedo is not an unmixed blessing and the enemy command are beginning to feel doubtful about the authenticity of the numerous claims made for success with this weapon. Two recent orders have referred to their wish to collect data for assessing Gnat attacks and directed boats to make visual examination whenever possible of the site of supposed sinkings. . . . It thus seems that the policy of refraining from informing the enemy of the true measure of his Gnat successes in the hope that a greater disappointment would result from gradual disillusionment may be bearing fruit'.

Thanks to the speed and regularity with which B.P. were now dealing with the daily changes in the settings of Triton, we were generally current in our reading of U-boat signals and sometimes knew more about the true situation at sea than did B.d.U. In February, for example, the Tracking Room reported that 'from early on 14th February to dawn on the 19th, the enemy operated his North Atlantic U-boat pack believed by him to comprise 26 U-boats but actually totalling 20 against convoys ONS.29 and ON.224'.

Throughout the early months of 1944 Dönitz continued to strive to attack the North Atlantic convoys but with practically no success. The greatly increased Allied air cover now available prevented the U-boats from making the wide reconnaissance sweeps which had previously been possible: there was no longer any 'Black Pit'. Nor could the B.Dienst give much information. The German spy network had never produced anything from British ports, but had occasional successes from Iceland and New York and more frequently from Ceuta and Algeciras about Gibraltar movements. By and large, however, Dönitz had to rely on his own resources and what help he could obtain from the G.A.F. for information about British convoys. The combination of loss of mo-

† Probably U.377 and U.972, hitherto recorded as lost from unknown causes.

bility and lack of reliable intelligence compelled him to concentrate on a few focal points.

At the end of January, Winn discussed the new dispositions: 'A characteristic of recent strategy has been the co-operation of reconnaissance aircraft to find targets for U-boats and the close-in disposition has no doubt been dictated by the need to collect the U-boats on to any convoys detected whilst these are in a sea area where freedom for diversion is restricted. It is obvious that the North Channel is one conduit for all trans-Atlantic traffic and that the various convoys must mutually hamper each other's changes of direction. Furthermore the southern approach is to a material extent bitten into by the range arc of offensive bombers based in western France. Thus aircraft flying, as latterly has been the habit, close in the approaches to the North Channel have an excellent chance of finding outward-bound convoys and shadowing until the mean course is established up to a point sufficiently near the U-boat patrol to facilitate the establishment of firm contact by one or more U-boats. There is little doubt that when this technique succeeds in providing a good start for a pack operation, any well-fixed outward convoy will have the full weight of the group concentrated against it. The enemy are as eager as ever to find a convoy in a position and in conditions of weather and relative strength permitting them to develop a full-scale pack attack with the old tactics of co-ordinated and cumulative attack in mass designed to overwhelm the escorts and annihilate the convoy'. It was fortunate that British sea and air defences were now so strong. This was the time when Captain Walker's famous 2nd Escort Group sank six U-boats in one cruise of twenty-seven days.

Among Walker's victims was one of the two first U-boats to be fitted with the Schnorkel air intake, or Snort as we nicknamed it in the Tracking Room. We were as anxious as the Germans to learn how successful this new development would be and on February 21 the Tracking Room reported as follows: 'The U-boat sunk by EG.2 was one of two now at sea known to have been recently adapted by the addition of the "Schnorkel" to travel at periscope depth on diesel propulsion by the use of an intake and exhaust trunk extended above the surface. The commander of this boat who possessed twice the average operational experience and has in the past achieved considerable successes, had been ordered to report his experiences of the performance of this new device, and in particular whether it could be used simultaneously with the periscope and what safety margin there was in various seas.' From then onwards there were frequent references in U-boat W/T traffic to the difficulties of acquiring the technique of schnorkelling, but nevertheless it was obvious that these difficulties were being overcome and that the Snort was going to present Coastal Command with an extremely awkward problem. The submersible boat was, after nearly fifty years, at last becoming a true submarine.

However, despite the continuing attempts to attack the North Atlantic and Gibraltar convoys and the maintenance of the campaign in more distant American, African and Indian waters, both the Tracking Room and B.d.U. were now becoming preoccupied with the obviously imminent opening of the Second Front. On January 29 B.d.U. was involved in a full-scale invasion alarm, which the Tracking Room found both amusing and instructive. In the very early hours of the morning, a German aircraft reported two to three hundred landing craft on an easterly course 120 miles south by west of Lorient. By 8 A.M. all U-boats in the Bay of Biscay and in the North Western Approaches as far north as Rockall had been ordered to surface and proceed at top speed, regardless of the danger from air attack or from mines, towards the presumed invasion fleet. By 10:30 A.M., it was all over. The first U-boat had reached the scene and discovered that the 'landing craft' were harmless tunny fishermen. Denning and Winn, with memories of the 1940 report about a concentration of U-boats in Emden, which in the event turned out to be river barges, felt some sympathy for the luckless U-boat men, so needlessly endangered, but B.d.U.'s reaction had been interesting. It was 'vigorous and prompt and characteristic of a predetermined plan. The priority of the operation was plainly absolute and the concentration on the single objective complete. The emphasis on disregard of danger from aircraft and mines establishes the acceptance of the view that U-boats are expendable in a major military operation'.

Ten days later Winn issued an appreciation entitled: 'U-boats as a factor in the Second Front'. There was, he wrote, a total of 400 U-boats of which 225 were still in the Baltic engaged on training or working up. Of those outside the Baltic 130 were based in Biscay ports, but forty of these were 740-tonners and so unsuitable for operations in the English Channel. However, it seemed likely that fifty boats could quickly be despatched from the Baltic and a further twenty-five from Norway if attacks on the Arctic convoys were abandoned. 'It is appreciated that the enemy would regard an attempt to invade France as the crisis of this war and would utilize his U-boats to the full regardless of losses. On this view all U-boats at sea in the Atlantic east of, say, 30 degrees West and north of, say, 30 degrees North would be ordered to attack military convoys and reinforce anti-invasion patrols.' In his concluding summary Winn warned that 'a total of 175 to 200 U-boats will be used to prevent or impair landings and to reduce the forces conveyed and their stores and armour and to attack the Atlantic convoys necessary to maintain the build-up and renewal of men.'

Dönitz presumably decided that he could not afford to wait until the invasion had actually started to marshal his forces, and on April 10 the Tracking Room reported that 'the outstanding feature of the present U-boat dispositions is the process of collection into Biscay ports of 500-ton U-boats.' By May 1, forty-four 500-tonners were being held in the Biscay bases. At the same time new boats sailing from the Baltic on their first war cruise were proceeding no further than southern and central Norwegian ports and were referred to as the 'Centre' group which by mid-May totalled sixteen U-boats. As the Arctic strength was maintained at between twenty-five and thirty it was obvious that the Germans were highly nervous of an invasion of Norway as well as of France. In consequence, of course, the numbers in the North Atlantic fell sharply.

A fortnight before the planned date for the invasion, even more precise information became available as the result of our interception of a signal from the U-boat Command to their liaison officer with the Admiral Commanding Western France. The following were its essentials:

. '1. A number of U-boats have been assigned to a special group. It is estimated that this group numbers thirty-seven to forty of the 500-ton type with possibly three others of the 740-ton type.

'2. All boats of this group will sail on or before D Day or at the latest D+1.

'3. A patrol will be established off the English coast between the Scillies and a point east of Start Point by an unknown number of boats from Brest possibly only three in number.

'4. Another patrol probably of two or three boats which will sail from Lorient will be established off the coast of North Cornwall between Trevose Head and the Scillies.

'5. Four boats from Brest will take up waiting positions in the northern Bay of Biscay with a view to their employment in the Channel as a second wave.

'6. All other members of the group in any Biscay port will take up waiting positions in the central and southern Bay of Biscay in a disposition hinged on the Spanish coast suggestive of a fear lest an invasion may be attempted in the Bordeaux area. . . .'

The most obvious need was to prevent the U-boats reaching the invasion area at all, and plans were made for intensive patrols by sea and air forces in the south-western approaches to the English Channel. Four Support Groups were transferred to the Plymouth Command, with six more Groups and three escort carriers patrolling west of Land's End. 19 Group of Coastal Command also received reinforcements. The whole area from southern Ireland down to Brest was to be flooded with aircraft so that every square mile would be covered at least once every thirty minutes, twenty-four hours a day.

It was also felt that special measures were required on the Intelligence side. Neither the Plymouth Command nor 19 Group had previously had much direct experience of the Tracking Room's methods and procedures, nor of the handling of a large volume of Special Intelligence. To meet this need and to ensure that the Commander-in-Chief and the Air Officer Commanding were kept as fully informed as they would have been if their Combined Headquarters had been situated in the Admiralty, Winn's deputy was sent down to Plymouth to establish a 'branch office' of the Tracking Room there. The experiment was sufficiently successful to be maintained for many months and extended to Combined H.Q. Rosyth when the centre of U-boat activity shifted to the Scottish coast in the last phase of the war.

Winn characterized B.d.U.'s reactions to the invasion, when it came, as 'prompt and energetic but remarkably confused' with many modifications and several changes of mind from his original plan. All Snorts were ordered up Channel, but nineteen boats not fitted with schnorkels were sailed to patrol the Bay of Biscay, nineteen boats were disposed off southern Norway and twenty-four off northern Norway. Sixty-two U-boats were thus neutralized as a result of the enemy's uncertainty as to whether the Normandy landings were the only ones which they would have to repel. U-boats were, however, ordered to 'adopt reckless tactics and to be prepared to sacrifice themselves to achieve sinkings'.

Despite this injunction, Winn reported six days after D Day that 'liaison between Captain U-boats, Western France and Admiral Commanding U-boats has been bad, in the main no doubt because of delay in communications. A single example will suffice: On D+5 Admiral Commanding U-boats thought no U-boats were at sea in the Bay of Biscay until reminded by Captain U-boats that nineteen had been disposed in this area on D+1. . . . It will be recalled that it had been estimated that thirty-seven to forty U-boats would form the original anti-invasion force; in fact thirty-five sailed on D Day and three have sailed since. From Brest fifteen sailed on the afternoon of D Day, of which six were Snorts, and were ordered up Channel and are eventually to attack traffic to and from the beachhead. The nine other Brest boats were non-Snorts and were to attack shipping in an unknown area off southwest Cornwall or Devonshire. Of these nine not more than two can still be at sea, the remainder, except for one, having returned with damage or owing to personnel casualties. The one exception was discovered by U-boat Command on D+2 to have a Snort and was then ordered to proceed up Channel. There is 'Z' evidence‡ of two kills of anti-invasion boats in the northern Bay of Biscay and in all so far five such boats are considered sunk plus six damaged and commanding officers wounded'.

In fact the U-boats were now faced with an almost impossible task. For the non-Snorts it *was* impossible: after four days Dönitz sailed no more of them, and two days after that recalled those already at sea. Even the Snorts could only make a snail's progress, so that it was nine days before the first of them managed to reach its designated operational area.

On June 19, Winn reported that 'three U-boats are known to

‡ i.e. Special Intelligence.

have called at St. Peter Port [in the Channel Islands] and it must be conceded a heroic achievement to have penetrated so far through the immensely powerful concentrations of surface and air forces which have been continuously searching the western Channel'. A little later he recounted that 'reports have been intercepted from two of these three boats in both of which stress was laid on the severity of the ordeal for the crews and on the menace of accumulating CO_2 and of ever failing batteries. One of these boats risked a couple of brief periods on the surface but the other remained continuously submerged for seven days and complained of the impossibility of snorting in daylight. The average rate of advance of 1.5 knots over the ground . . . is not considered adequate by U-boat Command who are clearly apprehensive that the crews of boats advancing so slowly may be so exhausted if and when they reach the Spout* as to be unfit to compete with dangers of operations there'.

It was impossible under such conditions to attempt to track U-boats with any great degree of precision either in the English Channel or in the Bristol Channel, but Dönitz himself was no better informed about the whereabouts of his boats. On July 3 Winn had to admit that 'the situation in the Channel is obscure and the obscurity is worrying Dönitz who, on 2nd July, somewhat plaintively informed the boats thought to be in the Spout that owing to the lack of reports from them it was impossible for him to estimate the situation'.

There were now signs that 'the enemy are not confident of the survival of the Biscay bases as operating centres', and the Tracking Room thought that 'the majority of 500-tonners . . . not fitted with Snorts will be sailed to operate against the Atlantic convoys. . . . It will be borne in mind that after one cruise in the Atlantic these boats would then have to return to Norway. . . .'

It was moreover evident that U-boats not fitted with schnorkels no longer had any hope of successful operations anywhere in the waters round the British Isles. Just over a month after D Day, Winn noted that, out of a total of forty-three U-boats which had operated or tried to operate directly against the invasion, eighteen or forty-two per cent, had been sunk. In no case had the average

* Code-name for the area between the Isle of Wight and the Baie de la Seine through which all the invasion traffic passed.

speed over the ground in the Channel exceeded two knots. One U-boat, we were interested to learn, had even drifted quite unintentionally into Spithead and counted herself extremely fortunate to have been able to get out again.

By the end of August, Brest, Lorient and St. Nazaire were being evacuated by all U-boats capable of putting to sea. At first some of them only moved down to La Pallice and Bordeaux, but although Lorient and St. Nazaire remained in German hands until the end of the war they could no longer be used as bases. Occasional calls were made by U-boats with supplies or in an emergency, but from now on Bergen and Trondheim became the main bases for the Atlantic boats. To cover the evacuation, diversionary attacks were made in the North Channel and Bristol Channel and the Biscay boats all, unfortunately, succeeded in reaching Norway safely. The Tracking Room found that in the new conditions it was far more difficult to estimate the speed which U-boats on passage would make good. An analysis of the cruises of twenty-seven U-boats which proceeded direct from the Bay of Biscay to Norway showed that their speed had been correctly forecast in eight cases, but that in eleven cases it had been over-estimated and eight cases under-estimated. The introduction of the schnorkel was certainly going to make the work of the Tracking Room as well as that of Coastal Command more difficult.

At the end of August Winn issued the following appreciation: 'The next phrase of the U-boat campaign will be very different and there is reason to hope that the loss of the Biscay bases will greatly handicap its development. One feature, probably the dominant one, will be the operation of U-boats in coastal areas off the coast of England and Scotland where focal traffic points exist. The evolution of the Snort U-boat will be found to have affected profoundly the balance of power between hunter and hunted in such areas. The U-boat will be able to remain submerged for up to ten days without presenting any target detectable or visible except at close range. It is probable that in addition to the operations which have begun in the Moray Firth, the North Minch and the approaches to Reykjavik and the impending patrols in the North Channel, B.d.U. will send U-boats close inshore in the Bristol Channel and St. George's Channel and near Land's End'.

Winn was right. The schnorkel was now permitting U-boats to

resume operations in waters from which they had been driven in 1940. They were virtually immune from detection and attack by aircraft, and only the deployment of very strong surface forces in the focal areas in the approaches to the main British ports could prevent shipping losses rising again. The continued successes which American hunter-killer groups were having against the larger 740-tonners in more distant waters, successes due to the extremely accurate and up-to-date information still available from Special Intelligence, tended to obscure the potentially very dangerous situation with which the Allies could be faced. The U-boat had regained its cloak of invisibility; if it were also to be given seven league boots in the shape of high underwater speed, not only the Allied air but also the surface defences would be rendered helpless. Nor was this a remote possibility: new types of U-boats, true submarines, not just submersible torpedo boats, were now being commissioned in large numbers.

Ever since the beginning of the war the Germans had been experimenting with the Walter U-boat, fuelled by hydrogen peroxide and theoretically capable of twenty-five knots under water. However, by the end of 1942, Dönitz, who had already seen the writing on the wall for the existing type of U-boat, had realized that the Walter U-boat could not be perfected in time. He had decided instead to use its revolutionary streamlined hull, in combination with greatly increased batteries for ordinary electric propulsion, to produce U-boats capable of maintaining a speed under water of eighteen knots for an hour and a half or of twelve knots for ten hours. In the end two types were built: Type XXI of 1,600 tons with the performance given above for ocean work and a smaller class, Type XXIII, of 300 tons with a submerged speed of ten knots for coastal operations. Prefabricated mass production was organized by Albert Speer, thus minimizing the effects of Allied bombing, and no fewer than ninety-eight of the new types were laid down in the second half of 1944 and as many as eighty-three in the first three months of 1945. The underwater speed of the larger type was greater than that of the Allied corvettes and only slightly less than that of the later frigates. Only destroyers would be able to deal with such formidable adversaries, but just as Nelson never had sufficient frigates, the British never had enough destroyers.

In the autumn of 1944 it seemed to many that the war in Europe was almost over, and the Admiralty began to push ahead with their plans to send very large reinforcements to the Far East and the Pacific. Winn became increasingly alarmed that the British anti-submarine forces in Home waters and in the Atlantic would be so reduced that they would be unable to cope with the still very considerable number of conventional U-boats, let alone with the far more dangerous new types, about which we were well informed.† We were also conscious of the dedication and discipline of the U-boat Arm and perhaps over-estimated the extent of its Nazi indoctrination. It seemed to us highly probable that, even if Germany itself were overrun, a fanatical last stand might be made in Norway and that the U-boat war might be prolonged for as much as three or four months with heavy sinkings and loss of life among the inadequately protected convoys.

In consequence Winn began, from October onwards, to emphasize more and more strongly in his verbal and written reports the dangers which might still lie ahead and the folly of prematurely lowering our guard. It seems probable that, for once, he may even have broken the first rule for any good intelligence officer and have deliberately painted too black a picture in an effort to counter the prevailing euphoria. His reputation was now so high that his opinions certainly carried great weight with the Naval Staff. An estimate which he produced at the beginning of November suggested that by December 1 there would be a total of 185 operational U-boats of which 15 would be Type XXI and 10 Type XXIII; by February 1945 the figure could rise to 267, including 52 Type XXI and 21 Type XXIII; by April the respective figures might be 275, 74 and 25. It is a little difficult to justify these estimates. On December 1, the Tracking Room's own records only showed an operational total of 155, none of them new types; in fact our lists only gave 35 Type XXI and 18 Type XXIII as actually commissioned. Although the numbers did continue to increase month by month, the figure on April 1 was 102 short of Winn's November estimate. Moreover the first two Type XXIII boats did not become operational until the third week in January

† Thanks, among other things, to a very full report to Tokyo, on 13th September 1944 by Vice-Admiral Abe, Head of the Japanese Naval Mission in Germany, made after a visit to Danzig at the end of August.

and it was the third week in March before the first Type XXI reached Norway. Only two of the larger boats were operational by the end of the war and neither of them in fact completed a full war cruise.

On the other hand it was hard to realize, after four years during which Bomber Command's efforts to restrict U-boat building had been very largely ineffective, that the situation had now changed dramatically. In particular the breaching of the Dortmund-Ems and Mittelland canals in November greatly hindered the transport of the prefabricated sections of the new types to the shipyards. Perhaps equally important was the fact that the Germans had been compelled to go into production without carrying out sufficient trials and experiments. There were inevitably teething troubles. This situation was made worse by Bomber Command's increasingly effective mining of the training areas in the eastern Baltic and then by the advance of the Russian armies. The new U-boats simply did not complete their working-up programmes with anything like the speed to which we had become accustomed.

There was, however, another very worrying development. The new pattern of the inshore campaign, with U-boats operating individually and mostly submerged, had greatly reduced the amount of signalling. There were far fewer opportunities for obtaining D/F fixes and there were also far fewer sightings than there had been in the days of Wolf Packs. The whole volume of signalling had fallen off, and although we might sometimes discover patrol areas from decrypts, even this source of information began to dry up. As far back as March 1944, the Tracking Room had reported that 'two rendezvous . . . between a supply U-boat and two outward-bound 740-tonners and a torpedo carrier were ordered by U-boat control in a special cipher. Thus it is plain the enemy suspects, probably as the result of the sinking of a tanker in the Indian Ocean‡ and of a freighter U-boat off South Africa, both near a rendezvous, that we have gained physical possession of his current settings, perhaps by capture of a U-boat. At present the enemy traffic is being read despite the subterfuge employed'. By

---

‡ *Brake* was sunk by the destroyer *Roebuck* after being sighted by aircraft from the escort carrier *Battler* south of Mauritius. Fears concerning this type of operation by ourselves and the Americans were therefore justified.

the middle of December the situation was becoming even more serious and Winn reported that 'the continued use of one ship cipher for transmitting the more important operational orders to U-boats has introduced a substantial element of hypothesis into the picture presented by the U-boat plot, and it has further transpired that a practice had been adopted—curiously enough as an innovation—by the enemy supplying to departing U-boats in their sailing orders all necessary patrol instructions which are accordingly supplemented or modified by W/T only so far as may become essential. The corresponding reduction in the value of Special Intelligence intercepts is substantial compared with the days when patrol orders were almost invariably despatched by W/T after a boat had sailed. In general communication with U-boats at sea has been progressively reduced as the U-boats now spend so much of their time submerged.'

As recently as 1973 Dönitz was still loath to admit publicly that his ciphers had been compromised. However, neither he nor his staff appear to have been as happy about the security of cipher Triton as their signal experts were, but it seems rather a tame excuse to claim that the Commander-in-Chief of the Navy could not overrule them. It remains something of a mystery why even more radical changes were not introduced.*

We were, of course, aware that the German services were now suffering from an acute shortage of oil, but it was not easy to calculate the amount which might be scraped together for continued operations from the Norwegian bases if this were to be ordered. The hard facts were that the U-boat fleet was still increasing, that the new types would certainly prove very formidable opponents if they became operational, and that the intelligence, both conventional and 'Special', on which the Tracking Room relied, was drying up. Winn was right to sound the alarm and the Naval Staff were justified in paying attention to his warnings.

At the beginning of 1945, Captain Roskill records, 'the First Sea Lord sent a gravely worded memorandum to the Chiefs-of-Staff Committee. He anticipated a renewed offensive on a substantial scale in February and March with large numbers of the new types of U-boats loose on the Atlantic convoy routes as well as in our coastal waters. Shipping losses might, he considered,

* See also footnote p. 169—Chapter 10.

even surpass those suffered in the spring of 1943, and if that happened the land operations in Europe were bound to be adversely affected'. As a result, three hundred flotilla craft destined for the Far East were held back, and air mining and other anti-U-boat operations intensified.

At the beginning of February messages from Dönitz to his U-boat commanders were intercepted in which the Gross-Admiral quoted Hitler's directive that 'the U-boat war was to be strengthened by all means and speedily intensified'. A week later we noted the departure of the first Type XXIII boat from Christiansand and we also learned of the intention to transport forty-five tons of diesel oil per month by U-boat to the Biscay fortresses. In the third week in February we intercepted messages from Dönitz giving instructions that 'dockyards are to continue to work at full pressure. The main thing is for as many boats as possible to be ready to proceed'. By the end of the month there was a sudden increase in the number of U-boats at sea and we learned that maximum priority was being given to the provision of sufficient fuel for Atlantic operations.

Despite the advance of the Allied armies into Germany from both east and west, there were no indications that the U-boats were ready to throw in the sponge. On the contrary, all the signs seemed to point to the intensification of the U-boat war which Winn had predicted. The only puzzling feature was the continuing delay in the emergence on operations of any Type XXIs and the fact that only two or three Type XXIIIs had left the Baltic. At last, on March 19, a patrol vessel reported the departure from Kiel of the first Type XXI, U.2511. The Tracking Room noted that she was commanded by 'a hand picked officer', Lieutenant-Commander Schnee, who had been awarded the Oak Leaves in 1942 and who, until recently, had been serving on Dönitz's personal staff. This seemed to be it—the long-awaited campaign in the Atlantic was about to open. The Tracking Room heaved a collective sigh of relief when, eight days later, Schnee reported that he was having to put back into Horten with periscope defects. We continued to watch his movements anxiously.

At the end of March Winn reported that it would be 'premature to assume any relaxation of morale. U-boats on operations, as contrasted with base staff and training flotillas, appear on the whole still determined and courageous', and the movement of boats away from the Baltic and the ports threatened by the advance of the Allied armies was resulting in considerable traffic up the Belts and in the Kattegat.

This movement presented the R.A.F. and the U. S. Air Force, who had by now gained almost complete control of the air over Germany and Denmark, with greater opportunities than they had enjoyed since the 'Bay Offensive' in 1943. Because of the R.A.F.'s mining campaign and the comparatively shallow depth of water the U-boats had to proceed for most of the time on the surface. The passage from Kiel to south Norway, which for almost five years had been a very easy introduction to a U-boat's first war cruise, now became increasingly hazardous. Strikes by Mosquitoes and Typhoons with rockets and bombs began to take a heavy toll, and one of them in the middle of April not only demonstrated the staggering increase in the Allied ability to take the war right into the enemy's home waters, but also the remarkable accuracy of our D/F organization. On April 16 the Tracking Room reported as follows: 'By good fortune, shortly before a party of thirty-eight Mosquitoes of 18 Group were due to take off on an anti-shipping strike, a D/F fix was obtained of a U-boat transmission in the Kattegat and as this was judged to mark the progress of a party of U-boats known to be northbound it was suggested that the Mosquitoes be briefed accordingly. They found and very gallantly attacked two northbound U-boats . . . outward-bound on their first war cruise, and a southbound 740-tonner still laden with cargo successfully carried by this U-boat from Batavia. All three U-boats were sunk'. It was a good example of the value of a combination of two different sources of intelligence.

Even as late as the 30th April it still seemed possible that the U-boat war would be continued. Schnee's boat had not left Bergen (it actually sailed that night), but a second Type XXI, under another experienced officer, Schröter, was outward-bound in the North Sea. Winn's Deputy stated that 'evidence of the intention to continue the U-boat war is provided by the transfer during the month of thirty U-boats from the school boat category to the force being made ready for operations. It is impossible to forecast how these plans will be affected by the reported negotiations by Himmler for unconditional surrender. A great deal will depend on the attitude of Dönitz and on the reserves of U-boat fuel in Norway. There is unfortunately no reliable evidence on either of these vital questions'.

By May 4, however, the end was clearly in sight. Just after 4 P.M. we intercepted a long signal on the U-boat frequency. Although we could not decrypt it, Winn considered 'that it was almost certainly to U-boats ordering them to cease hostilities and make away to their ports'. It was indeed. After five years and eight months the Battle of the Atlantic was over and the work of the Tracking Room finished.

Epilogue

THE WORK of the Tracking Room was not quite finished. There was no certainty that all the U-boats had received or would obey the surrender orders and the last British merchantman to be torpedoed by a German U-boat was in fact sunk by a Type XXIII boat, U.2336, on May 7. There were rumours that Hitler, Himmler, Bormann and other high-ranking Nazis were attempting to escape, or had already escaped by U-boat to South America. A number of U-boats failed to report their positions and some made for neutral ports, two of them eventually reaching the Argentine. It was essential to have a completely accurate list of every U-boat ever built with cast-iron evidence of its eventual fate or final location so as to ensure that no 'rogues' were missing. Winn's deputy, who had been posted to Germany, was able to secure the co-operation of Admiral Godt, Dönitz's successor as B.d.U., and of Commander Hessler, Dönitz's son-in-law. By the end of June he brought back to the Admiralty a comprehensive list starting: 'U.1. Commanding Officer—Deecke. Lost south of Stavanger. April, 1940.', and finishing: 'U.4712. Commanding Officer—Fleige. Lost in dock at Kiel by air raid. 4th May, 1945.' The last U-boat had finally been tracked. Every one of the 1,170 boats built since 1935 had been accounted for.

Some Personal View

O.I.C. WAS a team—a point repeatedly stressed to the author by Vice-Admiral Sir Norman Denning—and its success was due to the patient accumulation by many individuals of hundreds of scraps of information from many different sources. This information had to be scrutinized, analysed, indexed and filed. No matter how carefully and scientifically this was done, when a critical situation arose, a great deal still depended on the ability of a particular expert to assemble the relevant facts, to judge, possibly, what was abnormal and to fill in the gaps which even current Special Intelligence almost always left.

Then again, no maritime operation, whether it was something on the scale of Operation Neptune (the Invasion of France) or the landing of an agent in Brittany, a commando raid in Norway or an attack on a German convoy off the Low Countries, ever took place without preliminary and detailed consultation between its planners and some member of the staff of O.I.C. The painstaking analysis of the German U-boat building programme, the reconstruction from the original small fragment of the German Naval grid and then the solution of the transpositions with which the U-boat Command sought to disguise their references to it, the selection of the best areas for Bomber Command's four-year minelaying campaign: all this required continuous and often laborious work without which little else would have been clear or effective operational action possible. The handling of this mass of unexciting detail and the often dull and monotonous work of the teleprinter operators, typists, filing clerks and watchkeepers was just as essential as the flashes of inspiration of Denning and Winn.

Nevertheless, an immense debt was owed to these two men. Many well-earned tributes have been paid to Rodger Winn—fewer to Ned Denning; but the latter's contribution, both in respect of pre-war planning and war-time control of surface ship intelligence, was of no less importance than Winn's great work against the U-boats. Denning, throughout the whole war, spent six days and nights a week in the Admiralty. He was almost continuously on call. At Bletchley Park, at Bomber Command, in the Ministry of Economic Warfare, on the joint Intelligence Committee or in S.O.E.,* when people thought of O.I.C., they thought of Denning as the man most likely to supply the answers to their intelligence problems. Denning, the professional, was the better administrator and, in some ways, the easier man to work for; Winn, the amateur, was possibly the more skilful advocate with the flair for what would now be called 'public relations'; both of them were, in the words of Clayton's deputy, Captain Colpoys, 'the intelligence officers de luxe of all time'.

Less mention has been made in these pages of Jock Clayton, the Deputy Director Intelligence Centre, but Clayton, in his own way, exerted a profound influence on O.I.C. He was not a man to seek the limelight. Perhaps he lacked that extra touch of ruthlessness which might, otherwise, have brought him to the top of his profession. He was, however, an ideal personality to control the varied collection of people who made up O.I.C.'s staff—regular naval officers on the active list, others recalled from retirement, reserve officers young and old, men and women, the prima donnas and the ambitious, the disillusioned and the lazy. Working conditions were not altogether easy—long hours in artificial light and air, over-crowding and no wardroom mess in which to relax and recover equilibrium, with the Blitz and the Buzz bombs to contend with when off duty. Clayton's kindly and far-seeing personality smoothed away incipient clashes of temperament and was largely responsible for the fact that O.I.C. was a

* Special Operations Executive.

'happy ship'. He had also a very acute brain and, although he obviously recognized the great talents of his two principal subordinates and was generally content to leave them to expound their views to the senior members of the Naval Staff, he was always there to give advice and support if his juniors seemed in any danger of being over-borne by the weight of gold lace confronting them. Clayton would often appear when one had been wrestling all day with some intractable problem and, after listening quietly to the difficulties, suggest a solution which, in nine cases out of ten, would prove to be the right one. At the time, some of us may have felt that he was perhaps a shade too easy-going and tolerant. In retrospect, it is clear that he was the perfect 'Chairman of the Board'.

O.I.C. would, undoubtedly, have made a useful contribution even without any Special Intelligence, but obviously a large measure of its actual success was due to the work of the cryptanalysts at B.P. On the other hand, it seems probable that B.P. would not entirely have avoided the faults and weaknesses of Room 40 if O.I.C., or something very like it, had not existed. As it was, the extremely close and fruitful co-operation of the two organizations undoubtedly played a very significant part in the Allied victory at sea over Germany.

The question inevitably springs to mind, what would have happened if B.P. had failed to crack the German naval ciphers? But what would have been the result if, on the German side, the B.Dienst had equally had no success? The sinking of the *Scharnhorst* in 1943 was certainly made possible by Special Intelligence. Nevertheless, but for the work of the B.Dienst, it is more than possible that she would have been intercepted and sunk by Sir Charles Forbes in 1940. The U-boats were defeated in 1943 because, at long last, the Allied forces were supplied with sufficient ships and V.L.R. aircraft, equipped with the right weapons and, above all, with 10cm radar. But, without Special Intelligence, the victory might not have been achieved until much later and at far greater cost. Who can say what the consequences would have been if such a delay had prevented, as it most certainly would have done, an invasion of France in 1944? Would Russia have remained in the war? Would the V. weapons have knocked out Britain? Would the new types of U-boats have arrived in time to

SOME PERSONAL VIEWS

turn the tide in the Atlantic? But could Dönitz have achieved all he did between 1941 and 1943 without the help of the German cryptanalysts? Such speculation is fascinating. If Napoleon had not dined off fried onions on the night before Waterloo, he would, according to his devotees, have won the battle: they ignore the fact that Wellington might have reacted differently to other circumstances.

Wars, in the end, have to be won by men in ships, aircraft, tanks or trenches—men who may have to pay with their lives because the politicians, and the electorate, have in peace-time failed to provide them with the right weapons in sufficient quantity. The author would like to think that Special Intelligence and the way in which O.I.C. handled it at least made the task of the Allied seamen and airmen less difficult. Admiral Edelsten, the Assistant Chief of Staff (U-boats and Trade) from 1942 to 1944, wrote to the Director of Naval Intelligence when he relinquished his appointment. 'After two years' very close association with the Tracking Room, I feel it would be most ungracious of me not to record my very great appreciation of the work carried out in this section of your department. Admiral Clayton has been admirable at keeping his finger on the U-boat pulse and I have found his ever-ready advice and counsel of the greatest help in appreciating the anti-U-boat war and in many difficult decisions which I have had to make. For the Tracking Room staff itself, I can only speak in the terms of the highest commendation. Under the masterly leadership and guidance of Captain Winn, this section works as a team in perfect accord and co-operation under difficult conditions. I have seen, time and time again, convoys and independents guided out of danger as the result of the intelligent anticipation, sound appreciation and foresight of these officers, ably assisted by Commander Hall and his hardworking movements staff belonging to Trade Division.' Captain Roskill, writing in 1976, concluded that the contribution of O.I.C. 'to the victory in the Atlantic battle was vital'.

The Admiralty

A note on its operational functions and responsibilities as they affected O.I.C.

F R O M 1709 until the creation of the unified Ministry of Defence in 1964, the Royal Navy was administered by The Commissioners for Executing The Office of Lord High Admiral of The United Kingdom, or the Board of Admiralty as they were collectively known.

The Board was presided over by the First Lord of the Admiralty, the political head of the Navy responsible for it to Parliament. It was one of the most important posts in the Cabinet and was occupied from September 1939 until May 1940 (for the second time in his life) by Mr. Winston Churchill. When he became Prime Minister he was succeeded by the Labour politician Mr. A. V. Alexander.

The professional head of the Service was the First Sea Lord, a position held from June 1939 until shortly before his death in October 1943 by Admiral Sir Dudley Pound, and from then until the end of the war by Admiral Sir Andrew Cunningham. The other Sea Lords, the Second, Third, Fourth and Fifth, were responsible for various aspects of administration, personnel, material, etc., and during the war a number of other senior officers, usually of Vice-

Admiral's rank, were also appointed to the Board, which was completed by two other politicians, the Civil Lord and the Parliamentary Financial Secretary, and one Civil Servant, the Permanent Secretary, who was Secretary of the Admiralty and head of its civilian staff.

As well as being responsible for the administration of the Navy, the Board of Admiralty was, under the King, its supreme authority, and all orders and instructions to the Navy were issued, usually over the signature of the Secretary, in the name of the Board. However, the collection and dissemination of intelligence, the preparation of war plans, the development of tactical doctrines, the day-to-day allocation of ships and the control of operations was a function of the Naval Staff, some of whose most senior members were, during the war, additionally appointed to the Board. The Chief of Naval Staff was the First Sea Lord himself, but in practice he delegated much of the routine day-to-day control of the Staff to the Deputy Chief of Naval Staff (D.C.N.S.), whose title was changed in May 1940 to Vice-Chief of Naval Staff (V.C.N.S.), an officer of Vice-Admiral's rank. The V.C.N.S. was a frequent visitor to O.I.C.

Under the V.C.N.S. came the Assistant Chiefs of Naval Staff, eventually six in number. Three of these were intimately concerned with the work of O.I.C.: two, responsible for operations, A.C.N.S. (Home) and A.C.N.S. (Foreign), and A.C.N.S. (U-boat Warfare and Trade). The Assistant Chiefs of Naval Staff were Rear-Admirals and between them they were responsible for most of the various Divisions of the Naval Staff. The Intelligence Division was one of the exceptions to this rule: the Director of Naval Intelligence (D.N.I.) reported direct to the V.C.N.S. The D.N.I. from February 1939 to December 1942 was Rear-Admiral (later Admiral) J. H. Godfrey. He was succeeded by Commodore (later Rear-Admiral) E. G. N. Rushbrooke.

The Directors and Deputy Directors of the other Staff Divisions were Captains. Four of these Divisions were in constant touch with O.I.C. Plans Division was responsible for the preparation of plans for all future operations. Operations Division was divided into two; Home, covering the North Sea, Arctic and North Atlantic, and Foreign, covering all other areas of the world. Between them they allocated the necessary forces and issued the appropriate instructions, in the name of the Admiralty, to the commanders-in-chief, flag officers, fleets, squadrons or ships required to carry them out. They were also responsible for the routing and diversion of military as opposed to trade convoys and for the routing of warships on passage from one command to another. On special occasions, such as the pursuit of the *Bismarck*, or the PQ.17 operation, the Admiralty assumed direct control and this was then exercised by the appropriate Director, D.O.D.(H) or (F), unless and until the A.C.N.S., V.C.N.S., or First Sea Lord himself took charge. Trade Division, under its Director (D.T.D.) was responsible to A.C.N.S. (U.T.) for the movements of all Allied merchant shipping under British control and prepared the routes and issued diversion orders for all trade convoys and ships sailing independently. The Director of the Anti-Submarine Warfare Division (D.A./S.W.), who also reported to A.C.N.S. (U.T.) did not control the actual operation of the anti-submarine forces, but was responsible for doctrine, tactics, the development of new weapons and their correct employment.

All these officers and their subordinates were vitally affected by the work of O.I.C. One can in consequence appreciate the foresight of the D.N.I., Godfrey, in appointing someone of Clayton's seniority to take charge of O.I.C. as Deputy Director Intelligence Centre (D.D.I.C.), leaving the Deputy Director Intelligence Division (D.D.N.I.) responsible for the rest of the Division. The significance of Winn's promotion to the acting rank of Captain should also be viewed in this context. Just as the Intelligence Division was the senior Division of the Naval Staff, so O.I.C. can be regarded as the most important half of N.I.D. It should however be emphasized that O.I.C. had no executive authority: it merely provided information and appreciations in the light of which other departments took action. Plans, Operations and Trade Divisions were, in theory, perfectly entitled to ignore the advice proffered to them: the fact that they so rarely did so is an indication of the influence which O.I.C. exerted.

Although the Admiralty retained overall control of operations at sea, the responsibility for their execution rested with the commander-in-chief concerned. Thus C.-in-C. Home Fleet was responsible for operations against the major German warships unless and until they moved outside his area of command, when control would pass to the appropriate C.-in-C. for that area. C.-in-C. Home Fleet was also responsible for the running of the Arctic convoys to Russia. The C.-in-C. Western Approaches was responsible for the operation of all the escort vessels under British control in the Battle of the Atlantic, although, as noted, the routing and diverting of the convoys was done by Trade Division. The two authorities, of course, worked in very close co-operation with each other and with O.I.C. Other commanders-in-chief or flag officers, such as C.-in-C. Mediterranean, C.-in-C. South Atlantic, Allied Naval Commander-in-Chief Expeditionary Force (A.N.C.X.F.), Vice-Admiral Dover or Flag Officer Submarines (F.O.S.) exercised command over specific areas or forces. All of them had to be supplied with intelligence by O.I.C.

Coastal Command, on the other hand, was one of the three home operational commands of the Royal Air Force, the other two being Bomber and Fighter Commands. Although Coastal Command controlled all maritime aircraft (except the ship-borne aircraft of the Navy's Fleet Air Arm), the Admiralty had, at first, no authority over its operations, but could merely make requests with which, to be fair, the Air Officer Commanding-in-Chief (A.O.C.-in-C.) always did his best to comply. By the spring of 1941, however, a measure of operational control had been conceded to the Admiralty. Coastal Command nevertheless remained an integral part of the R.A.F. and responsibility for the provision of its personnel, aircraft and all other resources was always retained by the Air Ministry, who, for far too long, had to give priority to the demands of the other two Commands. The main link between O.I.C. and the A.O.C.-in-C. Coastal Command was the Naval Liaison Officer at his Headquarters, but urgent intelligence was increasingly passed direct to the Groups into which the Command was divided or, when they were established, to the Combined Naval and Air Headquarters at Liverpool, Plymouth and Rosyth.

Sources

FOR THE strategic and operational background to this book I have relied very largely on some of the many published accounts of the maritime war against Germany. I give below a short list of those which I have found most useful, and if I have, quite unconsciously, been guilty of plagiarism, I apologize to those concerned. After reading and re-reading their works so often I have found it difficult to separate my own thoughts and even words from theirs. I hope they will regard it as a compliment. A few of them deal specifically with intelligence problems, but, because of the security restrictions imposed until recently by the British Ministry of Defence, their accounts have necessarily been incomplete and in some cases, misleading.

It is in connection with the intelligence aspect of the war at sea that I do claim to have broken fresh ground. Here I have relied on two main sources. The first has been memory, my own and that of my old colleagues and others with specialist knowledge whom I have consulted. Their names and my thanks to them are recorded at the beginning of this book. I must, however, again mention Vice-Admiral Sir Norman Denning, who made available to me certain of his private papers, and Professor Dr. Jürgen Rohwer, who has supplied me with a great deal of help and information. It has not always been possible to indicate this in the text.

SOURCES

My second main source has been those O.I.C. records so far released to the Public Record Office, where they are filed under reference ADM 223/1 to 67. These records disclose a very great deal of information, but they are, unfortunately, incomplete. Much, including apparently O.I.C.'s War Diary and copies of the innumerable 'Out' signals made by O.I.C. were destroyed shortly after the end of the war in the mistaken belief that this was essential in the interests of security. Others still exist and will, it is understood, be released in due course. The reason for their continuing retention by the Ministry of Defence is, to say the least, obscure; it certainly cannot any longer have anything to do with national security. Duplicates of some, if not all of them, exist in the National Archives in Washington, where, it seems, they must also remain Classified until such time as the British authorities, in their wisdom, see fit to release the originals.

Some words of warning are necessary in connection with the ADM 223 files. Through no fault of the staff of the Public Record Office they are not always put together in a completely logical or comprehensive form. Copies of some papers appear in more than one file and very rarely is it possible to be sure that all the material bearing on a particular subject is contained in one place. Many of the files consist not of O.I.C.'s own papers, but of reports of Naval Section at Bletchley Park to O.I.C. These are often summaries or appreciations which were made weeks or even months after the events to which they refer; care must be taken not to be misled into supposing that the information which they contain was available absolutely contemporaneously to O.I.C. Others were obviously written at or after the end of the war, in some cases, one must suppose, by people without personal experience of the events they describe and not, therefore, always complete or entirely accurate; ADM 223/50, a Report on German Surface Raiders, is a case in point. It must also be remembered that a great deal of intelligence came to O.I.C. by telephone and telex and was recorded only in the War Diary, in the original telex message or just in the 'Out' signals made by O.I.C. Here one can only rely on the memory of the dwindling band of survivors, and this, as I know from my own experience, is not always a reliable source.

I have done my best to check the accuracy of all the statements I have made. I do not believe that there are any major errors, but that there may be one or two of detail remains a possibility. If any reader can detect them I shall be more than grateful for correction.

The English edition of this book was published in March 1977. In October 1977 the British authorities began to release to the new Public Record Office in Kew, London, the file copies of the telexes of translated decrypts from B.P. to O.I.C. They are filed under reference DEFE 3. Due to the need to meet my American publishers' deadline, I have only been able to examine some of the earliest of these releases. I have made one or two changes in the original text and added footnotes as appropriate in the American edition. U.S. authorities have similarly begun to release some of their records. The most important so far made available are two volumes of the OP 20G History of the battle against the U-boats. These were written soon after the conclusion of the war and are based almost entirely on the relative Special Intelligence. They are likely to prove the most complete record of the Battle of the Atlantic from the German point of view. As with the British records, they do not invalidate, in any major way, my original text.

BIBLIOGRAPHY

C. Babington-Smith. *Evidence in Camera*. Chatto & Windus.

R. Barker. *Aviator Extraordinary*. Chatto & Windus.

C. Bekker. *Hitler's Naval War*. Macdonald.

J. Broome. *Convoy Is to Scatter*. Kimber.

W. S. Chalmers. *Max Horton and the Western Approaches*. Hodder & Stoughton.

K. Dönitz. *Memoirs*. Weidenfeld & Nicolson.

L. Farrago. *The Tenth Fleet*. Obolensky.

J. H. Godfrey. *Memoirs*. Typescript.

D. Irvine. *P.Q.17*. Cassell.

W. James. *The Eyes of the Navy*. Methuen.

P. K. Kemp. *Victory at Sea*. Muller.

P. K. Kemp. *Escape of the Scharnhorst and Gneisenau*. Ian Allen.

D. Kahn. *The Code-Breakers*. Weidenfeld & Nicolson.

L. Kennedy. *Pursuit*. Collins.

A. J. Marder. *From the Dreadnought to Scapa Flow*. Oxford University Press.

SOURCES

A. J. Marder. *From the Dardanelles to Oran*. Oxford University Press.

D. McLachlan. *Room 39*. Weidenfeld & Nicolson.

J. Rohwer. *Geleitzug Schlachten in März 1943*. Motorbuch Verlag.

S. W. Roskill. *The War at Sea*. H.M. Stationery Office.

S. W. Roskill. *Naval Policy between the Wars*. Collins.

B. B. Schofield. *Russian Convoys*. Batsford.

H. G. Thursfield. *Brasseys Naval Annual 1948*. Clowes.

P. Von der Porten. *The German Navy in World War II*. Arthur Barker.

F. W. Winterbotham. *The Ultra Secret*. Weidenfeld & Nicolson.

Index

Its work was so secret that until 1975, thirty years after World War II, nobody not connected with it had ever heard of something called the Admiralty's Operational Intelligence Centre.

The German admiral Karl Dönitz, against whom so much of the OIC's activities were directed, was unaware of its existence, as was Admiral Raeder and the captains of a number of unfortunate German battleships and submarines. In fact, so secret — and so vital — were the intelligence secrets OIC passed on to the British Navy and the Royal Air Force that it is no exaggeration to say that without OIC Germany might have won World War II.

This is the story of that remarkable organization, told by a man who served in it from 1940 to 1945 and who, for the first time, reveals the full extent of its operations. The pursuit of *Bismarck*, the escape of *Scharnhorst* and *Gneisenau* through the Channel, the tragedy of Convoy P.Q. 17 and the German equivalent, the Battle of the North Cape, and above all the crucial war against the U-boats are only some of the events which are seen here in an entirely new light and from a unique angle. The development of OIC's techniques, as the many sources of intelligence are perfected, the various ciphers broken, and "Special Intelligence" flows out from the group's headquarters — it is the raw material of adventure fiction.

VERY SPECIAL INTELLIGENCE is, however, more than just a thrilling story. Based on material and personal knowledge not available to the authors of a number of recent best-selling books on this subject, it sets the record straight and is a vitally important contribution to the history of naval warfare and intelligence.

Patrick Beesly served in the Royal Naval Volunteer Reserve from 1939 to 1959 and did war service in the Naval Intelligence Division of the Admiralty in the Operational Intelligence Centre.

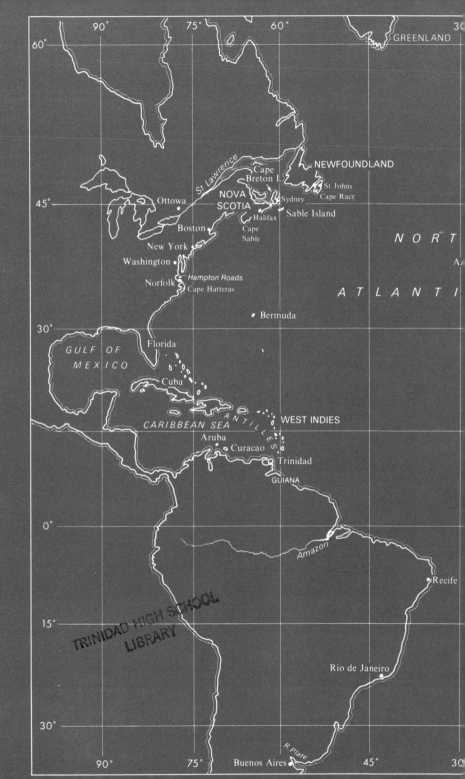

GREENLAND

90° 75° 60° 30°

60°

NEWFOUNDLAND

Cape
Breton I.   St Johns
NOVA   Sydney   Cape Race
45°   Ottawa   SCOTIA   Sable Island
                          Halifax
                 Boston   Cape
                           Sable
           New York   N O R T
        Washington   A
                                                 A T L A N T I
           Norfolk   Hampton Roads
                      Cape Hatteras

                              • Bermuda

30°
                Florida
    GULF OF
    MEXICO
                Cuba
                              A N T I L L E S   WEST INDIES
           CARIBBEAN SEA
                   Aruba
                     Curacao
                           Trinidad
                    GUIANA

0°
                              Amazon

                                                 •Recife

15°
    TRINIDAD HIGH SCHOOL
            LIBRARY

                              Rio de Janeiro

30°
                        R Plate
    90°   75°   Buenos Aires   45°   30